NO WALL TOO HIGH

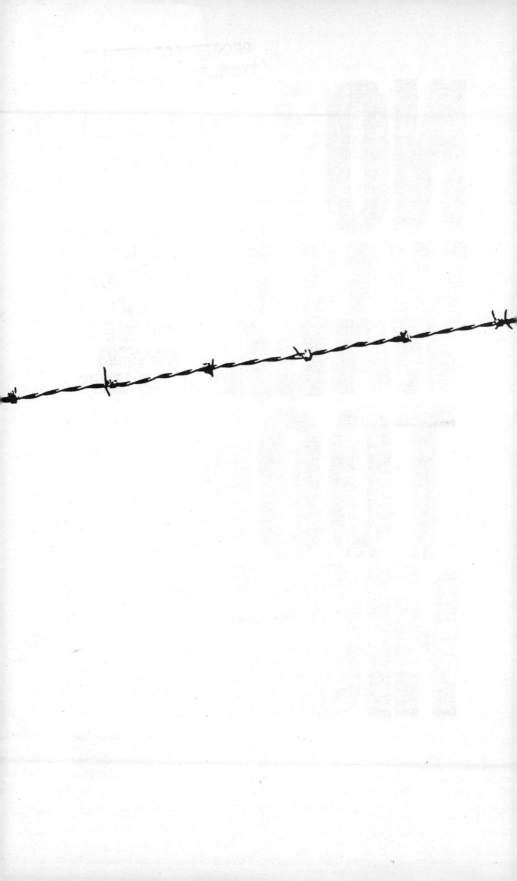

NO WALL TOO HIGH

XU HONGCI

TRANSLATED AND EDITED BY
ERLING HOH

ONE MAN'S
EXTRAORDINARY
ESCAPE
FROM MAO'S
INFAMOUS
LABOUR CAMPS

RIDER
LONDON · SYDNEY · AUCKLAND · JOHANNESBURG

1 3 5 7 9 10 8 6 4 2

Rider, an imprint of Ebury Publishing,
20 Vauxhall Bridge Road,
London SW1V 2SA

Rider is part of the Penguin Random House group of companies
whose addresses can be found at global.penguinrandomhouse.com

Penguin
Random House
UK

First published in Great Britain by Rider in 2017
Published in the United States by Sarah Crichton Books, an imprint
of Farrar, Straus and Giroux www.fsgbooks.com

www.penguin.co.uk

A CIP catalogue record for this book is available from the British Library

Hardback ISBN 9781846044960
Trade paperback ISBN 9781846044977

Printed and bound in Great Britain by Clays Ltd, St Ives PLC

MIX
Paper from
responsible sources
FSC
www.fsc.org
FSC® C018179

Penguin Random House is committed to a sustainable future for
our business, our readers and our planet. This book is made from
Forest Stewardship Council® certified paper.

In memory of the men and women who perished in the camps

Thus, with the first shout of insurrection in free Budapest, learned and shortsighted philosophies, miles of false reasonings, and deceptively beautiful doctrines were scattered like dust. And the truth, the naked truth, so long outraged, burst upon the eyes of the world.

—ALBERT CAMUS, "Kadar Had His Day of Fear"

Contents

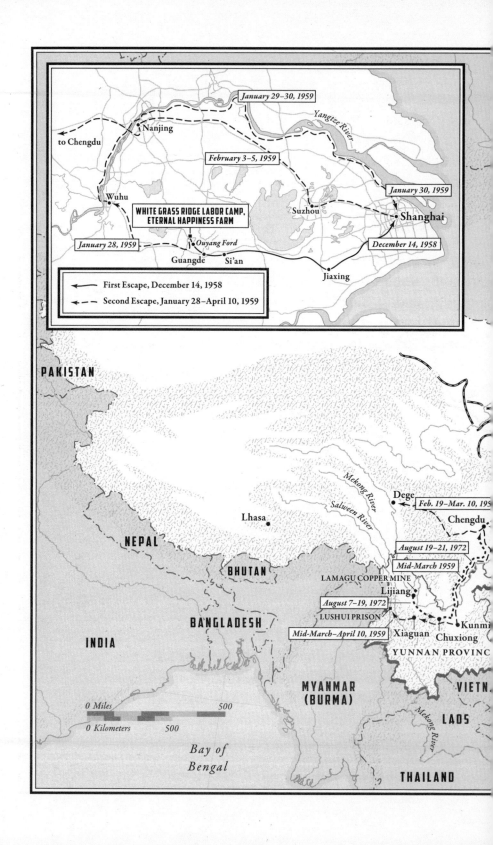

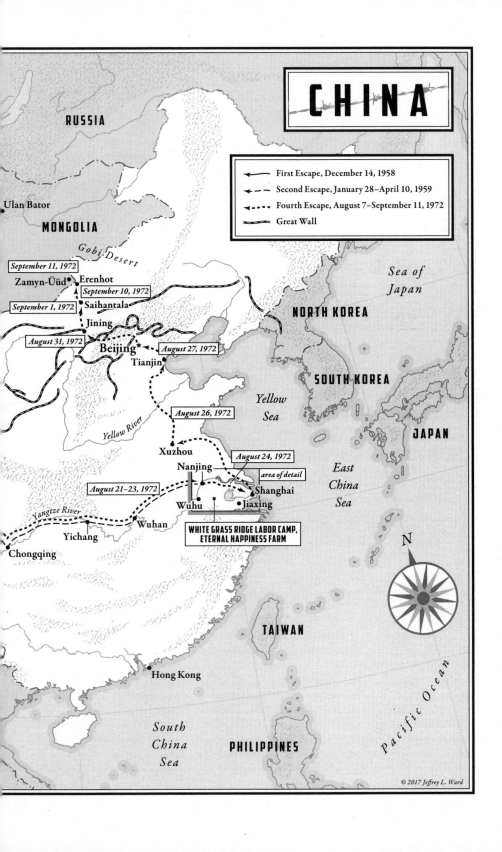

How This Book Came to Be

I was planning a novel that involved a breakout from a Chinese labor camp and had just reread *The Count of Monte Cristo*, looking for ideas. At Hong Kong's Central Library, I typed the word *laogai*, "labor reform," into the computer catalog. Among the books listed, to my surprise and excitement, was the title *Chongchu laogaiying*, "Escape from the *laogai*."

I retrieved the book from its shelf. The cover showed the silhouette of a man scaling a prison wall topped with barbed wire. The blurb read "*The Gulag Archipelago* + *Papillon*: the true account of an escape from hell." It was the chronicle of Xu Hongci, one of the 550,000 men and women unjustly dispatched to the labor camps for, on Mao's insistent behest, having spoken their minds in the spring of 1957. In 1972, after three failed escapes and fourteen grueling years in the camps, Xu Hongci had finally regained his freedom with a carefully planned, epic prison break.

"If there is a real-life story, why write a novel?" I asked myself. There and then, I decided to translate his book.

It had been published by Art & Culture, one of the many small presses in Hong Kong that cater to the millions of visitors from mainland China starving for a good, uncensored read. Paul Lee, the publisher, told me that *Chongchu laogaiying*, an oral account of Xu Hongci's story as told to the Shanghai journalist Hu Zhanfen, had sold eight hundred copies. He had never met the two but promised to see if he could find their contact information.

In early 2012, I called Hu Zhanfen and was saddened to learn that Xu Hongci had passed away in 2008, shortly after the publication of his book. Hu Zhanfen and I decided to meet in Shanghai, where he introduced me to Xu Hongci's Mongolian widow, Sukh Oyunbileg. Rummaging among her belongings, she brought out her husband's lifework: a 572-page autobiography, handwritten, with maps, little drawings, and many events not included in the Hong Kong edition.

Fortunately, the manuscript had been typed as a more legible Word file. The work to translate and condense it has been an eye-opening, engrossing odyssey through modern Chinese history, a journey to the heart of its darkness, always buoyed by the humane, brave voice that illuminates every page of Xu Hongci's stark testimony, written by the solitary campfire of remembrance.

Whether Xu Hongci was the only man to escape from the labor camps of Mao's China is an academic question. Considering the millions who were incarcerated, probability would indicate that he was not alone. Nevertheless, when I asked Harry Wu,* a highly respected historian of the Chinese labor camps and himself a *laogai* survivor, if he had ever heard of a successful escape, he replied, "No, it was impossible. All of China was a prison in those days."

One thing is for sure: by the time of the Cultural Revolution (1966–1976), a failed escape spelled certain death. Gu Wenxuan was a student at Beijing University who, like Xu Hongci, fell prey to the Anti-Rightist Campaign of 1957. In 1966, he escaped from a labor

---

*Harry Wu passed away on April 26, 2016.

camp in Shandong Province, made it across the border to North Korea, but was caught, extradited, and executed. Ren Daxiong, a Beijing University professor, was sentenced to life in prison for translating Khrushchev's "secret speech." After staging a failed mass escape, he and twelve other convicts were made to stand before the firing squad on March 28, 1970.

In the spring of 2015, I traveled to Yunnan Province, where Xu Hongci had been arrested on the border with Burma in 1959 and subsequently spent thirteen and a half years in the labor camps. Many of the places he described have been transformed beyond recognition; the mighty, tempestuous rivers he traversed have been dammed to a standstill, and some of the dirt roads he trekked have become four-lane highways. In the picturesque town of Lijiang, the 507 Agro-machinery Factory, Xu Hongci's last prison, has been razed, while the cobblestoned streets where he was paraded now stand lined with endless tourist shops. The only discernible landmark is his beloved Jade Dragon Mountain, still towering majestically to the north.

One day, I decided to find Yang Wencan, Xu Hongci's fellow inmate from his last prison. All I knew was that Yang Wencan came from Jianchuan, a county with 170,000 inhabitants, some fifty miles southwest of Lijiang. Walking down the county seat's main street, wondering where to start, I caught sight of an old man with a grizzled look, standing in the sun in front of a shop.

"I am looking for a man by the name of Yang Wencan," I said.

"Oh, Yang Wencan, he was Xu Hongci's friend," the man replied, as if he had surmised my purpose.

"You knew Xu Hongci?!" I said, taken aback.

"We were together at the Dayan Farm labor camp in the early sixties. He was a tall man from Shanghai," the old man said.

We chatted for a while. I could hear that Xu Hongci was a local legend. The old man gave me complicated directions for finding Yang Wencan and began a rambling explanation of the politics and factional battles that had propelled Xu Hongci to make his final escape in 1972. Lost in reverie, he spoke in a heavy Bai dialect, and I struggled to catch his meaning. I never managed to find Yang Wencan, but that didn't really matter. A few days later, trekking along Xu Hongci's final escape route in the mountains south of Lijiang, I realized that the old man's wistful words were all I had come looking for:

"He made it."

ERLING HOH
Hemfjäll Skola
October 6, 2015

NO WALL TOO HIGH

1

The French Will Protect Us

(1933–1945)

In 1931, Japan annexed the vast region abutting the Korean Peninsula known as Manchuria—the first step in its avowed historical mission to liberate China from Western imperialism, establish itself as the hegemon of Asia, and monopolize the continent's natural resources. The following year, thirty-three days of pitched battles between Japanese and Chinese forces in the streets of Shanghai left 14,000 Chinese and 3,000 Japanese dead. In the summer of 1937, the hostilities escalated into full-scale war as Japan launched a massive invasion of the Chinese heartland. The first major battle stood in Shanghai, where the Chinese generalissimo, Chiang Kai-shek, deployed his best-trained troops to repel the aggressors. From mid-August to late November, fierce fighting raged in the city and its environs, before Chiang, having lost some 190,000 men, ordered a retreat. The Japanese army marched on the capital, Nanjing, and for the next eight years China was engulfed in one of the most lethal conflicts of World War II, with a death toll of up to 18 million people.

I was born in Shanghai on September 10, 1933. My parents had two daughters, but both of them had died hastily of disease during the Japanese attack on the city the previous year. So I became their oldest child.

My grandfather passed away when my father, Xu Yunsun, was five years old. After that, Grandmother and Father lived with her older brother, Wu Cuiwu, an able man who worked as an agent for a Swedish trading firm. In time, he started mines and factories and belonged to China's first generation of industrialists. Wu Cuiwu adopted Father as his own son, gave him a solid education at a college of commerce, and helped him find a good-paying job.

An orphan raised under another family's roof, Father grew into a timid man. In our family, it was Mother, Wang Yamei, the pampered, headstrong daughter of a capitalist, who made the important decisions. Although she attended the Eliza Yates Memorial School for Girls, she never adopted Catholicism, which was just one example of her independent character. She ruled the family with an iron hand.

Having suffered dearly during the Japanese attack on Shanghai in 1932, my parents moved the family to the city's French Concession. Father worked in the Customs Tax Bureau, earning five hundred silver dollars a month, a high salary, and with the addition of Mother's money we were comfortable.

My parents dreamed of maintaining this middle-class life forever, but the war intervened. In the winter of 1941, following the attack on Pearl Harbor, the Japanese army entered the Western concessions in Shanghai and took control of the customs office. Father lost his job. Because my parents had an active social life and needed to keep up appearances, the loss of Father's salary put great pressure on our family. We were unable to make ends meet.

Finally, to get away from their bourgeois acquaintances, my parents made the difficult decision to move to Kunshan, then a small town thirty-five miles west of Shanghai, where we moved in with my maternal grandmother. Grandfather had once owned a lot of real estate in Kunshan, but having discovered the encumbrances of landowner-ship, he had sold all of it except for some ten *mu** on the western side of Kunshan, with eight single-story houses and two fishponds.

Unable to abide her husband's young concubine, Grandmother lived in one of these houses together with relatives from her huge clan. She was a generous, meek woman, and we got along well.

It took some time for me to get used to life in Kunshan. In Shang-hai, we had lived in a Western-style villa. Now we lived in a simple house, without even a bathroom. There was also a charm and serenity to Kunshan in those days. The fertile countryside around our house was dotted with rivers and lakes—the typical Jiangnan† landscape. To the north stood the beautiful Ma'an Mountain. In the east, a small river connected to Bai Lake. On the western side, rice paddies mingled with groves of mulberry trees, and south of us were the Puji Hospital and General Bu's Temple. All of that is gone now, replaced by asphalt roads and endless rows of concrete apartment blocks.

Together with friends, Father started a secondhand plank and beam business on a plot of vacant land by our house. They would buy old wooden houses in the countryside, dismantle them, and transport the lumber back to Kunshan, where it was either sold or used to make cof-fins. I often went to the coffin workshop to play with the tools and learned a bit of carpentry.

The income from this business was limited. Mother, who had always lived well, couldn't tolerate our newfound poverty and hectored Father to seek an official position again. By then, the Japanese invaders had set up a puppet government headed by Wang Jingwei.‡ So if you

---

*1 *mu* = 0.16 acres.

†The region encompassing the Yangtze River's lower reaches, one of the most fer-tile and prosperous in China.

‡In 1905, Wang Jingwei joined Dr. Sun Yat-sen's Revolutionary Alliance, and rose to national fame following a failed plot to assassinate Prince Qun, next in line to the throne of the collapsing Manchu Qing dynasty (1644–1911). A founding member of the Kuomintang, Wang Jingwei worked with Mao Zedong in the

wanted to serve in the government, you had to become a Japanese collaborator.

One of Mother's old classmates was married to Fang Huanru, a northerner who had joined the Communist Party in the early 1920s. In 1927, when Chiang Kai-shek launched his campaign against the Communists in Shanghai, Fang Huanru had fled to the Soviet Union, only to be classified as a Trotskyite during Stalin's purges in the 1930s. Forced to flee again, he had returned to China, thrown himself into the arms of the Kuomintang (KMT),* and been assigned to underground work against the Japanese in Shanghai. There, he was ferreted out by Wang Jingwei's agents and had become a Japanese turncoat to save his skin.

In January 1944, the Japanese established Huaihai Province with Xuzhou as its capital and Hao Pengju as the puppet governor. Fang Huanru was given a job as chief of the puppet administration. He and his wife often played mah-jongg with my parents, and Fang Huanru encouraged Father to come with him to Xuzhou.

Mother supported the idea. Around that time, a pest in the hatchery that Father had started with a friend killed all the chickens, leaving Father bankrupt. Desperate, he had no alternative but to accept Fang Huanru's offer and was assigned as director of logistics in Su County, where he supplied the Eighth Route Army† and apparently made some

---

Kuomintang's propaganda department during the KMT's short-lived "united front" with the Communists (1924–1927). Following Sun Yat-sen's death in 1925, Wang Jingwei lost the power struggle for the KMT leadership to Chiang Kai-shek, with whom he maintained an uneasy relationship for the next thirteen years. In November 1938, Wang Jingwei defected from the Nationalist government, initiated negotiations with the Japanese, and established a puppet government in Nanjing. He died in 1944.

*In late 1911, the Manchu Qing dynasty, hounded by uprisings across China, collapsed under its own decrepitude. Shortly after, Dr. Sun Yat-sen, the figurehead of the revolution, founded the Kuomintang, the Nationalist Party, an amalgamation of several revolutionary groups, which became the dominant political force in China for the next thirty-seven years. After Sun Yat-sen's death in 1925, the party's new leader, Chiang Kai-shek, launched his successful Northern Expedition against the three principal warlords, conducted a bloody purge of Communists in Shanghai, and established a fragile national government in Nanjing.

†One of the Communist Party's two main fighting forces, nominally within the

money. Although he resigned after only one year, this black mark haunted him the rest of his life and was the seed of his destruction.

Father's attitude toward the Japanese torments me. I was young and didn't understand what was going on. But if I had been an adult, I'm sure we would have had a fight. The Japanese invasion affected me deeply and, to a certain extent, determined my future path.

My first memories are of the atrocities committed by the Japanese. In 1937, when I was four years old, we were living in the French Concession on Pushi Road.* I remember my paternal grandmother holding me as we watched fires rage during the Japanese attack on Zhabei and the Southern Market. The fierce flames streaked toward the sky, and the air filled with thick black smoke and ear-shattering gunfire and explosions. People stood on the street watching this horrific scene for a long time, their faces dark with terror and anger.

"The Japanese will pay for their evildoing," Grandmother said to me.

"Will they burn down our house too?" I asked her, terrified.

"No, this is the French Concession. They don't dare to come here."

"Why?"

"Because France is a strong country, like Japan. The French will protect us."

The war against Japan grew protracted. It wasn't until we moved to Kunshan that I actually encountered Japanese soldiers and tasted the bitterness of belonging to a subjugated people. On my way to school, I had to pass a Japanese garrison with soldiers standing guard by the main gate. According to the Japanese rules, every person had to stop before the soldiers, stand at attention, remove his hat, and bow. Anybody showing the slightest sign of disrespect in his posture or expression was punished immediately.

KMT government's command structure during the Sino-Japanese War (1937–1945). Weapons, medicine, and other supplies were clandestinely traded between the Chinese parties to the conflict.

*Rue Bourgeat, now named Changle Road.

Every day, I passed that sentry post four times, bowing to the Japanese soldiers on each occasion. If I wanted to go into town, I had to bow at several other sentry posts. During those four years, I bowed to the Japanese devils thousands of times. Although I never saw the Japanese soldiers kill anybody with my own eyes, I heard countless stories of how they looted, burned, raped, and killed.

In fifth grade, I was forced to study Japanese. The teacher was a Japanese officer in the propaganda section by the name of Kobayashi. He was conscientious, but not a single student wanted to learn Japanese. Our scornful attitude infuriated him. Once, he caught me whispering to another student and ordered us to stand in front of the class. Suddenly he grabbed our hair and banged our heads together as hard as he could three times, almost knocking us unconscious. The results of his instruction were nil: although I studied the language for three years, I never learned to speak one full sentence of Japanese.

There were frequent guerrilla attacks around Kunshan, and the Japanese controlled the town with an iron grip, often knocking on people's doors in the middle of the night to check resident permits. Japanese soldiers would fish in our pond, swaggering off with the biggest carp without paying a single penny. Once, they accused my younger brother of scaring away the fish by talking too loudly and gave him a savage beating. We hated them from the bottom of our hearts.

Father followed the war closely, subscribed to a newspaper, and often studied the current situation on a map. I studied with him, learning how to read newspapers and maps at an early age. Sometimes I would listen intently as he and his friends discussed national affairs and the war until late at night. A boundless world opened itself before my mind. I wanted to grow up quickly and join the war against the Japanese devils. Inner images of bloody battlefields made me boil with indignation. In fifth grade, I wrote a long essay, saying I wanted to enlist in the army and serve my country. This frightened my teacher Duan Ruiying, who warned me not to write such sharp papers again. Our nation's tragedy awakened my political consciousness at a young age, and service to my people and my country became the guiding principle of my life.

When I was almost twelve, the Japanese capitulated. We celebrated the victory and looked forward to a bright future. People lined the streets to welcome the returning "National Army." Fervent young people joined the KMT's youth organization. Tens of thousands of Japanese POWs passed through our town. The U.S. Army visited Kunshan. People shouted, "Jiang Zhuxi wan sui!" "Long live Generalissimo Chiang!" But I also became aware of the struggle between the KMT and the Communists and was confused by the letter* written by Zhu De, commander of the Eighth Route Army, to Chiang Kai-shek. I had never realized China still had so many problems left to solve.

In secondary school, I never paid attention to my classes but read historical novels in secret under the table, until it became an addiction, absorbing me to the point where I forgot to eat and sleep. I must have read almost all the famous historical novels of China. Perhaps this is why I consider almost every problem from a historical perspective, trying to pinpoint its origins and foresee its future development. This, in turn, has made it impossible for me to simply drift with the tide and accept reality without questioning and made me a restless man, never at peace.

A person's disposition is basically inherited. Because I am a typical choleric, my traits are energy, poor self-control, straightforwardness, enthusiasm, irritability, courage, and resolve. As such, I am completely different from Father, who was introverted and cowardly, and similar to Mother, who was also quick-tempered and irascible. But Mother and I had differences too. Spoiled with love and attention from her earliest days, Mother was a conceited, domineering person who didn't know how to respect other people, especially within her own family. As for

---

*On August 17, 1946, Zhu De sent a cable to Chiang Kai-shek, demanding that Communist forces be allowed to accept the Japanese army's surrender in the areas under their control.

others, she only respected those who had more money and power than herself. Scoldings, beatings, and quarrels were daily occurrences in our family.

My paternal grandmother had a good influence on me. She was a traditional Chinese woman who loved her grandchildren and worked for us tirelessly. I have always tried to emulate her kindness, industry, loyalty, patience, simplicity, tolerance, and other qualities. In our family, there were two invisible fronts, and from beginning to end I stood on Grandmother's side.

Our house was frequented by all kinds of people: capitalists, landlords, politicians, officials, detectives, gangsters, and riffraff, who drank, gambled, whored, smoked opium, blackmailed, and speculated. I always looked at them with disdain. Every night, there would be a mah-jongg game in our house, but I never watched, and to this day I can't play the game.

The years in Kunshan brought me in close contact with the reality of people from all walks of life and gave me a better understanding of the working class. Living among peasants, I could see how hard they had to work simply to maintain the most basic standard of living. They considered my parents to be educated people, were respectful, and treated us well. I had great sympathy for them, especially seeing their helplessness when faced with diseases such as snail fever and tuberculosis, which killed many people. I always prayed for them, wishing they could have a better life.

I remember in particular the hunchback Hong Sheng, a skillful carpenter who could turn old pieces of wood into beautiful coffins. He never haggled and quibbled but kept his head down and worked diligently. Influenced by him, I fiddled about with the tools and learned to appreciate the meaning of work. I also met bricklayers, blacksmiths, fishermen, and other laborers and observed their toil firsthand. In this way, I got to know more about life than I would have in Shanghai.

My childhood passed under the shadow of the war against Japan. Seeing the weakness of my country, I wanted it to become strong and powerful. In my own family, I personally experienced the injustice and darkness of the old society. Our conflicts filled me with grief and doubts. The war taught me politics and geography and gave me an understanding of history. By the age of twelve, my head was full of clashing thoughts and feelings and countless unanswered questions.

2

A Heart Is Always Red

(1945–1949)

With Japan's capitulation on August 15, 1945, the Chinese people looked forward to peace for the first time in decades. But after a brief lull, the uneasy alliance between the KMT and the Communists unraveled, and the conflict escalated rapidly into outright civil war. Inept, corrupt, and demoralized, the KMT buckled under the Communist onslaught, and following a string of victories in Manchuria, Communist troops entered Beijing in January 1949. Shanghai fell in May that year. On October 1, Mao Zedong proclaimed the founding of the People's Republic of China, and on December 10, Chiang Kai-shek fled from the last KMT stronghold in southwestern China to the island of Taiwan.

In 1946, the KMT government took over the Kunshan Middle School and, thinking we had all been Japanese collaborators, conducted a screening. I didn't really understand the purpose of this and simply filled in the forms.

The KMT's paratrooper unit was stationed in Kunshan. Some of the younger soldiers came to our school to play basketball and flirt with the girls. I made friends with a second lieutenant by the name of Tan Fangzhong. He came from Guang'an County in Sichuan Province, had joined the army at the age of fourteen, and had fought in the Burma War. Only eighteen years old, he was open-minded and outspoken and seemed experienced.

He often took me to his camp, where he talked about military affairs, told war stories, and taught me how to shoot. Once, the gun went off by accident, and I almost killed him. We became inseparable, and because the paratroopers were educated and well mannered, my parents didn't object to our friendship. Fangzhong wasn't interested in politics, but he was worried about the intensifying civil war and had a premonition he would soon be sent into action.

In the fall of 1946, he was dispatched to the front. On the eve of his departure, Father held a farewell dinner for him. We couldn't bear to part. Later, he wrote to me, saying he was fighting against the Communists in the northern part of Jiangsu Province. Then, in the fall of 1948, he suddenly showed up in Kunshan to visit me. He told me that Long Ming, another paratrooper whom I knew well, had been killed in battle by a bullet to his head. His friend Gu Guochun had lost all his teeth from a bullet, and he himself had been injured. He said he was giving up his lieutenant rank, leaving the army, and going home to till the fields. I never heard from him again.

Fangzhong's grim stories from the battlefield forced me to reconsider the country's future, as well as my own. The victory against Japan had inspired us all. Everybody had thought there would be peace so we would be able to focus on rebuilding our country.

Initially, I believed the KMT's propaganda and thought the Communist Party was fomenting chaos with the help of the Soviet Union. In 1946, I supported a big demonstration organized by the KMT in Shanghai to protest against the Soviet Union. Eventually, though, my thinking changed. First, the corruption within the KMT made me lose confidence in it. Second, the Communist Party's underground organization was active in Kunshan and gave me a strong ideological education that set me on the road to revolution.

Fangzhong's departure had left me feeling lost. I was sure I would never be able to find a friend like him again. Soon after, however, I met two new boys I'll always remember—Zhang Benhua and Wang Yanxiong. Benhua was three years older than I and often took me to the home of Pastor Johnson, an American Baptist missionary, to participate in the Baptist youth organization's gatherings and have a taste of the American lifestyle. Yanxiong and I were in the same class. He came from a poor family, and after finishing primary school, he had been a Buddhist monk for three years before returning to school. An outstanding student, he loved art and was the chief editor of our class's wall newspaper. He encouraged me to write articles, gave me difficult books to read, and discussed current affairs with me.

Benhua and Yanxiong were members of the Communist underground organization and in their different ways were trying to educate me. Several of my schoolmates joined the underground organization. One of them, Yu Ming, had a sister, Yu Qin, who was a nurse at the Baptist hospital. With the help of people like her, the underground organization recruited young students, ostensibly to become members of the Baptist youth organization.

I was young and full of righteousness. Early on, the underground organization had taken note of me and assigned Benhua and Yanxiong to recruit me. Benhua and I became the zealots of the Baptist youth organization, attending every meeting. The Johnsons liked me and invited me to their house to study English and play the piano. I went alone a few times, but Father objected in the strongest terms. He said all the missionaries were spies, and he warned me against falling into their trap. To calm him down, I agreed to seldom go there.

In 1947, negotiations between the KMT and the Communists collapsed, and China descended into full-scale civil war. To finance its army, the KMT printed money hand over fist, causing hyperinflation and further economic hardship. The Communist underground became extremely active. Student and worker movements roiled the nation. By proclaiming its opposition to the civil war and waving the banner of democracy, the Communist Party won the hearts of students and intellectuals, bringing young people like me into its fold.

I often brought progressive periodicals and books back home and also wrote some critical articles, which upset Father. He warned me I would get myself killed if I continued on this path and urged me to change my opinions and focus on my studies. While paying lip service to his admonitions, I continued my activities with even greater intensity. Only fourteen years old, I was as politically engaged as my older classmates and, being more naive, even more fervent.

Chen Xianmin lived in South Street. I can't remember exactly how we became friends, but it happened quickly. We called him Shorty. His bright eyes seemed capable of penetrating everything. He was a serious student, knew many things, had a lot of good sense, liked to help people, and naturally became a leader. I was proud to have a friend like him.

In contrast to my previous friendships, this one was founded solely on politics. In the spring of 1948, Xianmin invited me to his house for a long talk. I was taken aback by what he told me. He was speaking to me as a representative of the Communist Party. The party I worshipped!

"The revolution is progressing quickly," he said. "The Communist Party will defeat the corrupt KMT government within five years and establish a new China. I hope you can join the party and dedicate your life to the great cause of liberating our country. If you agree, you shall write a letter of application to the Communist Party and give it to me within two weeks. If you do not agree, you must promise to keep this conversation a secret."

His words filled me with conflicting feelings. I was excited that the party had called on me and scared because I would be risking my neck. I was just starting out in life and had to think about this carefully. Finally, my revolutionary fervor conquered all misgivings and hesitation. In great secrecy, I wrote my application letter and gave it to Xianmin.

After this, we became even closer friends and spoke for a long time each day. Often, we would walk from school to the Sanli Bridge, braving the freezing wind, talking about the future of our country, life, school, hobbies, family, and friends, everything you can think of. And because I knew he was a party member, our conversations became even more frank, full of warmth and hope. I had never experienced this kind of happiness before.

On March 28, I was instructed by Xianmin to go to Banjian Park on the east side of Kunshan and establish contact with the underground party organization. When I arrived, I caught sight of a familiar figure in the pavilion: the mysterious Lu Bingzhong, party member and professional revolutionary. He smiled and shook my hand.

"Congratulations. Your application for membership in the Communist Party has been approved."

I was excited and realized that joining the Communist Party meant being prepared to sacrifice myself for the liberation of mankind. Bingzhong was also moved. Steadying himself, as an official representative of the Communist Party, he explained the domestic and international situation, the political scene in Kunshan, and the objectives of the underground party's struggle.

"The party's student organization must make greater efforts to rally and unify the masses, speed up progress, isolate reactionary forces, and prepare for liberation," he said.

I listened carefully. It was my first assignment as a party member. Bingzhong emphasized the importance of secrecy, put me in the party group led by Dai Peiji, and separated me and Xianmin from an organizational point of view.

Bingzhong was constantly on the move. Every few months, he would appear, make an appraisal of the situation, issue instructions, and then vanish in smoke. Peiji was a lively boy from Taicang, never shaved his mustache—black and downy on his upper lip—and seemed older than his seventeen years. The two other members in Peiji's party group were Yang Hesheng and Zhao Pigang. Hesheng was my old classmate, introverted and taciturn. Pigang was his exact opposite, outgoing and straightforward.

Our group met once a week to exchange ideas and study. Sometimes we met at my home. My parents never suspected we were doing underground work. Forty years on, I still have fond memories of this group, and what hurts me the most is that Pigang would be branded a Rightist and commit suicide. Hesheng, on the other hand, would rise to become deputy mayor of Suzhou.

The political situation at our school was complicated. The principal, Zhu Nan, was a major landlord and an opponent of the Communist Party. The assistant principal was a reactionary, and according to rumors our sports teacher, Song Kuangting, was a KMT agent. Among the students, Wei Yougen, the son of an herbal doctor, was said to have close relations with the KMT. Other than that, there were some small-time hoodlums of undecided political color.

My task was to rally and unite the masses and to keep a close eye on Yougen. To this end, I organized a harmonica group, calling it Liaoyuan, "Set the Prairie Ablaze," which attracted many members. I did a duet with Wu Baokang that became famous. Later, we added a bass harmonica and a bronze drum, gave street performances, and became so well-known we were often asked to perform at various functions.

By then, my studies existed in name only. Once, Father gave me an English book and asked me to read it aloud. Hearing me recite the text in halting English, he scolded me severely. My other subjects were also a mess. The party eventually became aware of the situation and required us to study diligently in order to improve our reputation among the public. Later, realizing I was no longer under his control, Father simply left me alone. In the second half of 1948, I often slept at Baokang's house, and Father didn't even come to look for me.

At that time, with the devaluation of the Chinese *fabi* currency causing him great losses, Father was in serious financial trouble. Racking his brains, he tried everything from saving gold to hoarding rice. Our problems kept Mother in a constant state of anger and irritation, and she hurt a lot of people. My antipathy toward her continued to grow. In 1948, I asked to be sent to the liberated area* but was denied permission by the local underground organization.

Following the liberation of Jinan, the KMT went into a tailspin, losing battle after battle, and, instead of the five years generally antici- pated, collapsed in six months. Everybody in the Communist Party was in high spirits as we awaited the arrival of the People's Liberation Army. With Lu Bingzhong in the north to participate in the first Na- tional Youth Congress, the party put Wang Yuanding in charge of us. He was a serious thinker and operated with caution. I liked him, and we often exchanged ideas for hours on end. After liberation, he voluntarily went to Xinjiang in Chinese central Asia to work but was branded a Rightist in 1957 and sentenced to twenty years of hard labor.

We were young and inexperienced. As the revolution gathered steam, our heads swelled, and we did stupid things. During one debate, Pigang slapped the assistant principal. I was disciplined for quarreling with our military instructor. At the beginning of 1949, after the term exami- nations, my classmates smashed windows at our middle school in protest against its leadership. For this, we were criticized by Wang Yuanding for violating the party's policy of respecting property in enemy areas and ordered to make a self-criticism.†

The underground party member Bian Genyin argued with the party secretary and threatened to go to the police station and report us. Because he knew too much, nobody dared to offend him. We also made some other mistakes, attracting the attention of the KMT, which was preparing to arrest all of us Communists. Du Jie, chief edi- tor of the *Kunshan Morning News*, caught wind of the pending action and informed Father, who immediately told me to go to Shanghai and hide at my maternal grandfather's house on Xi'an Road. I, in turn,

---

*The area around Yan'an in Shanxi Province, which had served as the Communist Party's base since the end of the Long March in 1935.

†The practice of self-criticism originated in Bolshevik Russia. By turning the disobedient party member into his own inquisitor, it evolved into one of the most important tools of political control and psychological terror employed by Com- munist regimes around the world.

informed the other underground party members, and we all went into hiding.

My parents also sent my sister Hongming and my brother Hongnian to my grandfather's house in Shanghai, while they stayed on in Kunshan together with my other sister, Yunqing, and my paternal grandmother. From Shanghai, I followed the development of the civil war on tenterhooks, especially for news of Kunshan's liberation.

One day, I discovered a big wooden box in the pavilion of my grandparents' house. To my surprise and joy, it contained the works of Marx and Lenin. From the chop, I saw that the books belonged to Fang Huanru. Although I wasn't really able to understand these deep, theoretical works, just leafing through them made me feel more learned and wise. The sea of knowledge had no limit, and if I wanted to make a contribution to my country, I would have to study diligently. Three days after the liberation of Shanghai, I hurried back to Kunshan and reported to the party for duty.

3

In Cold Blood

(1950–1951)

The Chinese Communist Party was founded in Shanghai in 1921 to overthrow the capitalist class and establish the dictatorship of the proletariat, with the ultimate aim of creating an egalitarian society. Following Chiang Kai-shek's execution of some two hundred Communist Party members in Shanghai in 1927, the party was forced underground and established its first community based on the Soviet model in the rural areas of Jiangxi Province, five hundred miles southwest of Shanghai, where it confiscated the land of rich peasants and redistributed it to the poor. Dislodged from Jiangxi by KMT forces in 1934, the Communists, led by Mao Zedong, set out on the legendary Long March, a six-thousand-mile, twelve-month trek to Yan'an, situated on the loess plateau of northwestern China, where the party established its new base, steadily growing in numbers and strength. After it had defeated the KMT and established itself as the new ruler of China, the Communist Party's first priority was to implement its land reform program on a national scale.

By the time I returned to Kunshan, the big meeting between the northern cadres and the underground party members had already taken place. Most of the northern cadres came from Haiyang and Yaqian County in Shandong Province and were basically peasants, with no more than a primary school education. They assumed leadership, while the local underground party members were either transferred to other places or made deputies. Being young, I wasn't particularly concerned with these matters but often heard unhappy stories about power struggles.

Revolutionary fervor was at its peak, and many students joined the army. Even young masters and ladies from landlord families put on their rucksacks and left home. Hearing Father's talk about how advanced Manchuria was, Baokang, my harmonica partner, volunteered to go to Jilin to work with wireless radio. At the first student federation meeting in Kunshan, I was elected chairman.

In August 1949, exhausted from study and work, I collapsed with an acute inflammation of the kidneys. My parents had to spend lots of money on doctors, and it took me three months to recover. But the doctor said it was extremely difficult to cure this kind of disease completely and predicted I would only live until thirty.

At the time, Father's business had failed completely, and we were living on savings. Hyperinflation was still rampant, and the constant worrying brought Mother to tears. Father urged me to continue studying and get a university degree. But because I had joined the Communist Party, this was no longer my own decision.

At the beginning of 1950, I was assigned to a work group set with the task of finding ways to reduce rents and interest payments for the peasants. After a few days of training, we drove south about twenty *li** to Hewangge in the Qiandeng District, where we were lodged in

---

*One *li* = one-third of a mile.

peasant dwellings. We organized *sukuhui*, "grievance meetings," and *douzhenghui*, "struggle meetings," to denounce the landlords and rich peasants and raise the standing of the middle peasants and poor peasants, waived or greatly reduced that year's land rent, analyzed our experiences, and shared them with other villages in the county.

One day, the county party committee informed me that I was being sent to the East China Youth League School in Shanghai to study. I was happy to get out of Kunshan, away from the northern cadres. During the past year, I had learned many things, begun to fathom the complexity of society, and, through my dealings with the northern cadres, become aware of the Communist Party's peasant origins and authoritarian, closed, narrow-minded, and factional character, which ran completely contrary to my ideals of democracy and freedom. Nevertheless, to survive, I forced myself to adapt and make concessions and was rewarded by the party for every little sign of submission.

In October 1950, I began my studies at the East China Youth League School, an old Japanese school located on Sida Road in Shanghai, where some one thousand students from the five eastern provinces had gathered to study. Most of the students in my group came from Anhui Province and northern Jiangsu. The school's facilities were virtually nonexistent, with no tables, chairs, or beds. We studied seated on the floor and slept on reed mats. The school's principal was Rao Shushi,* secretary of the East China Bureau.

As soon as I arrived, I committed a *cuowu*, "mistake." We ate our meals in a temporary thatched shack buzzing with flies, and there were dead bugs in our food too. I wrote an article on the school's blackboard newspaper, criticizing the administrator Zhu Wei for treating us like pigs. This caused a ruckus, and I was condemned for expressing hostility toward the Communist Party and lacking class awareness. Some people demanded I be expelled from the party. I insisted Zhu

---

*A veteran Communist Party activist, Rao Shushi (1903–1975) rose to become head of the party's Organization Department. In 1954, he was implicated in the Gao Gang Affair, the first major power struggle after liberation, and spent the rest of his life imprisoned or in custody.

Wei had done a poor job and deserved criticism and that he was not the Communist Party. But in the end, I was forced to recant and conduct a thorough self-criticism.

Our study term was six months. The curriculum consisted of the party's guiding principles and policies and instruction in the Youth League's mission. The teaching method never varied. Every day, we listened to reports, discussed, made summaries, and wrote essays about what we had learned. After my initial clash with Zhu Wei, he had improved his work, and we became friends. Overall, the school upheld the traditions of the revolution, and the atmosphere was good.

At the beginning of the term, Rao Shushi gave a speech. He was a short man, square-faced, sported a Stalin mustache, and wore an earthen-yellow military overcoat. When speaking, he had the habit of sticking his hands into its pockets. He spoke in a gentle, unhurried manner, the words flowing from his mouth as from a master's pen.

One day, we heard the news that the Chinese People's Volunteer Army had crossed the Yalu River into North Korea. Everybody was excited and jointly wrote a letter to Rao Shushi, asking to be sent to North Korea to fight the war. I told Father I was going there, ignoring his advice against it. But just as we were about to depart, Rao Shushi came to our school and gave another speech.

"The present domestic situation is tense," he said. "Land reform has not yet been completed, counterrevolutionaries are conducting cease-less military activities, and public order in the cities is poor. To resist U.S. imperialism and assist Korea, we must first consolidate our rear. Therefore, the East China Bureau has decided to organize you into land reform teams and dispatch you to the countryside to assist in the land reform process."

The students greeted the decision with thunderous applause. That evening, the school held a swearing in for new party members. Not yet formally inducted, I too participated in the ceremony, pledging my allegiance in front of the party's flag with tears in my eyes. My motives were pure, and I was prepared to dedicate my life to the glorious cause of Communism.

Two days later, the school announced the list of land reform teams. To everybody's surprise, I was assigned to the land reform inspection team of the East China Bureau's agricultural committee. Even in my wildest dreams, I hadn't imagined I would be given the opportunity to work at such a high level. Everybody envied my good luck.

At the East China Bureau, I was given the job as secretary in the land reform inspection team headed by Feng Qi, a tall, solemn cadre* with white hair who spoke Mandarin. In November 1950, we arrived at the agricultural committee for northern Jiangsu Province in Yang-zhou, where a local cadre by the name of Shi Ping gave a report. "The masses have many misgivings regarding the redistribution of land and fear future retribution from the landlords. To strip the landlords of their prestige, we must execute some of them. Otherwise, the masses will not rally to the cause," he said.

Gao Feng, the local party secretary, proposed a big denunciation rally in Fairy Temple of Jiangdu County, to see if the execution of a few landlords would embolden the masses. Everybody, including Feng Qi, supported the idea, and orders were sent to Jiangdu County to make the necessary preparations, whereupon Gao Feng and Shi Ping traveled to Fairy Temple with a large group of cadres.

I went there with Feng Qi. Fairy Temple was a small, run-down town. The denunciation rally was being held on an empty plot of land near a few old, dilapidated houses. Well aware that several high-level cadres would be in attendance, the Jiangdu party committee had chosen with great care the peasants who were to take part in the meeting and organized them scrupulously.

The rally proceeded in a tidy, theatrical fashion as waves of indignation, wrath, and hate rose and subsided in succession. The high-ranking cadres weren't seated among the people but observed the events from

---

*"Cadre" is a French word with the original meaning of "frame" and the derivative meaning of "one who sets things in order." The Bolsheviks adopted it to denote a person with a high level of political consciousness who was thereby qualified to carry out specific political tasks. It eventually assumed the meaning of Communist Party official.

behind the stage. I saw two men with their hands tied tightly behind their backs standing under a tree, guarded by PLA* soldiers, and walked closer to have a look. Both of them, one older and one younger, were wearing traditional dark cotton-padded robes. The old man was close to eighty, tall and robust, his face full of wrinkles, his eyes devoid of expression. The younger man was about thirty. Frail and ghostly pale, his whole body was trembling with fear.

Seeing the assembled peasant masses, hearing the harsh slogans echo, they probably realized what was in store for them. I could see they were making a great effort to keep their backs straight. The old man even appeared composed. Having lived his life, perhaps it was easier for him to accept death.

Time passed, minute by minute, second by second, until their final moment arrived. Standing in front of the masses, the county's party secretary announced that the two landlords, being guilty of heinous crimes and having refused to reform themselves, would be executed. The two were brought by soldiers to the side of the field. The younger landlord, fighting for his life, tried to scream, but the rope tightly tied around his neck prohibited him from uttering a sound.

My view was blocked by other people. Shots rang out. As the peasants dispersed, I walked over to look at the corpses. Both men had been shot in the head and were lying in puddles of fresh blood and white brain matter. The old man's eyes were still open. This was my first brutal lesson in class warfare. Nineteen years later, having been brought by PLA soldiers to my own denunciation rally in Lijiang, facing the mad, raving crowd, I kept seeing those two corpses before me.

I worked in northern Jiangsu for about a month before returning to Shanghai, where I wrote a report about our land reform work. Soon after, I was dispatched on a second assignment. When we arrived at our destination, Taizhou, not far from Yangzhou, the land reform movement was in full swing, and landlords and rich peasants were being killed in droves.

---

*Acronym for the People's Liberation Army.

On a single day, seventeen people were executed. The street was jam-packed with people crowded along a procession of rickshaws—each one carrying a tightly bound prisoner with a *zhanqi*, "execution flag," sticking up from his back—being escorted by PLA soldiers in full battle gear to the execution grounds. Convulsed with fear, some of the prisoners struggled desperately and almost fell off the rickshaws. Their frantic fight to live deeply unsettled me. But resistance was futile, and finally they arrived at the execution grounds.

There, the soldiers pulled a few of the prisoners off the rickshaws, pushed them onto their knees, and executed them with a rifle shot to the head. Their skulls shattered, the prisoners dropped to the ground into pools of their own brain matter. Seeing this, the remaining prisoners went out of their minds, their bodies shaking with spasms of absolute horror. Fighting, kicking, resisting, they were dragged away and shot. In the scramble, I saw people approach the corpses and soak steamed bread buns in the brain matter flowing from their heads. Recalling Lu Xun's short story "Medicine,"* I was overcome by nausea. It was too barbaric, too cruel. But this was revolution, and if I wanted to be a revolutionary, I would have to toughen up. On the way back to our hostel, I kept telling myself, "Be strong."

On May 25, we were transferred back to the Youth League School. In many ways, my work at the East China Bureau had been valuable. I had met several high-level cadres, learned how the party worked, and become much more politically mature. But I had also seen the negative side of the party. In particular, the memory of the wanton executions sent shivers down my spine.

On the third day of returning to the Youth League School, I went downstairs to fetch my clothesline and was shocked by what I saw. Every classroom was filled with prisoners sitting curled up on the floor with their hands tied behind their backs. Even my clothesline had

---

*In this short story by Lu Xun (1881–1936), a major contemporary writer, the main characters are a consumptive boy and his mother, who early one morning brings a bun of steamed bread to the town's execution grounds and dips the bun in the brain matter of an executed man, believing it will cure her son.

been used for this purpose. Apparently, the Communist Party had rounded up Shanghai's "hoodlums, despots, and counterrevolutionaries" during a mass arrest that morning and, with the city's jails overflowing, turned the Youth League School into a temporary detention center.

A few days later, all these people were executed. *Liberation Daily* published a long list with the names of the several thousand people who had been put to death, together with their purported crimes. All over Shanghai, relatives of those arrested ran their fingers down that list to find the name of their dead father, son, or sister.

This was the first high tide of the Campaign to Suppress Counter-revolutionary Activities. According to the stories that circulated, the prisoners had been taken to the Longhua execution grounds, where they had simply been mowed down with machine guns. Those who didn't die immediately had been finished off with a bullet to the head.

In the summer of 1951, we received instructions to greet an international student delegation and were put up in rooms at the Jinjiang Hotel, the most fashionable, expensive hotel in Shanghai at the time. The delegation was headed by the chairman of the Italian Student Federation, Enrico Berlinguer, who later became the secretary-general of the Italian Communist Party. I admired his debonair style, especially the effortless flow of elegant words with which he charmed everybody.

Arrangements for the delegation's visit had been made with great care. I was responsible for the Dutch delegate. He was even taller than I, had blond hair and blue eyes, and dressed casually. At our first stop, Hujiang University, he was given a grand reception. After that, we went to the Asia Iron and Steel Factory, formerly run by the Japanese, where they were in the process of casting molten iron, with sparks flying in all directions. Little did I know that the head of the factory was the father of my future girlfriend, Tang Ximeng.

By July, all the students at our school had returned from their land reform work in the eastern provinces, tanned, tougher, and stronger. Several of them had guns, which they said had been seized from the enemy. Fortunately, nobody from our school had been killed during the land reform movement and the Campaign to Suppress Counter-revolutionary Activities.

In this manner, what had started as a student movement to join the war in Korea against the United States came to its close.

Frankly, I had only been a bystander in the land reform movement. I never took part in the process of categorizing people into different classes or confiscating and redistributing land and property. Nor did I ever arrest or kill anybody. But observing the movement from the side-lines enabled me to see things clearly and objectively. Later, I told people that the official policy for land reform and what had actually taken place on the ground were two entirely different matters. If land reform had been conducted according to the directives of Liu Shaoqi,* Mao's right hand at the time, it would have been peaceful. In reality, land reform didn't follow any laws or decrees. Violence was used, and countless innocent people were killed.

---

*Liu Shaoqi (1898–1969) was a veteran revolutionary, the author of *How to Be a Good Communist*, and, as president of the PRC from 1959 to 1968, the country's second most powerful man. Having criticized Mao for the Great Leap Forward, he was the main target of the Cultural Revolution and was denounced as China's "No. 1 Capitalist Roader." ("Roader" is a word that has been minted to translate the Chinese expression used to excoriate Liu Shaoqi: "dangnei zuida zou zibenzhuyi-daolude dangquanpai," "the No. 1 person in the party who is taking the road of capitalism.") Attacked by Red Guards, he was cruelly persecuted, was denied medical care, and died in captivity on November 12, 1969.

4

I Saw the Chairman

(1952-1953)

Organized like its Soviet mentor, the Chinese Communist Party had 4 million members in 1952 and ruled a nation of 580 million inhabitants. By then, Mao, having elevated himself to the status of a demigod, wielded absolute power. The highest formal body is the Politburo, at the time composed of thirteen veteran Communists, including Zhou Enlai, the foreign minister, and Liu Shaoqi. The party's Youth League is a mass organization that inculcates its members with the party's tenets and prepares them for future careers as cadres. One of the most powerful organs is the secretive Organization Department, which keeps a dossier on every party member, controls all top positions, and has a key role in assignments, promotions, and demotions.

Huang Xinbai was the leader of the United Front* of the East China Youth League's work committee. About thirty years old,

---

*The United Front Work Department is an agency responsible for managing relations with the eight political parties ("democratic party factions") that are

he was of medium height, a bit plump, lively, and cheerful. After study-ing lots of personal dossiers, he chose me and assigned me to do social work among young people.

For a few months at the end of 1951 and the beginning of 1952, I worked in Shanghai's Luwan District, trying to learn about the situ-ation of unemployed youths there. But because they were jobless and spread out all over the place, simply finding them was difficult. Our leaders told us to take care of them, but I thought the task impossible, hated it, and quarreled several times with the comrade in charge of my section.

Although Father was not a landlord, his political instincts had told him the confiscation and redistribution of land wouldn't be a dinner party, and to steer clear of the land reform movement, he and Mother had moved to my maternal grandparents' old house on Xi'an Road in Shanghai, leaving my paternal grandmother and my sister Yunqing behind in Kunshan. My brother Hongnian went to Yuci in Shanxi Province to do metalworking in the Jingwei Textile Machinery Plant, and my other sister, Hongming, passed the entrance examination for the Shanghai Theatre Academy.

Having endured several unhappy years of quarrels and disagree-ments with my parents, I was glad to see that my job at the East China Bureau had raised my standing in their eyes, and we got along better than before. Of course, they were also considering their old age and the necessity of maintaining good relations with their children. Father let me use his Blue Bell bicycle, which I rode all over the city.

In 1952, I was classified as a grade 19 cadre in the new administra-tive system, with a monthly salary of thirty yuan. Because Father didn't have a steady job, I agreed to pay the living expenses of my younger sister, which made my parents happy. With the Korean War still raging, Father often listened to the Voice of America and sometimes talked

---

allowed a nominal existence under Communist rule, as well as with other promi-nent non-Communist individuals and groups.

about the war with me. Although I disagreed with his opinions, I didn't argue with him, preferring to keep the precarious family peace.

As I was doing social work in the Luwan District, there was some turbulence on the domestic political scene. Following the execution of the high-ranking leaders Liu Qingshan and Zhang Zishan in Tianjin for mass embezzlement, Mao Zedong launched the *sanfan*, "three antis," campaign against corruption, waste, and bureaucracy. Xiao Yusheng, a leader of the East China Youth League, was ferreted out for pocketing illicit money, denounced, and expelled from the party. This was followed immediately by the *wufan*, "five antis," campaign, to crack down on bribery, tax evasion, jerry-building, and the theft of state property and classified economic information, which uncovered the shady dealings of lingering capitalists.

In Shanghai, Xinbai was put in charge of the *wufan* campaign in the Laojia District, Shanghai's major commercial area, and he assigned me to Manting Lane, where all the hardware stores were located.

In the two years since my transfer from Kunshan to the East China Bureau, I had made great progress in the art of politics and quickly established my authority among the district's grassroots cadres. I gave my first political speech in front of two thousand people at the Grand Theatre* on Nanjing Road. Later, I gave more than ten speeches in places like Heping and Jincheng and did well each time. I was grateful to Xinbai for giving me these opportunities. He told people I was his disciple, and I acknowledged him as my teacher.

When Xinbai got married to Qian Zhengying in Shanghai later that year, I lived in a pavilion by their building, and we were always together. Zhengying, also a high-ranking cadre, liked me and poked fun at me for wearing a pair of U.S. Army leather boots, calling me *Meiguobing*, "Yankee soldier." To this day, she still calls me *Meiguobing*.

---

*Designed by the Hungarian-Slovak architect László Hudec (1893–1958), the Grand Theatre is a fine example of Shanghai's prewar Art Deco architecture.

Although Xinbai taught me a lot, one thing I never learned from him was how to conform, toe the line, and go with the flow. Xinbai knew exactly where the boundary for politically correct speech and action lay and never stepped beyond it. Sometimes, he even concealed his real thoughts and said things contrary to his convictions. During the Anti-Rightist Campaign,* I witnessed him join in the denunciation of the physicist Ceng Zhaolun, stepping on a man who had already been brought low. It was just one more example of how high-level cadres violated their principles and muffled their sense of justice to escape becoming victims themselves.

During the *wufan* campaign, Xinbai had another assistant by the name of Tong Yizhong, who, having been the Youth League secretary of the Laojia District, knew the area well. Accused by the party of having shielded his capitalist father, he was actually on two years of internal probation. Physically weak and gentle, he worked efficiently, and we were good friends.

I also became good friends with his girlfriend, Yan Hong, who worked in the municipal Youth League and often came to Laojia. They eventually got married and were assigned to work at the state sports committee. Many years later, I would learn that Yizhong had thrown himself in front of a train during the Cultural Revolution.

Not long ago, Yan Hong came to see me in Shanghai. Reminiscing over our youth, I reminded her, "You said that by the time we were old, China would definitely be a just and fair Communist society. Now we are old, but where is the just and fair Communist society?" Her silence held all the broken dreams of our generation.

At the end of 1952, Xinbai was transferred to a job at Jiaotong University, leaving me feeling stranded. I realized I needed an education and wrote a letter to the Organization Department asking for permission to take the university entrance examination but received a negative reply. It was the first time I had put forth a personal request to the party, and because it was completely reasonable, I couldn't under-

---

*This campaign took place in 1957–1958.

stand why it had been refused. "Where are my individual rights?" I asked myself.

In May 1953, the new head of the United Front, Qiao Shi,* who later became a member of the Politburo, dispatched me to the Youth League central committee in Beijing to participate in the preparations for the second National Youth Congress. This was one of the most memorable occasions in my life. The preparatory meetings were held in the Huairen Tang, "Hall of Remembered Benevolence," in Zhongnanhai,† where Mao Zedong and the other top leaders lived and worked.

One day, I and a few other youths walked up on the podium and caught sight of a row of chairs with high backs.

"Let's sit on every chair. Mao Zedong must have sat on one of them!" I said.

Taking the lead, I sat down on every chair in turn. We were beside ourselves with joy.

The congress was held in the middle of June. The East China Bureau sent a delegation of about sixty comrades led by Qiao Shi. Hu Yaobang,‡ the future general secretary, several Central Committee members, and comrades from the democratic party factions§ all made reports and gave speeches. Everybody's ardent wish was to see Chairman

---

*Qiao Shi (1924–2015) was a member of the Politburo from 1987 to 1997. In May 1989, he abstained from a Politburo vote on whether to clear Tiananmen Square with military force.

†Zhongnanhai, "the Middle and South Lake," is an imperial garden just west of the Forbidden City, where the emperors of the Ming (1368–1644, with Beijing as capital 1425–1644) and Qing dynasties (1644–1911) resided. Since the Communist Party's assumption of power in 1949, its top leaders have lived and worked in Zhongnanhai.

‡Hu Yaobang (1915–1989) was general secretary of the Communist Party from 1982 to 1987 and a major force in the rehabilitation of the millions of people who were unjustly persecuted during the Anti-Rightist Campaign of 1957 and subsequent Cultural Revolution. It was his death on April 15, 1989, that sparked the protests that culminated in the bloody crackdown on Tiananmen Square on June 4.

§The eight democratic party factions, founded before 1949, which are allowed a nominal existence under Communist rule: the China Zhi Gong Party (1925), the Chinese Peasants' and Workers' Democratic Party (1927), the China Democratic League (1941), the China Democratic National Construction Association (1945), the China Association for Promoting Democracy (1945), the September 3 Society

Mao, and the request was raised at every meeting, but the leadership didn't give a definite answer.

On the final day of the congress, with the official closing ceremony concluded, we still hadn't seen Chairman Mao and were extremely disappointed. That night, the Youth League central committee and the National Youth Federation hosted an acrobatics performance in the Huairen Tang for all the congress delegates. Just as it was about to begin, everybody suddenly stood up, clapped their hands, and shouted, "Mao Zhuxi wan sui!" "Long live Chairman Mao!" There, in front of the rostrum, were Mao Zedong, Liu Shaoqi, and Zhu De, waving to us and shaking hands with people in the front row.

Seated in the eleventh row, I stood up on my chair to have a better view, clapping my hands and shouting, "Mao Zhuxi wan sui!" He had a lot of white hair and looked older than in the photographs. The turbulence continued for more than ten minutes as Mao paced back and forth by the rostrum, waving and telling us to sit down. Gradually, the delegates' euphoria subsided, everybody was seated, and the acrobatics performance began.

But the delegates were too excited, took no interest in the show, and just wanted to see Mao, if only a glimpse of his back. At the end of the performance, we stood up, clapped our hands, and shouted until Mao had left the venue through a side door. Our wish had come true. We could return home and tell our families, "I saw Chairman Mao in Beijing." I worshipped him as the people's savior and the founder of a new China and could never have dreamed that in just a few years I would collide with him head-on.

After our return to Shanghai, China's first five-year plan was announced, and Comrade Tan Zhenlin gave a rousing speech to more than ten thousand cadres in Culture Square. I sat in the first row, looking at his familiar, short, sturdy silhouette, remembering the previous year,

---

(1945), the Taiwan Democratic Self-Government League (1947), and the Revolutionary Committee of the Chinese Kuomintang (1948).

when we had worked together on the Shanghai party committee. Zhenlin spoke with a strong voice, gesturing forcefully: "China will become a superpower! If the enemy attacks, we will drown him in the sea!"

The crowd was ecstatic. Fired by his grand visions, overcome with revolutionary passion, I applauded with all my strength. It was a magnificent speech. Back home, I contemplated his words and took stock of my future. To be able to make a contribution to my country, I realized I needed an education and began to review my middle school courses.

At the beginning of 1954, the ambitious Qiao Shi finally attained his objective and was transferred to become head of design at the An'shan Steel Factory, although he knew nothing about design. He left without even holding a farewell banquet, and was replaced by Liu Jiannong, a zealous but incompetent Youth League cadre. Making use of the disorder, I studied as much as I could. Wang Yanxiong, my old friend from junior middle school who was working as a cadre in the Hongkou District, encouraged me. "There are many outstanding comrades in the party, and the party always appoints the best comrades to leadership positions. It will be hard for you to succeed in such a competitive environment. You must study and learn a skill," he said.

His words strengthened my resolve. Father was delighted to learn of my plans and supported me wholeheartedly. In June 1954, the party announced its decision to allow cadres with a middle school education to take part in the university entrance exam. This time, the Organization Department couldn't stop me. With only one month to go, I gathered every night with ten other young cadres to cram for the test.

On July 7, nervous and excited, I took part in the university entrance examination and did all right. But because I had had tuberculosis, the enrollment committee wouldn't allow me to study engineering, the most prestigious, sought-after field, and instead assigned me to the Shanghai No. 1 Medical College. Initially, I was unhappy with this and didn't even participate in our celebration dinner. But Father did everything he could to persuade me, explained the worthiness of medical studies, and urged me to enroll. I decided to give it a try and went to the Organization Department to request a change of status. The responsible cadre, Zhao Fahai, looked pale, treated me coldly, and, although he conducted the formalities, criticized me for individualism. In his opinion, it was a crime to want to study.

5

Khrushchev's Secret Speech

(1954–1956)

I n the grave silence of the Kremlin's Great Hall, you could feel the Siberian wind howling through the threadbare garments of a Gulag chain gang. Dmitri Goriunov, chief editor of *Komsomolskaya Pravda*, fumbled for his bottle of nitroglycerin. Stony-faced apparatchiks sat dumbstruck, staring blankly into the vortex of horror and perfidy, beads of cold sweat glistening on their foreheads.

It was February 25, 1956, the last day of the Soviet Communist Party's Twentieth Congress, and Nikita Khrushchev had just finished his historic "secret speech," a four-hour firebrand denunciation of his mentor, Stalin: the barbaric tortures; the odious falsifications; the despicable maltreatment of Comrade Eikhe; 383 execution lists signed by Stalin in person during the Great Terror of 1937–1938, sending 44,465 party, state, and other personnel to their deaths; 1,920,635 people arrested between 1935 and 1940; 688,503 shot.[*]

A dark brew of complicity, remorse, and calculation, Khrushchev's

---

[*]William Taubman, *Khrushchev: The Man and His Era* (London: Free Press, 2003), 279–80.

speech sent shock waves roiling through the Communist world. Hospitalized in Moscow with pneumonia, Bolesław Bierut, Poland's Little Stalin, read the transcript, had a heart attack, and died. In Beijing, Mao Zedong pondered the speech with equal gravity. His personal relationship with Stalin had always been touchy, but the Chinese Communist Party ruled with the same iron fist as its Soviet sponsor, and Mao himself had boasted that he was a hybrid of the Red Tsar and Qinshihuangdi, the most notorious in China's long line of tyrants. "This year the number of arrests must be greatly reduced from last year," Mao ordered his police chief on February 29. "The number of executions especially must be fewer."*

I n August 1954, I was enrolled as a transferred cadre student at the Shanghai No. 1 Medical College, a famous university with several decades of history and first-rate teachers and facilities. The main buildings, housing the medical college and the affiliated Sun Yat-sen Hospital, hovered like two city gate towers over the campus, lending it a solemn atmosphere. I was assigned to the Department of Medicine. Altogether, there were about seven hundred students in our freshman class, most of them in the Department of Chinese Medicine.†

With the college in a stage of rapid expansion, there was a severe lack of dormitories, and we were more than ten students in each room. My first friend was Bi Jicai, who, respectful of my underground past and party membership, called me *lao qianbei*, "the veteran," which became my nickname at the college. I also made friends with Zhuang Derun and Zhou Qinzong.

There were few party members among the new students, and like me they were all transferred cadres, accepted to the college almost solely

---

Jianguo yilai Mao Zedong wengao (Manuscripts of Mao Zedong since the founding of the People's Republic), 13 vols., ed. CCP Archive Study Office (Beijing: Zhongyang Wenxian Chubanshe, 1987–1998), 6:45–46.

†Traditional Chinese medicine, based on an herbal pharmacopoeia, acupuncture, massage, *qigong*, and dietary therapy.

on the basis of their party affiliation. In my class, the only other cadre student was Li Changchun, a thirty-year-old man from Shanxi. Peasant-like and slow-witted, he struggled desperately with his studies.

The party members in the first four freshman classes formed the second party branch, with Zhang Quanyi as secretary. As a grade 16 cadre, almost thirty years old, he had entered the college with his wife. He was a sturdy, robust, and rough man who never shaved his full beard, and also a skillful political operator. During the three years we worked together, I consistently underestimated him and finally came to grief at his hands during the Anti-Rightist Campaign.

Because I hadn't studied seriously in middle school, I was no match for the students who had been accepted on the basis of their academic achievements, and I fell behind at the start. My first midterm exam was a disaster.

But I remembered some advice from Chen Nianyi, a young chemist at the Academy of Science who considered conceptual thinking to be the key skill. I realized I had a problem with this and decided to review all my previous courses to ascertain definitions, contemplate their contents, compare concepts to reveal their differences, and thereby deepen my understanding.

I had a breakthrough. At the final exam of the first semester, I surprised everybody by placing in the top ranks. In those days, students were extremely ambitious, competition was intense, and high achievers were admired. Because the transferred cadres were usually weak academically, their status, despite their party membership, was quite low. My results raised the standing of the cadres, and people looked up to me as somebody who was an excellent student and knew politics.

Besides studying hard, I had to do a good job on my party work. Burning with revolutionary zeal, I slept as little as possible and tried to make the best use of my time. Every morning, as soon as I had gotten out of bed, I reviewed my Russian vocabulary. After a full day of classes, I did political and social work in the evenings. Sometimes our meetings continued after the bells announcing the end of the self-study period had sounded. According to the rules, we were supposed to rest after 9:00 p.m., but I often studied until 11:00 and worked extra on Sundays. Eventually, the strain began to take a toll on my health.

The students were full of confidence in the future of the new China and had great hopes for their professional futures. Everybody respected the old professors, taking them as models. We competed quietly but fiercely. Outstanding results were glorious; poor results, a disgrace. An atmosphere of concentrated study pervaded the college, and in the evenings the students hurried to finish their meals in order to find a silent place in the library. The most ambitious not only reviewed the simple mimeographed teaching materials but also studied thick Russian textbooks, even reading the long footnotes in small print.

In the first period after liberation, the party was rather successful in educating young people ideologically, and many pure-hearted students had a strong desire to join the party or the Youth League. Taking our cue from the class categorization conducted during the land reform movement, we carried out an informal classification of all the students. The three most basic categories were *jinbu*, *zhongjian*, and *luohou*, "progressive, moderate, and backward." Within these groups, we classified the students according to their class background, their parents' political problems, and any particular personal issues.

As an example, Tang Shijing, a student from Wenzhou, had been a member of the party's Trotskyite faction and was kept under constant surveillance. I was considered one of the *tian zhi jiaozi*, "heavenly elect," and respected as a representative of the party. Other party members also had a strong sense of privilege. Students who were not interested in politics kept a safe distance from us.

During my freshman year, there were three beautiful, seemingly inseparable girls I often saw walking together on campus—Tang Ximeng, Gao Er'ling, and Yang Ling. All three were dressed fashionably, carried themselves gracefully, and were the subject of much attention from the other students. Not knowing why they were such close friends, I simply assumed that like attracts like.

Tang Ximeng was the tallest of the three. She wore her hair in the latest fashion and had a square face and a straight nose. When she was happy, she twinkled with a kind of Western beauty. When she was thoughtful, her eyes were suffused with a deep, contemplative glow. Her father, Tang Hanzhong, was a steel expert who had served as a senior engineer in the KMT's munitions department during the war against Japan. After the war, he had returned from Chongqing to Shanghai to take charge of the Japanese Asia Iron and Steel Factory and gradually assumed ownership of it. In the *sanfan* campaign, he had been investigated and given a fifteen-year probationary sentence for "misappropriation of enemy property" but had been retained by the factory as a supervisor.

Gao Er'ling was a bit shorter than Tang Ximeng, always smiling, with regal features, soft eyes, a sharp, somewhat crooked nose, and freckles. Her father had been a Kuomintang major general and had served as commander for the KMT's Shanghai garrison command. After liberation, he had been sentenced to five years and was incarcerated in the Tilanqiao Prison.*

Yang Ling was the shortest of the three. She was exquisite. Her parents were separated, and she lived with her mother in a public housing estate on Huashan Road.

The party considered these three girls members of the bourgeois class and had classified them as "backward." Well aware of their despised status, they never took part in political activities and focused on their studies.

For a long time, I had little to do with them. If we happened to pass each other on campus, they would occasionally smile. When the Youth League began organizing social dances, we had more opportunities to meet. All three were skilled dancers, knew every dance, and

---

*Built by the British in Shanghai's International Settlement at the turn of the century, this prison, originally called Ward Road Gaol and nicknamed Alcatraz of the Orient, was the largest in the world until the 1940s.

moved with light steps. Yang Ling, in particular, danced with the grace of a swallow. Whenever I had the chance to dance with one of them, we exchanged a few sentences and gradually got to know each other.

Once, Gao Er'ling asked me, "I've heard you come from a 'good' background. Is that right?"

The question confused me, because in the party's view, people from the bourgeois class were "bad," while working-class people were "good." But it appeared Gao Er'ling was using the word "good" in its prerevolutionary sense and considered me to be "of the same cloth." I didn't deny this and nodded my head, even though my family was not really bourgeois—petit bourgeois at the most. My friendliness made her happy. She was no longer afraid of me, and there was a subtle change in our feelings for each other.

At the time, China and the Soviet Union were brothers in arms, and university education in China followed the Soviet model slavishly. Our college had three Soviet specialists in residence: Sibiryakov, a biology professor and a member of the U.S.S.R. Academy of Medical Sciences; Panov, a professor of epidemiology; and Ivanov, a professor of surgery. The Soviet professors emphasized a broad foundation, rote learning, and strict examinations, which gave us a solid body of knowledge and fostered intellectual discipline but failed to kindle a spirit of innovation.

The Soviet textbooks were dripping with nationalism and authority worship, and scientists like Pavlov and Lysenko* were the heroes. Everything they had written was infallible law, and every achievement in the medical sciences could be traced back to them, just as Popov was shamelessly accorded the honor of every significant innovation in wireless electronics. Hearing Pavlov's name repeated ad nauseam, I grew fed up and finally outright antipathetic.

---

*Ivan Pavlov (1849–1936), a Russian physiologist best known for his work on the "conditioned reflex," as demonstrated by "Pavlov's dog." Trofim Lysenko (1898–1976), a Soviet biologist whose harebrained science and false claims were elevated to state dogma by Stalin, who imprisoned or executed some three thousand biologists for daring to question "Lysenkoism."

Nevertheless, I took my Russian-language studies seriously, and by the second year I was able to read books in Russian with the help of a dictionary. For the purposes of scientific research, however, I discovered English was more useful and realized that by making Russian the first foreign language, our college and the whole country were committing a serious mistake.

In the second semester of our freshman year, the college adopted the Soviet system of oral examinations. Conducted face-to-face between the professor and the student, these exams were incredibly difficult, and although I did well, the burden they placed on our shoulders was too heavy. I felt the system was drowning us in trivial details, forcing us to become pedantic bookworms. Every day, I experienced the drawbacks of the Soviet education system, and my longing for reform only grew stronger.

Since I had entered the university, my relationship with my parents had greatly improved. They lived with my maternal grandmother in her old house on Xi'an Road, while my maternal grandfather lived with his concubine on Shaanxi Road. When Grandmother died in 1954, my parents took over the house and settled there permanently.

As a cadre student, I had a monthly salary of fifty-four yuan, more than enough for one person, and gave twenty yuan to my parents every month. Thankful for this filial gesture, they treated me better than before. Mother was over forty, had had her fair share of tribulations, and had eventually learned how to do housework. When I returned home on Sundays, she always cooked a delicious meal for me. Sometimes she even helped me wash my clothes and bed linen. Because I was both a party member and a good student, my parents would often boast about me to their acquaintances and had great hopes for my future.

Because Mother had always had a bad relationship with her mother-in-law, Grandmother was not willing to move to Shanghai and stayed in Kunshan with Yunqing, the younger of my two sisters. The older, Hongming, had made progress as an actress at the theater academy, but she was lazy, changed boyfriends all the time, and played tricks and games in politics.

For her ideology class, she once wrote a paper criticizing Mother and Father as being completely worthless. This essay found its way into the hands of my enraged parents. They discovered that Hongming often lied, disappearing for weeks on end without a word, and realized she was heading down the wrong path. My parents sent her essay to me, but to keep my good memories of her, I decided not to read it and burned it instead. Despite all this, we were tolerant and patient with Hongming and always tried to help her as much as we could.

Following the final exams of the first year, the college wouldn't allow the students to return home but kept us on the campus to conduct the *Sufan yundong*, "Campaign to Eliminate Counterrevolutionaries." The origin of this campaign lay in a 300,000-character report written by the author Hu Feng* to Mao Zedong, demanding reform of the party's policy on literature and art. On reading it, Mao had thrown a fit, accused Hu Feng of counterrevolution, and arrested him along with some of his supporters.

This incident grew into a nationwide witch hunt for lurking counterrevolutionaries. I was appointed head of the *Sufan* group in our class. First, we studied the insidious document. But Hu Feng's language was obscure, and it was hard to pinpoint any obvious counterrevolutionary content. Instead, blinded by our boundless trust in the party and worship of Mao, we accepted unconditionally the chairman's opinion that Hu Feng was a dangerous heretic and felt sure there were traitors hiding in our midst.

Nevertheless, I had a nagging feeling the evidence against Hu Feng was insufficient. A strange bifurcation took place in my mind. While the party's directives continued to steer me, thoughts contradicting the party line lay suppressed at a deeper level together with old grievances, such as my antipathy toward the northern cadres, my anger at the sup-

---

*One of the few Chinese writers to openly criticize the hairsplitting, suffocating dogmatism of the party's leading cadres in the field of literature and art, Hu Feng (1902–1985) was incarcerated for twenty-five years. An account of his life, *F: Hu Feng's Prison Years*, written by his wife, Mei Zhi, and translated by Gregor Benton, was published in 2013.

pression of intraparty democracy, and the criticism I had been subjected to for requesting permission to study.

The second step was to ferret out the fifth columnist traitors. Because nobody was walking around with "counterrevolutionary" stamped on his forehead, this was a difficult job. Having screened all the students, we analyzed and examined those who appeared to have some kind of problem, Trotskyites and others, but were unable to agree. A tense atmosphere of mutual suspicion settled over our class. Wang Zongdong, the college's political commissar, convened a meeting for the *Sufan* group heads, where he criticized our inability to dig up any renegades and accused us of being Rightists.

This frightened me, because I knew that if I didn't produce a counterrevolutionary, I would have to bear the brunt of this political witch hunt myself. Finally, having discussed the matter nervously with the other members in my group, we decided to ferret out Bi Jicai. Although we had little evidence against him, he was constantly making cynical remarks and would have to suffice as a target for a round of criticism.

The news that Jicai had been identified as a counterrevolutionary had an unexpected, strange effect on our class. Even students who ordinarily had nothing to do with politics, such as Ximeng, stood up and denounced him fiercely. When Jicai refused to acknowledge any fault, some classmates got excited and started pushing him, and I had a hard time maintaining order. But after two days of struggling and failing to produce proof that Jicai was a counterrevolutionary, the students lost their indignation.

Once again, I could feel the heat. At this time, Gu Pu, my first girlfriend at the college, told me that the girl sleeping next to her, Yang Deying, was behaving secretively, hiding things in her suitcase. The image of this dull girl appeared before me. "Is she a thief?" I asked myself. At the next *Sufan* group meeting, I put forth this suspicion and told Gu Pu to go and look in Deying's suitcase. She returned with news that it was full of stolen goods: clothes, shoes, instruments, stethoscopes, gloves, makeup . . .

Confronted with the evidence, Deying was forced to confess. The students hated thieves more than anything and struggled with her fiercely for several days. This time, Ximeng was even more zealous, took every opportunity to be close to me, and even expressed a wish to join the Youth League.

She lived on Lintong Road, not far from my parents' house on Xi'an Road, and one day she suggested we walk home together. We talked a lot on the way. Her sincerity made me feel I had completely misjudged her, and I was struck with guilt. I told myself to stop looking at her through the prejudiced blinkers of class struggle and start treating her fairly.

At the time, I was having problems in my relationship with Gu Pu and was thinking of leaving her. Now, all of a sudden, Ximeng appeared by my side, warm, eager, and friendly. But I had no thought of falling in love with her. Her reputation as a bourgeois beauty and the daughter of a shamed capitalist was simply incompatible with my position as a Communist Party member.

After two weeks of fretting, the college leadership declared the *Sufan* campaign concluded, and the students were allowed to return home. Wang Zongdong, the political commissar who had been so insufferably bossy at the height of the campaign, vanished into thin air, without even giving a work report. Personally, the campaign had left a bad taste lingering in the mouth. Although I had caught a thief, I hadn't been able to uncover a single counterrevolutionary. In the process, I had subjected my old friend Bi Jicai to humiliation and could only feel remorse at these mistakes, committed under heavy political pressure.

Around this time, I went to the Huashan Hospital for a lung examination. The doctor told me I had a tubercular infiltration in the tip of my right lung and required complete rest. This was bad news for me, because if the tuberculosis couldn't be cured, the college might order me to terminate my studies or at the very least force me to take a year off. Because I was already older than my fellow students, I couldn't afford to delay my studies any further.

The doctor said that in order for me to be able to continue, the infiltration would have to be basically cured within three months. I was convinced the tuberculosis had returned because of my heavy work-load. While Gu Pu offered little sympathy, Ximeng gave me support and comfort. She herself had been cured of TB and felt sure I too would defeat the disease. I spent the summer in Kunshan convalescing under the care of my paternal grandmother and my younger sister, leaving my books and political work behind, and enjoying the countryside.

Returning to Shanghai at the end of August, I visited my college and walked straight into a struggle meeting against my fellow student Qiu Weiqin, who was standing in the middle of the lecture hall, surrounded by a mob of raving people. Apparently, Weiqin had been a member of the Army of the Virgin Mary, a supposedly counterrevolutionary organization set up by the recently arrested Catholic priest Gong Pinmei.* But Weiqin was stubborn and refused to reveal any information. In the end, not a single member of the Virgin Mary's Army was arrested at our college. A few of them immigrated to Canada, but most of them graduated, and as I write this, Weiqin is a chief physician in Shanghai.

On this occasion, I met Ximeng for the first time since the beginning of the summer. We were happy to see each other again. She told me the party had changed its attitude toward her in the six weeks that I'd been gone and had invited her to various activities and meetings. She said she was much happier than before. She had even begun to dream of being granted political equality. I was touched by her enthusiasm, felt a strong sympathy for her, and wanted to help her as much as I could. From that day on, we always walked home together, and our feelings grew deeper.

No matter how I pleaded, the doctor wouldn't allow me to return to college at the beginning of the fall semester. Instead, to give me one last chance of not losing a whole year, he issued a sick leave certificate for six weeks. If my illness showed signs of remission within this period,

---

*Ignatius Gong Pinmei (1901–2000) was the Roman Catholic bishop of Shanghai. Arrested in 1955 along with several hundred priests and church leaders, he spent thirty-one years in the Tilanqiao Prison. In 1979, Pope John Paul II named Gong Pinmei a cardinal *in pectore*—that is, secretly—in order to protect him and his congregation.

I could resume my studies; otherwise, I would have to wait until the following year. Miserable, I returned home to rest.

My parents gave me nutritious food and limited my reading. But the main reason for my quick recovery was Ximeng. During these six weeks, she came to my house several times. At her first visit in the middle of September, she wore a dark suit and was elegantly made up with her hair in the latest fashion. When Father brought her to my room, I could see how taken he was with her. Ximeng brought me sweets and the Swiss author Romain Rolland's book *Jean Christophe*, saying it would help me defeat the demons of my illness. She urged me to rest. I could feel her love for me and realized our relationship had gone beyond ordinary friendship.

After she left, I became agitated. I could not believe the feelings she expressed were simply a political calculation. I thought she had fallen in love with me, with my intelligence and open, adventurous character. I was completely taken with her beauty, gentleness, nobility, understanding, and good sense; I began harboring thoughts of making her my wife.

I realized that many obstacles lay before us. Her family background was a major problem. Not only had her father been a bigwig capitalist, but he was serving a fifteen-year probationary sentence. If I were to have a relationship with Ximeng, the party would surely consider this an act of disloyalty and criticize me for adopting a wrong position on class relations. During the land reform campaign, I had heard many stories about party members who had been prohibited from marrying girls from landlord families.

The biggest problem, however, was Ximeng's personal life. There were rumors she had a boyfriend studying in East Germany, and I recalled having seen her walking together with a short, ugly man in an intimate manner earlier that year. At the time, I hadn't known her very well and hadn't thought about it, but looking back, I realized this man was probably her boyfriend. I wanted to ask her but, because our relationship had just begun, thought it would be rude and kept silent.

In mid-October, an X-ray examination showed that my TB had

regressed, and the doctor allowed me to resume my studies. Overjoyed, I returned to the college. Having been absent for more than six weeks, I had lots of catching up to do. Once again, Ximeng helped me, gave me all her lecture notes to copy, and explained the knotty points. Her handwritten notes were small but neat and clear, and they saved me a lot of effort.

As the first-semester exams approached, I was still far behind and was forced to postpone my anatomy exam until after the winter break. Every day during the holidays, I went to the anatomy room to study the laid-out corpses, sometimes till late at night, the sharp smell of formalin burning my nose. Using a probe and a pair of tweezers, and struggling to overcome my discomfort, I identified blood vessels, nerves, and muscles. The night before my exam, I studied in the anatomy room until three o'clock in the morning. In the oral exam, I was able to identify all the twelve cranial nerves, answered every question correctly, and received the highest mark.

During a morning break at the end of February 1956, I opened the newspaper and drew a gasp of astonishment.* In a "secret speech" to a closed session of the Communist Party's Twentieth Congress, Khrushchev had denounced Stalin for his despotism, brutality, and abuse of power. Enraptured, I ignored the bell calling us back to class and continued reading until I had finished the article. Khrushchev's astonishing action had a profound effect on me. In a flash, I saw the similarity between Stalin and Mao, and in my mind the dream of reforming the Chinese Communist Party was born.

---

*The news of Khrushchev's "secret speech" was not immediately reported in the Chinese newspapers. Most probably, Xu Hongci is referring to the full-page article in the *People's Daily* titled "Why the Cult of Personality Violates the Spirit of Marxism-Leninism," but this article was not published until March 30, 1956.

6

Not of This World
(1956)

In Poland, Khrushchev's speech was reprinted and spread far beyond its intended audience, fanning the flames of anti-Soviet sentiment. On June 28, thousands of workers in the Stalin Locomotive Factory in the city of Poznan marched in protest, shouting, "Down with the Red bourgeoisie!" The Provincial Party Committee was sacked, and as the demonstration transformed itself into an insurrection, the authorities sent in four hundred tanks and ten thousand soldiers, leaving scores dead and hundreds seriously wounded.

Four months later, on October 22, five thousand students crammed into the main auditorium of the Budapest Technological University, where, following a heated debate, they adopted the Sixteen Points—the beginning of the Hungarian Uprising. That same night, Soviet tanks entered the city. On the streets of Budapest, men, women, and children battled the tanks with rifles and Molotov cocktails. After five days of fighting and political maneuvering, Imre Nagy, the new, reform-minded prime minister, announced a cease-fire. The Soviet troops began retreating, and for the next few euphoric days, the

Hungarian people allowed themselves to believe that they had van-
quished the Soviet Goliath and reclaimed their freedom.

On the evening of October 30, Khrushchev met with the Chinese
vice-premier, Liu Shaoqi, who had flown to Moscow at the Soviet
leadership's request to consult on the Polish and Hungarian uprisings.
Earlier in the day, Imre Nagy had announced the end of Hungary's
one-party system, reigniting the crisis. Liu Shaoqi relayed Mao's latest
opinion: the Soviet army should stay in Hungary. "I don't know how
many times we changed our minds back and forth," Khrushchev wrote
in his autobiography. "Every time we thought we'd made up our minds
what to do, Liu Shaoqi would consult with Mao Zedong. It was no
problem for Liu to get in touch with him on the telephone because
Mao is like an owl; he works all night long . . . We finished the all-
night session with a decision not to apply military force in Hungary."

The next morning, Khrushchev informed the Central Committee's
Presidium of his discussions with Liu. A heated argument ensued. If
Hungary was lost, what would happen in the other Eastern Euro-
pean satellites? The whole Communist bloc would unravel, and
the imperialists would be standing on Moscow's doorstep. Again, the
vacillating leadership swung in favor of military intervention. In the
early hours of November 4, the Red Army reentered Budapest with
devastating force—150,000 troops, 2,500 tanks, and air support—
launching savage attacks that transformed Budapest into a heap of
debris, firing into breadlines, and littering the streets with corpses.
The final death toll stood at twenty-five hundred.

In six months, Ximeng and I had grown inseparable, causing a lot of
talk at our college. By now, I knew for sure she had a boyfriend:
Bao Yougen, a graduate of the Dalian Marine College who was training at the Halle steam turbine factory in East Germany and expected
to return to China in 1958. The son of Sister Bao, Ximeng's wet
nurse, he had grown up with the Tang family and been educated at
their expense. Following liberation, as the Tang family's social standing

had dropped like a stone, the political status of Yougen, the child of a worker, had shot up in equal measure. This had emboldened him to court Ximeng, who had accepted his advances, while her parents tacitly acknowledged the relationship.

Ximeng was not a woman of easy virtue. She had fallen in love with me, and I with her. It was that simple. Now, with all the cards on the table, there was nothing she could say. All I could say was "Let's end this here."

At the time, she was busy organizing a student trip to Hangzhou for the spring break and was excited about the excursion. I told her I wouldn't go. I didn't want to see her more than necessary and cause even more gossip. She didn't cry and make a scene like other girls— Ximeng never cried—but I knew she was hurt. She pleaded with her eyes, hoping I would change my mind, but I steeled myself. Finally, she broke down and begged me to come along on the trip, agreeing to talk about everything after our return. My willpower evaporated. I could not live without her. Seeing her heartbroken expression, I agreed to join the excursion.

Most of our class went on the trip. We slept at Zhejiang University, strolled about, and saw all the famous sights of Hangzhou. To this day, I still remember the wonderful meal Derun, Meihua, Ximeng, Weiyu, and I shared at the Louwailou (House-Outside-the-House) Restaurant by the West Lake. Ximeng doted on me, happy as a child. Sometimes I walked with Er'ling and Weiyu, ignoring her on purpose, but instead of being angry, she just looked for the next opportunity to be close to me.

On our way back to Shanghai, I fell ill, probably because I had drunk too much cold water at the Running Tiger Spring. As soon as we had gotten on the train, my stomach began to ache, and the pain grew worse and worse. I felt so sick I rested my head in Ximeng's lap. She made no sign of opposition to this and braved the sharp glances of surprise. When our train arrived back in Shanghai at ten o'clock in the evening, Ximeng hailed a pedicab and took me home.

In that era of extreme puritanism, our open display of affection on the train caused a commotion on the college campus. Ximeng pretended not to hear the tattling and whispering and continued to walk with me as usual. Finally, Zhang Quanyi, the party branch secretary, unable to restrain his indignation, summoned me to his office and criticized me for my lack of Communist morality, having sunk so low as to be stealing my lover from another man.

Convinced that Ximeng really loved me, I disagreed with his rebukes. Angrily, Zhang Quanyi stormed off to see her, demanding she make a choice between Yougen and me. When Ximeng told him that she only loved me, he ordered her to write a letter to Yougen and formally end their relationship. After she had agreed to do this, he returned and informed me of their conversation.

"Ximeng and Yougen are not married, and their relationship has no legal standing. Now, because she has chosen you of her own free will, we will let this matter rest, and the party will not interfere anymore. But you must be mindful that she is not playing a double game."

Ximeng never wrote that letter to Yougen but kept corresponding with him as usual while keeping our relationship a secret from him. She was candid with me about this and said she was doing it in order not to hurt Yougen. And all the while, she grew bolder and more intimate, until I was unable to extricate myself.

On May 4, 1956, we had been to see a movie and were walking home late at night. By the time we reached Ximeng's house, it was already 11:00. She opened the front gate and walked into the dark, small gatekeeper's house. I followed her. We stood there in the pitch dark, holding each other tightly for a long time. From her rapid breathing, I knew she was waiting for me to kiss her. I mustered the courage and kissed her gently. Having waited in vain for more, she whispered, "Go away!"

People in love do not belong to this world. I remember once when a typhoon had struck Shanghai, flooding the campus. Ximeng had seen an ad for a new Soviet movie, *Gadfly*, playing at the Hengshan cinema and told me to buy tickets for the evening show.

"The streets are flooded. How are we supposed to get there?" I asked her.

"Who cares?" she replied.

So we walked hand in hand, splashing through the knee-deep water all the way to the Hengshan cinema. Another time, after a movie one Saturday night, we walked from Huai'an Middle Road to the Tilanqiao Bridge in the pouring rain, wild with happiness. As long as we were together, we could have walked until the next morning without being tired.

To mollify me, Ximeng showed me a few letters Yougen had written to her, together with photographs of him from East Germany, Poland, and the Soviet Union. I recognized the short, thirty-year-old man I had seen with her in the summer of 1955. Ximeng told me he insisted on writing to her every week, but since the beginning of our relationship she had replied only rarely, which had made him worried. In his letters, Yougen intimately called her Xixi, but the contents were plain, without excess of ardor. I was tolerant and didn't pressure Ximeng, confident that in the end she would be my wife.

Our classmates gossiped about our relationship with great interest, mainly because I was a Communist Party member and a top student while Ximeng was a beauty from the bourgeois class. Weng Fuping, the Youth League secretary at our college, thought I was doing a disservice to myself politically by falling in love with Ximeng. And the love triangle with Yougen added to the titillation.

One of the few who supported me was my old friend Zhuang Derun. He told me to ignore the gossip and walk my own path. I realized that the party might well lose faith in me, but because all I wanted was to graduate and become an assistant professor, I felt sure I would manage. As time passed and my relationship with Ximeng became steadier, the backbiting abated, and people accepted our love affair as a fait accompli.

Ximeng told me it would be hard for me to win her family over. In the early summer of 1956, on the occasion of her father's birthday, she invited me to her house for the first time and introduced me to her parents, brothers, and sisters. They lived in a three-story British-style villa at 49 Lintong Road near the Tilanqiao Bridge. Before liberation, they had occupied the whole house, but after Tang Hanzhong's heavy probationary sentence, the Asia Iron and Steel Factory's deputy director, Li, had taken over the third floor. Their living space reduced by one-third, the Tang family used the first floor as their drawing room, with all the bedrooms on the second floor.

Because it was my first visit to Ximeng's house, I didn't take part in the activities of her family and friends in the drawing room but retreated to her bedroom to chat with her. She was the oldest child, with two sisters and four handsome brothers who observed me suspiciously and made me feel embarrassed. Sensing my discomfort, Ximeng brought me a piece of cake and played the piano to make me relax. As I was walking down the staircase, I saw a dark, emaciated woman around fifty years old sitting in the small back room above the kitchen, glowering with hostility. My intuition told me this was Yougen's mother, Sister Bao, and my suspicion was soon confirmed.

Ximeng's father came from a wealthy family that had once owned half of Wusong, then a town just north of Shanghai. A bit more than fifty years old, he was a dignified, amiable iron and steel specialist who had studied in France for seven years, and then worked in the iron industry in England for another three, before returning to China and marrying Jin Ruifang. On the eve of the Communist takeover, he and his older brother had considered leaving for Taiwan, but in the end they hadn't been able to tear themselves away from their factory and had decided to stay on. According to Ximeng, they hadn't actually appropriated the Asia Iron and Steel Factory from the Japanese but had been given it by the KMT government. Tang Hanzhong's political problems had put the family in a difficult economic situation, and they were relying on the meager savings of his wife, Jin Ruifang, to maintain a household of ten people.

A painter, around forty years old, Ruifang looked very much like

Ximeng, except for her penetrating glance, which spoke of her intelligence and strong spirit, more martial than feminine. She was a capable woman who cooked, sewed, mended clothes, and kept the family's life in perfect order. Ximeng had inherited many of her mother's virtues: she knew how to be frugal and never wasted a penny. She seemed to have many new clothes, but in reality most of these were old garments that her mother had altered. Although we had lots of homework, Ximeng still found time to knit. Once, she told me she was knitting a sweater for Deputy Director Li's housemaid. The dramatic transformation of their circumstances had really changed everybody in the family, and none of them displayed the least bit of haughtiness.

One Sunday morning, I went to see Ximeng, who asked me to stay for lunch. She brought me to the library on the second floor, where lunch was served. On the table, there were only two bowls and two pairs of chopsticks, and Ximeng and I ate a rather plentiful meal. Later, I discovered that the rest of the family was eating a simple meal of thin rice gruel downstairs. This made a deep impression on me, and after that I seldom visited.

Feeling sorry for Ximeng and being in a better position economically, I liked spending some money to cheer her up. On Sunday evenings, I usually invited her to my house for dinner. Mother always prepared something special for her, and Ximeng appreciated the kindness. For the Chinese New Year of 1957, she made a large batch of sticky rice dumplings for Mother, to show her gratitude.

After I had visited Ximeng's family a few times, she finally told her parents about her feelings for me. Initially, unwilling to break their promise to the Bao family, they opposed our relationship. Gradually, however, seeing that we were inseparable and realizing there was nothing they could do, they accepted the new reality. But they didn't say anything to Yougen and avoided the matter until it forced itself upon them. Of course, Yougen's mother could see that I was her son's rival, but ultimately she was a servant in the family, had no influence over Ximeng, and could only nurse her hatred for me in private. This situation frightened me. The more I thought about the future, the more confused I felt. Sometimes, I had the feeling that as soon as Yougen returned to Shanghai and moved back into the Tang family's house, everything would be turned upside down.

At the beginning of August 1956, Father proposed that I travel to Yuci in Shanxi Province, some eight hundred miles northwest of Shanghai, to visit my younger brother, Hongnian. I also wanted to see Huang Xinbai and Lan Cheng, my old friend from the Communist underground, in Beijing. After saying goodbye to Ximeng, I boarded the train to Beijing and stayed with Lan Cheng in his dormitory at Qinghua University, before continuing to Yuci. But at Hengshui, 170 miles south of Beijing, a mountain torrent had washed away the railway bridge, and after waiting for two days and two nights, I was forced to return to the capital.

My classmate Jiang Weiyu was spending the summer in Beijing. Zhuang Derun also joined up, and together we visited all the famous sites. Lan Cheng and I talked about many new things, of which I remember two. First, he said that China should be governed by people with education and knowledge and that ultimately the Communist Party must relinquish power and become a looser political organization along the lines of the League of Communists of Yugoslavia.* Second, he said that while history had seen democratic revolutions by the bourgeoisie, it was now up to the proletariat to conduct a democratic revolution and allow competing political parties.

Although 1956 was the Communist Party's golden year, there were many such different political opinions circulating in the capital. We

---

*Under the leadership of Josip Tito (1892–1980), the Communist Party of Yugoslavia departed from the Soviet model by allowing self-management of workers in state-run enterprises and decentralizing political power, changing its name to the League of Communists of Yugoslavia to mark this shift.

talked about various absurd phenomena caused by the slavish adoption of Soviet-style university education; Khrushchev's secret speech; the similarities between Stalin and Mao Zedong; and the dubious case against Hu Feng that had triggered the Campaign to Eliminate Counterrevolutionaries in 1955. At the time, Lan Cheng, not yet admitted to the party,* wasn't subject to its disciplinary control, and the wings of his thinking were spread wider than mine. His opinions both fascinated and scared me. I felt that he was unusual but also that he put himself at great risk.

Being interested in Khrushchev's secret speech, I searched in vain for English-language newspapers to read about it. On the question of the party's leadership, remembering my experiences with the northern cadres, I completely agreed with Lan Cheng. With these uneducated people in charge, the party would never be able to modernize China. The country must be led by people with knowledge, and the proletariat would have to democratize its way of doing politics. My conversations with Lan Cheng awakened some ideas that had lain buried in my subconscious, but I was still under the control of mainstream political thinking and didn't dare to adopt all his opinions.

As Lan Cheng was seeing me off at the train station, I suddenly remembered some of the things we had spoken about and felt a bad taste in my mouth.

"Yugoslavia is taking the road of Martov's[†] revisionism, which Lenin criticized. You should be vigilant," I warned him.

---

*In 1948, Lan Cheng had gone to the liberated area in northern Jiangsu Province without permission from the underground organization and, lacking documents and contacts, had been arrested as an enemy agent. Huang Xinbai had gotten him out of jail, but Lan Cheng was still awaiting his formal induction to the party.

†Julius Martov (1873–1923) was a Russian revolutionary and for several years a close associate of Lenin. The two fell out at the second congress of the Russian Social Democratic Party, in 1903, whereupon Martov became a leader of the Menshevik faction, the liberal wing of the Russian socialist movement. Following the 1917 October Revolution, Martov walked out of the first meeting of the Council of Soviets in disgust at how the Bolsheviks had seized power, uttering the parting words "One day you will understand the crime you are taking part in."

"Yes . . . you're right . . . you're right," Lan Cheng replied haltingly, stunned by this warning out of the blue.

We said goodbye, not knowing that only one year later we would both be branded Rightists. I will always remember the discussions I had with Lan Cheng in Beijing, because they determined the rest of my life.

That fall, we began our junior year at the medical college, where all the students had been reorganized to accommodate the new Department of Pediatrics. I was in the same class as Ximeng, remained a member of the party branch, and lived in a dormitory room with thirteen other students. The new arrangements broke up the unity and good atmosphere of our old class, and it became harder to organize common activities.

This new setting dampened our enthusiasm and zeal, and as our social activities declined, Ximeng and I immersed ourselves deeper and deeper in love. We sat together in class, did our laboratory experiments together, studied together in the evenings, walked home together on Saturday afternoons, walked back to the college together every Sunday night, and saw at least one movie or play every week.

Gradually, Ximeng's parents became friendlier toward me. One night, they invited me to dinner, making a delicious soup with the mushrooms I had brought back for them from Beijing. I really enjoyed Jin Ruifang's cooking. After that, I no longer felt uncomfortable in their house and was even able to talk about family affairs with Tang Hanzhong. Encouraged by Ximeng, her younger sisters and brothers also became closer to me.

Two major events took place in October 1956. First, following Nasser's nationalization of the Suez Canal, Great Britain, France, and Israel attacked Egypt. Then the Hungarian Uprising took place. At the time, the Chinese people were strongly opposed to the attack on Egypt by Britain and France, and there were rumors of a volunteer army being organized to assist the Egyptians. I too was agitated and ready to join up, but following the intervention of the United States and the Soviet Union, things there quieted down rather quickly.

The Hungarian Uprising, on the other hand, made a deep, lasting impression on everybody. Due to the blinkered, selective nature of our country's news media, I could never get a clear idea of what was happening; nevertheless, it was obvious that the Hungarian dictator, Mátyás Rákosi, had committed grave errors, that the Hungarian people had risen to overthrow him, and that the Soviet Union had sent in its troops to brutally put down the revolt.

I admired Tito's speech at Pula, in which he condemned the Soviet Union and expressed his sympathy with the Hungarian people. In discussions with my classmates, I spoke of my dissatisfaction with the Soviet Union, and because the two events above took place at virtually the same time, people with sinister motives intentionally garbled my words, accusing me of having said, "If there is a Hungarian Uprising in China, I will be the first one to join it"—one of the false accusations leveled against me during the Anti-Rightist Campaign.

All told, 1956 was the best year since liberation. Not only was there peace and a measure of prosperity, but I was allowed to experience love. This happiness, however, proved short-lived—a mere prelude to unending, unmitigated disaster.

7

A Breath of Fresh Air

(1957)

Haunted by the specter of the Hungarian Uprising, Mao took to his bed, where he stayed for the next three months preparing a speech, "On the Correct Handling of Contradictions Among the People," to prove himself the greatest living Marxist theoretician and leader of the Communist world. The gist of the speech, delivered on February 27, 1957, before a closed session of China's Supreme Council, was a distinction between two different conflicts: "among the people" and "between us and the enemy." The success of the revolution depended on the party's ability to handle the two types accordingly. Hungary had erred by eliminating too few counter-revolutionaries. Stalin had treated all critics as enemies.

"Have we killed people we shouldn't have killed?" Mao asked his comrades. "Yes, at the time of the great Campaign to Suppress Counterrevolutionary Activities in 1950, 1951, 1952 . . . But basically there were no errors; that group of people should have been killed. How many did we kill? Seven hundred thousand were killed, and after that time probably over seventy thousand more have been killed. But fewer than eighty thousand. Since last year, basically we have not killed people; only a small number of individuals have been killed."*

Once again he reiterated his call to "let a hundred flowers bloom and a hundred schools of thought contend" and promised "long-term coexistence" with the eight democratic party factions. Delivered in the style of a soapbox orator, sprinkled with humorous asides, the speech was a tour de force, Mao at his political best. "I do not remember a moment in my life more exhilarating than when Mao Zedong's February 1957 speech to the State Council was released," wrote China's most prominent journalist of the period, Liu Binyan, who subsequently spent sixteen years in the labor camps.

On April 30, the Rectification Campaign, intended to demonstrate Mao's skill in handling conflicts among the people and avert a Hungarian Uprising, was officially launched. By then, China's intelligentsia had been cajoled by the state-controlled media's steady barrage of calls to speak up. Debate forums were convened in the major cities, and non-Communists were invited to state their opinions on national affairs, provide criticism, and discuss any topic of their choosing. "Many leaders of the Communist Party consider themselves to be the truth incarnate," Ma Zhemin, a leader of the Democratic League from Hubei Province, told a forum at Beijing University. Much of the criticism focused on the poor relations between the Communist Party and the people. Other speakers condemned the party's brutal methods during the recent Campaign to Eliminate Counterrevolutionaries.

It was the tip of an iceberg, and no sooner had Mao let the genie out of the bottle than his miscalculation became apparent: instead of defusing a Hungarian Uprising, he had started one. On the evening of May 14, he met with the Politburo to discuss the unfolding Rectification Campaign. "For the moment, we shall not refute the erroneous criticism of the nonparty people, especially the opinions

---

*Mao Zhuxi wenxian sanshi pian (Thirty articles by Chairman Mao) (Propaganda Department of the Beijing Special Steel Factory, 1967), 97.

of the Rightists, but let them speak their minds freely," Mao told the other leaders. While the subsequent Anti-Rightist Campaign was not his bloodiest in the sheer number of executions, the treachery embedded in these words has ensured its infamy in Chinese history.

On June 8, Mao sprang his trap. Overnight, on the cue of one editorial, "What Is This?," published in the *People's Daily*, the Rectification Campaign was transmogrified into the Anti-Rightist Campaign—a nationwide witch hunt to punish those who had spoken up on Mao's insistent behest and to smoke out any hidden resistance to his dictatorship. Debate forums became struggle meetings, where the men and women who had answered Mao's call were now treated to the iron fist of the people's "democratic dictatorship." One of them was Xu Hongci.

O n the Western New Year's Eve, the Youth League and the Student Union organized a big party, with an appearance by the traditional Russian Santa Claus, Ded Moroz, and his Snow Maiden, Snegurochka, as the main attraction. Invited to play the part of Snegurochka, Ximeng had spent a lot of time preparing for her role.

There were many dance parties in progress, and the atmosphere was buzzing with excitement. But without Ximeng, I felt a strange loneliness. As midnight approached, I hurried to the main assembly hall to wait for her appearance. Everybody wanted to see Ded Moroz and his Snegurochka, and in the crush of people I was pushed to the side.

Entering the hall at the stroke of twelve, Ded Moroz and his Snegurochka were engulfed by the crowd. From a distance, I caught sight of Ximeng, dressed in white, beautiful as an angel. Everybody clapped and cheered wildly. My eyes filled with tears. I was proud of Ximeng and happy that she was mine.

After Santa Claus had finished throwing presents to the crowd, he and his Snow Maiden concluded their festive circumambulation, and everybody returned to the dance parties. Ximeng was in an ecstatic mood, dancing without rest. She and Derun danced a fast waltz.

I wanted to dance with her too, but all the men were jostling to invite her, and I wasn't able to catch her attention.

My classmate Chen Jiuru was particularly entranced by her. On this evening, Ximeng's appearance as Snegurochka had made him lose his head completely. Casting aside his girlfriend, Li Lifen, a plump, earnest girl, and ignoring my presence, he refused to let go of Ximeng.

It was already past one o'clock in the morning. Seeing that Ximeng was not taking any note of me, and feeling very low, I stood up and walked out to get some fresh air, then headed toward our class activity room, where the dance party was petering out. Qin Junyu must have noticed my moodiness and reminded Ximeng not to forget me, because just as I was about to leave, the two of them came looking for me. Both Ximeng and I were reticent. We danced one dance, then went for a short walk before returning to our dormitories. This was our first little friction since falling in love. I didn't know what Ximeng was thinking, and I felt a bit lost.

The third-year course work was stimulating, especially the subject of pathological anatomy. As soon as a corpse arrived at the college, everybody crowded into the small anatomy theater to watch our professor perform the dissection. I learned as much from one dissection as I would have from reading ten books, and to this day I clearly remember some of the cases we studied.

Pathological physiology was also very interesting. Our lecturer, Zhou Huanwen, was a sharp, unconventional thinker. Later, he was transferred to the Chongqing Medical College, where he committed suicide during the Cultural Revolution. Several other top scientists at the Shanghai No. 1 Medical College, such as Professor Jia Gujing, a specialist in pathological anatomy, Professor Zhang Changshao, an authority in neurological pharmacology, and Professor Hu Zhekui, an anatomist, all ended their own lives during those cataclysmic years.

To my consternation, after a trip we made to Nanjing during the Chinese New Year of 1957, Ximeng's attitude toward me began to change. She said Yougen would be returning in the coming year and that her parents, Yougen's mother, and her relatives and friends were all pressuring her to maintain her relationship with him. Seeing that she was on the verge of going back to Yougen, I scolded her, "You knew this day would come! Why did we even start?!"

We quarreled. She accused me of being insensitive and rude. To avoid an outright fight, I wrote a long, emotional letter to her, which must have touched her, because she became friendly with me again. At the time, both of us were afraid that we would be criticized if our quarrel became public, and we therefore made an effort to keep up appearances, walking, eating, and studying together as usual. Nor did I report the matter to the party branch secretary or tell my parents. I didn't want the party to interfere, and I wanted Ximeng to have some breathing space when she visited my house.

I couldn't understand women. On the one hand, Ximeng had raised the matter of Yougen again. At the same time, she was drawing closer to me than ever before. I only talked about my love problems with my two best friends, Derun and Xu Xueren. One Saturday night, we went for a meal at a restaurant on Huaihai Road. Derun, who was bitter about his own breakup with Liu Meihua some time before, angrily admonished me to make a clean break from Ximeng. Xueren was a bit calmer and told me to wait and see.

On June 3, 1957, Ximeng and I walked back to the college from our homes and went straight to my laboratory to study. We were the only people in the whole building. We studied and talked about our relationship.

"Whatever happens, I can't live without your feelings for me," Ximeng said.

We held each other tightly. That night, there in the laboratory, we made love and did not return to our dormitories until the small hours.

The next day, we went together to the College of Orthopedics for our practice as interns, accompanying our instructor on his round of the wards. Ximeng stayed close to me, looking at me shyly. I couldn't take my eyes off her. Every glance sent a current of joy through our bodies. Feeling her breath and the warmth of her body, I didn't hear a word the instructor said.

"Will we ever be separated again?" I asked her on our way back to the dormitory.

She shook her head.

By the time Mao's latest political move, the *zhengfeng*, "rectification," campaign, had been under way for almost a month, I read in our college newspaper that the party committee was organizing debates among the democratic party factions and calling on intellectuals to speak their minds. On June 5, after a lecture at the Sun Yat-sen Hospital, Zhang Quanyi, the party branch secretary, asked all party members to remain, to give us the latest news on the campaign.

"The *mingfang*, 'airing of views,' has begun with great vigor at the universities in Beijing, and the masses have put forth many opinions to the party. Some of these views are very incisive and have touched upon the question of our political system. A female student in the Department of Law at the Chinese People's University, Lin Xiling,* has become the students' leader and is criticizing the *zhengfeng* campaign in Shanghai for being tepid and lifeless. In the next few days, she will be leading a group to Shanghai to launch the *mingfang* here and may very well visit our college. The party committee is calling on everybody to make the necessary ideological preparations," he said.

"We are completely capable of mobilizing the masses. There is no need for her to come here," I replied.

Actually, the situation in Beijing at the time was complicated: having opened the genie's bottle, the party had found itself unable to contain the "airing of views." To stop the wildfire from spreading to Shanghai, it had therefore disseminated information to party members here with the purpose of indirectly persuading us to suppress the movement. But I completely misread the situation.

"The party committee has not issued a unified directive. Everybody

---

*Lin Xiling (1935–2009) was a student leader during the spring of 1957 and spent fifteen years in the labor camps before her release on Mao's personal order in 1973. She lived in France from 1983 until her death. Her biography, *Lin Xiling, l'indomptable*, written by the French sinologist Marie Holzman, was published by Bayard in 1998.

should decide for themselves how to act," Quanyi said, and ended the meeting.

That evening at six o'clock, Wang Lesan, the third party secretary at the college, convened all party members and Youth League cadres at the college for a meeting in the main auditorium, where he explained the Beijing university students' participation in the *zhengfeng* campaign, praising their zeal in speaking their minds. By contrast, he said, we had not even managed to post a single *dazibao*.*

"Tomorrow, I want to see your *dazibao*!" he said.

After the meeting, I met Ximeng to prepare for our exams but couldn't concentrate on my studies. A sense of duty was compelling me to make a clean breast of the ideas, thoughts, and opinions I had been mulling and formulating for a long time.

At nine o'clock, I returned to my dormitory. A large group of people were gathered around our fellow student Chen Minwen, who was reading the Nanjing University student newspaper out loud. I grabbed a copy. The first-page news was all about the *zhengfeng* campaign and carried the texts of several *dazibao*. Having just heard Wang Lesan's call to action, I told everybody, "The party committee is waiting to see our *dazibao*! Now is the opportunity! Let's start right now!"

A lively debate erupted. As Zhou Qinzong took notes, we let a "hundred ideas contend" until one o'clock in the morning and then condensed our thoughts into a *dazibao* containing fifty-one articles. Reading it, I felt satisfied, convinced our poster would please the party committee.

On June 6, we didn't have morning classes and used the time to find a writing brush, an ink stick, an ink stone, and paper. As the best calligrapher among us, Qinzong was chosen to write out the *dazibao*. In our introduction, we pointedly referred to the Youth League cadre Weng Fuping, because she had stated that "the airing of views" among

---

*Translated as "big character poster," *dazibao* were an important medium of communication during the Maoist years. They were written with a Chinese brush on any large sheet of paper available, often old newspapers, and pasted on boards and walls in every workplace and school in the country.

students was not a problem. Proudly, Qinzong dashed off the poster in the blink of an eye.

Before mid-morning, we had posted our *dazibao* on the blackboard opposite the H-building, where many students and teachers passed every day, and very soon people began to gather around it. (Although our *dazibao* had the title "Fifty-One Articles," it actually contained only fifty, because in his rush, Qinzong had forgotten to copy Article 23.)* Among the articles, we criticized the Communist Party's "general elections" as fake and undemocratic. Denouncing these farcical single-candidate "elections," we demanded that candidates be nominated by the people, give election speeches, and conduct election activities. We also criticized Mao Zedong for his secretive inspection tours, saying that he should meet with the people. We attacked China's slavish attachment to the Soviet Union, and we proposed that students be allowed to choose their own foreign language.

After posting our *dazibao*, we went to the main auditorium to attend a lecture. I sat by a window overlooking the blackboard, watching the crowd swell around it, feeling pleased. What made me even more excited was that so many other people were putting up their own, freshly written *dazibao*, until they covered the entire length of the sixty-foot blackboard. The deluge of *dazibao* continued to grow, spreading to every wall on the campus. "Haven't we breathed some life into this dead old college?" I thought. Ximeng smiled too.

When the bell rang, the party branch secretary asked all party members to remain seated. Smelling trouble, Qinzong quickly snuck up to the next floor and found a corner to eavesdrop on the meeting.

"Who told you to put up the *dazibao*? Who gave you the permission?" Zhang Quanyi questioned me angrily. "Look! In less than two hours, more than twenty *dazibao* have been posted. The party committee had made careful plans for the *zhengfeng* campaign. You have upset them completely and will be held responsible for this!"

---

*See Appendix 1: "A Foul Wind in the Department of Medicine," p. 289.

"You heard Wang Lesan's report last night," I responded. "He called on us to take the lead in posting *dazibao*. I've merely answered his summons. Why haven't you done that? Where is your *dazibao*? The party has told us to speak up. Who else do I need permission from? You? Why are you afraid? Let people put up a hundred *dazibao*. What's wrong with that? The more, the better."

We were both flushed with anger. After we quarreled for about fifteen minutes, Quanyi, realizing that I wouldn't blink, waved his hand and told everybody to go and eat.

Having heard everything from his hiding place, Qinzong told the others about my argument with Zhang Quanyi. This frightened Yu Meiqi, who immediately posted a *dazibao* declaring that she was withdrawing her name from our *dazibao*. Qinzong also wanted to pull out but, having taken the notes, written the draft, and penned the final version, was in too deep and could only brace himself for the coming storm.

That same afternoon, I attacked Zhang Quanyi in a *dazibao* titled "Sincere Advice." Throughout the afternoon, more and more *dazibao* were posted, covering the sports field's perimeter wall. Lei Mou, an introverted lecturer in the Department of Public Health, hung a huge twenty-seven-article *dazibao* from the H-building's second floor that attracted a lot of attention. Cadres from the party committee were dispatched to take photographs of the *dazibao*, and as soon as a new one was posted, people rushed over to copy it by hand. Even Chen Tongsheng, the college president, showed up.

"You must boldly put forth your opinions to the party. There will be no retribution," he assured everybody.

The scene made me both happy and uneasy. Recalling Zhang Quanyi's words, I had a feeling he was being directed by powerful forces from behind the scenes. I sensed a conspiracy and that I, excluded from the inner circle, had foolishly and blindly fallen straight into their trap.

I tried to speak with Ximeng about my misgivings, but she had never experienced anything like this before and, lost in the excitement, didn't understand what I was trying to say. Although the whole campus was buzzing with an electrified atmosphere, I felt very, very lonely. June 6, 1957, was the longest day of my life. In truth, it would last twenty years.

The next morning, confused and agitated, I didn't go to class but sat alone in the library turning matters over in my mind. The more I thought about it, the more convinced I became that a secret plan lay buried beneath this unprecedented invitation to speak our minds. But I wasn't about to capitulate and steeled myself to continue the fight.

At around 9:00 a.m., I walked into the party committee's office, where Li Jingyi, the fourth party committee secretary, received me. She was about the same age as Mother and even resembled her. During the party committee elections, I had seen her curriculum vitae and knew she had become a party member in 1933, the year I was born.

"The party committee urged us to put up *dazibao*. Why then is Zhang Quanyi criticizing our actions? I want you to decide: Am I wrong, or is he?" I said.

"We haven't advocated posting *dazibao*. *Dazibao* are only a medium, and the medium is secondary. The contents are what matters. When you posted your *dazibao*, you should have considered its contents," Li Jingyi said slowly in her heavy Anhui accent.

"This is not what Wang Lesan said. He told us to take the lead in posting *dazibao*. The party committee is not in agreement. Who should we listen to?" I replied.

Li Jingyi stubbornly clung to her position, repeating the same few sentences again and again. In despair, I took leave of her.

After lunch, I spoke with Ximeng and decided to convene the party members in our class. All of them attended the meeting. I explained the differences between me and Zhang Quanyi and told them about my conversation with Li Jingyi. At this time, I was still respected among the students, and most of them supported me. We decided to ask Li Jingyi to come to our class the next afternoon to explain the party's policies and also invited representatives from the democratic party factions: Professor Zhuang Mingshan from the China Democratic League, Professor Fan Rixin from the Chinese Peasants' and Workers' Democratic Party, and Assistant Professor Ye Ying from the September 3 Society.*

That afternoon, Guo Xueqin, a new party member in our class, put up a *dazibao* criticizing our fifty-one articles. I could feel the heat from all directions. I knew many people were holding their fingers up in the air, waiting to see which way the wind would blow. Clearly, Xueqin had posted his *dazibao* on the instigation of Zhang Quanyi.

On the afternoon of June 8, the meeting was held in a small classroom. All sixty students in our class were there. Li Jingyi did not attend but sent Xiao Shuying, head of the party committee's propaganda unit, to act on her behalf. After I had once again described the events leading to the posting of our *dazibao* and explained the conflict with Zhang Quanyi and Li Jingyi, everybody turned his attention to Xiao Shuying, waiting for her to explain the party committee's position. About thirty years old, smart, pretty, and a bit plump, she was dressed in a Lenin uniform and looked serious.

"Today, Party Secretary Li has other matters to attend to, and I will answer your questions in the name of the party committee," she said, speaking slowly and deliberately. "This *zhengfeng* campaign was launched and is being led by the party, and the party welcomes everybody's opinions. You can rest assured that there will be no suppression of any kind. You may put forth your opinions to the party in any manner, whether in forum debates, essays, or *dazibao* . . ."

She spoke smoothly and evasively, leaving no room for criticism. Everybody, including me, applauded loudly. By forcing the party committee to explain itself, I felt we had won a big victory. What I didn't realize was that it was merely a strategic move by the party committee.

That same evening, throwing caution to the wind, we met in the biology lab to conduct a *mingfang*, venting the thoughts and feelings we had kept buried in our hearts and minds for a long time. We criticized

---

*The name refers to the date of Japan's capitulation to China in World War II.

the party's unjust classification of students according to its method of class analysis as "progressive, moderate, and backward." Chen Minwen delivered a firebrand speech. Huang Shengxue confessed that he had been a puppet for the regime and had betrayed our trust. Shen Junwen protested the unfair treatment of Christians. Niu Zhikui's speech was most unforgettable. With tears streaming down his cheeks, he accused the party of blowing the Campaign to Eliminate Counterrevolutionaries way out of proportion, driving one of his old classmates to his death.

There were fifth columnists among us, such as Li Changchun and Guo Xueqin, who wrote down our speeches and later used this evidence to incriminate us. The number of people this meeting destroyed! Of the sixty students in our class, thirteen would be branded as Rightists. Huang Shengxue would be expelled from the Youth League and dismissed as a delegate to the National People's Congress. Niu Zhikui would be branded as a counterrevolutionary, arrested, brought to court, and sentenced to ten years' imprisonment. And more.

On the morning of June 9, the party committee launched its counterattack by posting a *dazibao* to expose my dirty laundry, falsely signing the poster in the name of all the students in our class. It was the Communist Party's old trick: isolate your enemy through a smear campaign and gradually diminish his influence. Worst of all, they described my relationship with Ximeng as "a repulsive ménage à trois that debases Communist morality."

My classmates began to look at me with suspicious, doubtful glances and at Ximeng with contempt. She became depressed and distracted, obsessing over her love life and future instead of focusing on her studies. When Mao Zedong's article "The Bourgeois Direction of the *Wenhui Daily* Must Be Criticized"* was published, she knew for sure that I was finished.

At the beginning of July, on the instigation of her parents, she asked

---

*This article was published on the front page of the *People's Daily* on July 1, 1957. The *Wenhui Daily*, together with the *Guangming Daily*, enjoyed a certain amount of autonomy and published many critical articles during the six weeks of "airing of views." The two papers' editors were subsequently purged.

me to formally end our relationship. From the eavesdropping Qinzong, I had learned that Chen Tongsheng, the college president, had declared me a "traitor to the party." Realizing the severity of my situation, and to reduce Ximeng's suffering, I agreed to her request.

Nevertheless, she was still in love with me and despite our official separation continued to accompany me as if nothing had changed.

"Father says that you are about to be denounced and that the *zhengfeng* campaign is a conspiracy. His factory has repeatedly urged him to put forth his opinions to the party, but he has bitten his tongue and said nothing. Otherwise, he would suffer the same fate as you."

"I haven't done anything wrong!" I replied angrily. "In three hundred years, history will tell who was right, me or Mao Zedong. I haven't let the party down, I haven't let our country down, and I haven't let you down!"

Beset by all these worries, Ximeng and I did poorly in our exams. Zhou Huanwen, our lecturer in pathological physiology, had always liked me, but now, under the influence of the smear campaign, his attitude changed completely. He gave me a low grade, seemingly determined to ruin my perfect record. Ximeng and I needed each other more than ever and clung to the hope that the moment of our final parting would never arrive. But having lost the support of the party, I realized that soon she would also be separating herself from me.

Examining my participation in the revolution, I felt I had always been fighting for the truth. During the *zhengfeng* campaign, it was I who had given people the courage to speak up. Now the party I worshipped had branded me a traitor. Nevertheless, I still considered myself a Communist. My head boiled with plans and romantic notions. Recalling Lenin's words "The working class has no motherland," I decided that I must leave China, to continue the revolution abroad.

On July 6, after our final exam, Li Changchun informed me that a party branch meeting would be held the following day to discuss my serious mistakes during the *zhengfeng* campaign and ordered me to attend.

I walked home with Ximeng as usual. "The meeting tomorrow

bodes ill," I told her. "I may be expelled from the party, and we may not be able to see each other very often."

Ximeng was mute with grief. It was the last time we saw each other alone.

The party branch meeting was a *douzhenghui*, a "struggle meeting," pure and simple. As I entered the hall, a sea of eyes glistening with hatred fastened upon me. I could feel murder in the air. The look on Zhang Quanyi's face was particularly chilling. Having opened the meeting, he shouted, "Stand up and make a self-criticism!"

The gravity of the situation only redoubled my courage: "I was carrying out the directives of Third Party Secretary Wang Lesan! It was a correct decision to mobilize the masses to post *dazibao* . . ."

Even before I had finished, people started screaming at me. Zhang Quanyi then read a resolution prepared by the party branch, enumerating my errors. First, I had incited the masses to post *dazibao* and ruined the party committee's plans for the Rectification Campaign. Second, our fifty-one-article *dazibao* was an ultra-reactionary, crazy attack on the Communist Party, socialism, and Marxism-Leninism and opposed the Soviet Union and toadied to U.S. imperialism. Third, I had liaised with reactionary elements among the democratic party factions and engaged in clandestine activities. Fourth, I had mobilized the unknowing masses to oppose the party committee.

"Xu Hongci is a traitor to the party and must be expelled!" he concluded.

In the following "vote," every party member present raised his or her hand in favor of my expulsion.

"I will appeal to the municipal party committee's disciplinary commission," I said, holding up my hand in protest.

"You can appeal as much as you like, all the way to the Central Committee in Beijing," Zhang Quanyi replied viciously.

That same evening, I was required to attend yet another, larger *douzhenghui*. This time, I was neither afraid nor angry, and simply described the course of events.

"I have done nothing wrong," I said. "I am not opposed to the party or socialism. On the contrary, I have made a contribution to the *zheng-feng* campaign."

In an instant, the jeering and booing exploded. I didn't say anything more but stepped down from the podium and returned to my seat. One by one, my fellow party members took to the stage, vying with one another to denounce me. Finally, Li Jingyi, representing the party committee, declared that it had accepted the party branch's resolution and announced my formal expulsion from the Communist Party.

As soon as her voice had fallen silent, the whole auditorium screamed at me, "*Get out of here!*"

I stood up and, without looking back, hurried down the stairs, out through the college gates, returning home on the number nine bus. Mother and Father were waiting for me in the living room. I told them I had been expelled from the party. It seemed they had already guessed, because they showed no shock. We sat in silence for a long time, battling the confusion in our hearts. I knew my parents were very worried.

Finally, Father spoke: "During the *mingfang*, I thought about advising you not to say too much, but I was too late. You are in trouble now. Your expulsion shows they have decided to make an example of you. You will have to attend even more *douzhenghui*, and you must prepare yourself for this."

"What does Ximeng think?" Mother asked.

"It is all over," I replied.

Mother was angry with Ximeng and criticized me. "You've spent too much money on her," she said.

"What does money matter now?" I thought bitterly.

We sat silent some more, then talked some more, searching for a sliver of light. Our last hope was that I at least be allowed to continue my studies and graduate.

I lay sleepless through the night as thoughts and feelings raced through my head. For the first time, I felt I understood Father. Although he had only said a few simple things about the calamity I was facing, they fully expressed his love for me. He didn't castigate me or try to comfort me with empty platitudes. He simply told me to face reality and gave me the courage to carry on. I scolded myself for ever having belittled him. If I had spent more time with him, talked with him, and listened to his advice, things might not have come to this.

8

Rip Him to Pieces

(July 1957–April 1958)

With the country's future leader Deng Xiaoping in charge of its execution, the Anti-Rightist Campaign gathered steam throughout the fall of 1957 and the following spring. All over China, schools and workplaces were ordered to ferret out the Rightists and given percentage quotas to fulfill at any cost. Officially, 550,000 men and women were branded Rightists in 1957–1958, but some historians put the number as high as 3 million. Rightists were subjected to struggle meetings, denounced by colleagues and classmates, ordered to write self-criticisms, repudiated by their spouses, and fired from their jobs. Many were sent to do menial labor or packed off to a labor camp in some distant corner of the empire, where, if they survived, they would spend the next twenty years.

On July 16, I was the target of yet another, even larger *douzhenghui*, held in the medical college's new auditorium, with room for some three thousand people. Arriving punctually at 9:00 a.m., I was seated in the third row to the left. Chen Tongsheng, the college's president and party secretary, sat in the second row in the middle section. I saw Ximeng sitting nearby. She looked grave, kept her head down, and did not speak.

Wang Lesan opened the denunciation meeting, reiterated my crimes, and told me to make a self-criticism. I walked up to the podium, placed my notes on the table, and retold the course of events from my point of view. Because I showed no sign of guilt or remorse, the assembly grew agitated. Students began arguing with one another, and soon more than a hundred notes had been placed on the table in front of me. Responding to the students' questions in turn, I transformed my "self-criticism" into a rambling speech as the party committee leaders, unable to stop me, stared at each other.

I looked at my watch. Forty-five minutes had passed. I gathered the notes on the table, declared my self-criticism concluded, and stepped down from the podium. Wang Lesan called on the participants to expose me. Many people were eager to speak. I had already guessed Ximeng would be one of them, and knew the party committee had been busy brainwashing her, convincing her that I was a bad person, that I had fooled her, and that her only hope lay in separating herself from me once and for all. But I could never have imagined she would disown me so callously.

Exposing my innermost thoughts, she revealed the most incriminating, counterrevolutionary sentence I had ever uttered: "I haven't done anything wrong! In three hundred years, history will tell who was right, me or Mao Zedong." At the time, Mao was God, and to challenge him was to dig your own grave. Ximeng's betrayal broke my heart. The woman I loved faded away, transformed into the grim reaper, capable of anything, even killing me.

After the meeting, a special publication with articles criticizing me was distributed to every student. Most of them were vicious personal attacks laced with ludicrous exaggerations and sheer fabrications. According to one, I was a whoremaster who had been engaging in sexual relations with six female classmates during the same period. The descriptions of my relationship with Ximeng were even more disgusting.

Most serious, however, were the political defamations, all concocted out of thin air: my counterrevolutionary organization had cells over the whole country, as well as abroad; I had been planning to leave the Communist Party in order to become a member of the U.S. Democratic Party; in 1956, I had said, "If there is a Hungarian Uprising in China, I will be the first to join." Reading this hogwash, I realized that the articles criticizing Rightists published daily on page after page of the major newspapers were nothing but lies. To smear a person, the Communist Party and the newspaper editors seemed capable of any and every shameless act.

On July 23, *Liberation Daily* and *Youth Daily* both published articles attacking me. The headline on the second page of *Liberation Daily* ran, "A Rightist Pawn Attacks the Party. Xu Hongci's Shameful Betrayal of the Party." *Youth Daily* called me "a traitor to the party who happily kneels at the feet of Rightists," while *Liberation Daily* repeated the claim that I was planning to defect to the United States and join the Democratic Party* and that I was trying to foment a revolt in China modeled on the Hungarian Uprising. Because *Liberation Daily* was a prestigious national newspaper, people believed every word printed in it and kept asking me how I planned to make it to the United States and how I was going to become the Nagy† of China.

When Mao Zedong came to Shanghai at the end of July, he stayed at the Peace Hotel, where he met with student delegates from the city's universities, listened to their reports, and issued his directives. Our college sent a delegate nicknamed Big Tongue, who provided Mao with a detailed report on the struggle against me.

"Rip him to pieces," Mao is said to have instructed.

From July 7 to 31, I endured more than twenty *douzhenghui*. Ximeng participated in some of them. Depressed, exhausted, and pale, she didn't make any speeches but simply shouted along with the others and left immediately afterward to avoid me. By then, my freedom had been

---

*This is not borne out by the *Liberation Daily* article. It may have been in the *Youth Daily* article, but when I retrieved that day's issue at the Shanghai Municipal Library to confirm this, the first page of the newspaper was missing. See Appendix 2: "A Rightist Pawn Attacks the Party," p. 295. —Translator.

†Imre Nagy, the Hungarian prime minister who played a prominent role in the Hungarian Uprising of 1956. He was executed in 1958 on orders of Khrushchev "as a lesson to all leaders in socialist countries."

A young Xu Hongci

curtailed, and I was always followed by somebody. Old friends like Zhuang Derun didn't dare to speak with me. On August 1, the college party committee finally announced the summer break, and I was allowed to go home to rest. The following day, the *People's Daily*, the Communist Party's mouthpiece and the country's newspaper of record, reprinted an abridged version of the *Liberation Daily* article about me.

My friend Lan Cheng returned from Beijing to Shanghai. Having both been branded Rightists, we had many things to talk about. He advised me to leave China. But how? We discussed two methods. The first was legal: Father's old friend Lu Liangbing was an airfreight executive in Hong Kong. I would persuade Father to ask him for a job and move to Hong Kong so that I could follow. The second was illegal: to escape to India through Tibet. Lan Cheng's Tibetan girlfriend had told him that China's border control in the Pamir Mountains of western Tibet was lax and that the Tibetans passed in and out of the country as they pleased. Naturally, my priority was to leave the country legally, because I knew my chances of making it alive across the border to India would be slim.

We also discussed philosophical matters. The Anti-Rightist Campaign had made us realize that the present conflict was not only between the Communist Party and its opponents but, on a deeper level, between the individual and the collective. Five thousand years of tyranny had endowed the Chinese people with a miserly mentality that strangled individual initiative and creativity. Anybody who did anything unconventional and stood out in any way encountered the wrath of the masses and was destroyed. For the first time, we realized how superficial the Communist revolution had been and that it had barely scratched the surface of our country's real, deep-seated cultural problems.

At the end of August, Lan Cheng returned to Beijing. We didn't see each other again for twenty-eight years. I urged Father to look for a job in Hong Kong. After hesitating for a long time, he finally wrote a letter to Lu Liangbing asking for his help but received no reply.

Zhou Qinzong, the co-author and calligrapher of our *dazibao*, had also been branded a Rightist and expelled from the party. He had never exposed or criticized me during any of the denunciation meetings, and we still greeted each other in the street. Both of us were ostracized, lonely, and in need of companionship, and after hesitating for a few weeks, we became close friends again. We were both young, had never been the target of political persecution before, and had no experience in dealing with a dictatorship. Unable to restrain our thoughts and feelings, we began discussing our futures.

Qinzong's parents were in Hong Kong, and his older brother was studying physics at Beijing University. He lived by himself in an apartment on Shaanxi South Road. He also wanted to leave China, was planning to study biochemistry at a university in Switzerland, and asked me to go with him. It was a good idea, but China was a closed country at the time, and because we had both run afoul of the government, it would never let us go abroad.

In any case, Qinzong thought that knowledge of a foreign language would be useful and persuaded me to study English with him at an evening school on Shaanxi South Road. The teacher, Li Shande, about forty years old, was of mixed Chinese-American origin, looked like a foreigner, and spoke both the Shanghai dialect and English fluently. Classes were at 6:30 p.m., three times a week, and the fee was five yuan per month. Shande had his own special way of teaching English and promised us that we would have a good grasp of the basic grammar within one month. Initially, I didn't believe him, but after a few lessons I felt he knew what he was doing, and I started to study seriously.

To avoid attention, Qinzong and I always arrived at Shande's school separately. After class, however, we often walked together and talked until late at night. But these good times didn't last for long.

"Li Shande has been arrested. He has been accused of accumulating wealth by improper means. There will be no more classes," Qinzong told me one day.

I felt sorry for Shande. Although he didn't have a formal degree, he had been a better teacher than our university professors. A few days later, Qinzong brought me to an old man on Great Deer Road who had been a member of the Chinese military delegation dispatched to France during World War I. We paid him five yuan each per month to teach us French three times a week. I found the language impossibly difficult, especially its spelling and verb conjugations. Even though I had studied Russian and Latin, I was unable to make progress and gradually lost interest.

These clandestine French lessons lasted about four months, until one day in the winter of 1957–1958 we were discovered through yet another stroke of bad luck. On that day, I was meeting with Qinzong among some trees off Zhaojiabin Road when Xiao Shuying, the head of the college party committee's propaganda unit, suddenly walked by, staring at us with suspicious surprise. Realizing that our secret had been exposed, we grew nervous but forced ourselves to look calm. In the distance, Xiao Shuying turned her head again to look at us.

"We're in trouble," I said.

Qinzong nodded his head. After this, we never met during the day and took even greater precautions to maintain our secrecy. But Xiao Shuying didn't forget this matter, and we weren't able to elude her.

Xu Xueren and Gao Er'ling, still very much in love, never took part in any political activities and had been bystanders throughout the Anti-Rightist Campaign. One day, I ran into Er'ling in the staircase of the old main building. She smiled and said my name in a low voice: "Xu Hongci!"

That simple salutation and gentle smile were like a sip of spring-water. Having for several months been the subject of constant angry looks, hostility, and condemnation, I too was losing my humanity and becoming a wild animal ready to battle barbarity with barbarity. I'll never forget Er'ling for greeting me as an ordinary human being on that occasion, and to this day I have a warm feeling every time I see her.

I ran into Ximeng twice at the library. We didn't speak, but although the situation was awkward, she still smiled. I smiled back. It was a smile of love, hate, desire, bitterness, longing, despair . . . I don't think there is a writer who could describe it.

Father finally received a reply from Lu Liangbing, who said that Hong Kong's airfreight business was in the doldrums and that he was unable to arrange a position. This disappointed Father deeply because he and Liangbing were sworn brothers, and when Liangbing had been down on his luck, Father had done everything he could to help him. Perhaps he didn't realize the gravity of our family's situation. Later, when Father had died and I was in prison, Liangbing often sent money to Mother out of regret.

While 1957 caused me much suffering and pain, it was in 1958 that my real calamity began. After the Western New Year, just as we were preparing for our semester exams, the college announced they had been canceled. Instead, a second Anti-Rightist Campaign would be conducted, because the first campaign had not been sufficiently thorough. We had all known it was only a matter of time before the Communist Party dealt with us Rightists in earnest, but nobody knew exactly what was planned. A new law about *laojiao*,* "education through labor," had just been passed, and many people believed it would be used to punish the party's opponents.

In contrast to the first campaign, this new round of *douzhenghui* was not improvised and ad hoc. This time, the party committee did not entangle itself in empty conspiracy theories but rather seized on actual facts, digging up every last piece of the accuseds' dirty laundry. They launched an investigation into my friendship with Zhou Qinzong. After holding out for five days, Qinzong caved in and confessed to everything, leaving me with no other choice than to own up to our secret plans to study abroad.

Having been expelled from the party, I was now thrown out of the college. At a big *douzhenghui* held just before the winter break, Li Jingyi announced that I was being sent to a labor camp for *laojiao*. But because the Public Security Bureau wasn't ready to receive us yet, I was allowed to return home in the meantime. With my *laojiao* sentence already decided, there was nothing my parents could do. Mother blamed me for my friendship with Zhou Qinzong. The whole family passed the Chinese New Year in a state of despondency. Wang Ou, my sister's one-year-old daughter, was our only source of happiness and consolation.

---

*The *laojiao* system was formally announced on August 3, 1957.

On April 8, I was summoned to Li Jingyi's office.

"From your words and actions, it is clear that you are a class traitor. It was right to expel you from the party. You will now be sent to *laojiao*. Be on your way."

"Will I be allowed to return to my studies?"

"That depends on your behavior."

I was handed over to a plainclothes public security officer, who would escort me to the labor camp. The officer was short and wore a severe expression but still seemed human.

"I can't go just like this. I have to go home first and get my things," I told him.

He nodded his head in agreement.

Escorted from the medical college, I passed through its gates without turning my head.

"Where is the labor camp?" my parents asked.

"In a few days, he will write and tell you," the officer replied.

My parents and my sister Hongming brought out the blanket and suitcase that had already been packed in preparation and followed me out to the road. The officer hailed a pedicab and off we went. Looking back, I saw my parents and sister crying, waving goodbye, telling me to write home soon. Tears filled my eyes.

The pedicab gradually left the busy part of the city, twisting and turning along the narrow lanes, heading toward Zhabei. After about forty minutes, we arrived at a grand-looking gate of a large courtyard compound. The gate was unmarked—there was no sign whatsoever—but armed guards stood sentry.

We climbed down from the pedicab. The officer insisted on paying, then helped me carry my things inside, where he handed me over to the guard on duty. I was led into the courtyard, which I discovered was huge, like the house of the Jia family in *The Dream of the Red Chamber*.*

---

*Written by Cao Xueqin (1715–1764), *The Dream of the Red Chamber* chronicles the declining fortunes of the Jia clan and is considered one of the greatest Chinese literary works.

There was a guard at every gate we passed. When I had counted five gates, I was locked into a big room packed with people, some standing and some sitting. They were friendly and arranged a seat for me by the wall. There were no beds, only bedding placed on the floorboards. They told me we would sleep on the floor at night and roll up our bedding and place it by the wall during the day.

"Is this the labor camp?" I asked.

"No, this is the Courtyard of Four Lights. We are being kept here temporarily for a few days and will soon be sent far away."

9

The Forgotten Archipelago

(April–December 1958)

Modeled on the Soviet Gulag, the Chinese *laogai*, "labor reform," camps constitute a vast system of incarceration and forced labor. During the Maoist years, this system was founded solely on the political exigencies of the Communist dictatorship, with no regard for judicial concepts such as due process and a fair trial. A sarcastic comment or a postal stamp of the chairman pasted upside down was a crime that could send a person to the *laogai* for many years. Throughout the 1950s, the victims of the Communist Party's recurring campaigns swelled the number and size of the camps, from the enormous agricultural penal colonies of Xinjiang and Manchuria to steelworks, factories, and local prisons scattered across the land. With physical conditions as harsh as in the Soviet Gulag, the Chinese camps added the extra dimension of "ideological reform," conducted through endless study sessions to indoctrinate the convicts with the party's tenets, force them to memorize the writings of Mao, and transform them into model Communist men and women.

The Anti-Rightist Campaign marked a watershed in modern Chinese history—the beginning of the country's descent into twenty years of madness. In May 1958, Mao announced the Great Leap Forward, a delusional scheme to catapult China to superpower status within a decade. The collectivization of agriculture was accelerated, and the country's 550 million rural residents were forcefully organized into 26,000 people's communes, where private property was confiscated, work was regimented along military lines, and all meals were taken in huge free canteens. To double steel production in a single year, farm tools and cooking utensils were collected, thrown into "backyard blast furnaces" fired with wood from torn-down peasant dwellings, and smelted into useless metal clumps.

B efore liberation, the Courtyard of Four Lights had belonged to the Association of Fellow Townsmen from Ningbo, a port town on the other side of Hangzhou Bay, a hundred miles south of Shanghai, and served as a coffin depot for deceased Ningbo merchants awaiting transportation to their final resting place back home. Now it was being used as a transshipment point for Shanghai's labor camp convicts— progress of sorts—although the conditions were hardly fit for living human beings.

Our daily ration was two bowls of thin rice gruel, and our hot water was limited. Hungry and thirsty, all of us wanted to get out of this foul place as soon as possible. With nothing to do, we exchanged stories, walked about in the cell, did calisthenics, or stood by the door peeping through the cracks, trying to figure out what was going on.

After two weeks, we were told to write to our families and ask them to visit us. My parents, my sister Hongming, and her daughter, Wang Ou, came to see me. Mother had brought a lot of food. Again and again, Father told me to swim with the current and not stir up more trouble. Promising to mend my ways, I put all the money I had left, thirty yuan, into his trembling hand and told him this was my last filial gift. Half an hour passed quickly. The police ordered my family to leave. Crying, I watched their backs disappear. I never saw Father again.

On the morning of April 22, about two hundred labor camp

convicts were escorted by armed police onto four river barges. After an eight-hour journey, we reached Huzhou, at the southern end of Lake Tai, ninety miles west of Shanghai. There, we boarded buses and continued sixty miles farther west toward the Baimaoling, "White Grass Ridge," labor camp in southern Anhui Province.

The road grew narrower and narrower, the pavement worse and worse. The bus rattled violently. We entered a region of barren, low hills. On the occasional narrow strip of flat land, peasants toiled with simple tools. Their dwellings were made of mud and straw—a stark contrast to the brick houses in the prosperous countryside of Zhejiang and Jiangsu.

At dusk, the bus stopped on a mountain slope. We unloaded our belongings and looked around. It was a wasteland, with not a building in sight. The police told us that we would have to walk the remaining six *li* (two miles) to the labor camp. How was I supposed to carry my heavy bedroll and leather suitcase? Other prisoners also protested. The police told us to leave our things and come back for them the next day.

By the time we reached the camp, it was pitch-dark. Our barracks were made of *mao** bamboo. The camp guards lit oil lamps and gave us thin rice gruel. Exhausted, we ate hurriedly and fell asleep fully clothed on the bamboo bunks.

The next morning, we were awakened early and organized into groups. I talked with four students from the East China Normal University. One of them, Chen Xiangzai, was put in my group. He had also left his things on the mountain slope, so after breakfast we walked back to get them. Bookworms, we were both out of training and, using a carry pole between us, had to make four return journeys to retrieve our belongings. This was the first test of my physical stamina in the camps, and from that day on I did hard labor for twenty-six years.

Each of us was handed a four-tooth iron cultivator and set to the task of reclaiming wasteland. The quota was two *fen*† of land per day,

---

*A long, sturdy variety of bamboo used in construction and scaffolding.
†1 *fen* = 718 square feet.

which nobody was able to fulfill. Soon, my hands were covered with bloody blisters. My arms swelled, my back ached, and when I fell into bed at night, every limb felt as if it had been dislocated.

After one week of this kind of work, I began to adapt. But hunger was an even bigger problem. There was not enough food. The evening meal was a bowl of thin rice gruel, and at night our stomachs growled as we twisted and turned, unable to fall asleep.

The four students from the East China Normal University had all been branded Rightists and included Tian Jianmo, who had fought against the Americans in the Battle of Triangle Hill* in Korea. Chen Xiangzai was the youngest. He was also a veteran of the Korean War and had served as a radio operator on a bomber aircraft. But when his uncle, a Japanese collaborator, was executed during the Campaign to Eliminate Counterrevolutionaries, Xiangzai, incriminated solely on the basis of their kinship, had been expelled from the army and sent to study Russian at the East China Normal University instead.

Seeing us five Rightists hanging out together probably made the labor camp commanders nervous, because Xiangzai and I were soon transferred to another farm under the administration of the White Grass Ridge labor camp, the Eternal Happiness Farm, three miles down the road.

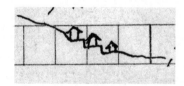

The camp sat on a mountain slope, with three terraces cut into its side and four single-story bamboo prison barracks on each terrace. Altogether, we were six hundred convicts, divided into four squadrons.

---

*Fought between Chinese and U.S./South Korean troops from October 14 to November 25, 1952, the Battle of Triangle Hill was the Korean War's bloodiest that year and ended in a failure of the United States and South Korea to capture the strategic ridge.

Xiangzai and I were assigned to the same squadron. Our commandant, Mao Kourong, came from Chongming Island in the Yangtze Estuary. Built like an ox, he had a grim, malicious face, glaring eyes, and a big mouth with a curled upper lip that revealed a set of uneven, protruding teeth. He walked like a tank and spoke with an earsplitting voice. According to the grapevine, he had previously been a prison guard on the Amoy Railroad but had been transferred to White Grass Ridge after he had shot and killed an inmate.

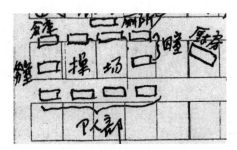

Eternal Happiness Farm setup

Curiously, Mao Kourong appointed me our team's deputy leader and Xiangzai secretary. Xing Zhilian, our team leader, was a slick character. About forty years old, he was thin but strong. With his sunburned skin, he looked like a peasant, but from his fastidious manner you could have mistaken him for an educated person. He always carried a little notebook, wrote down everything he saw and heard, and reported it to Mao Kourong. In the beginning we got along well enough, but gradually we became like oil and water.

Spring plowing added another stone to our backs. In addition to reclaiming wasteland, we had to build dams and dikes, harrow rice paddies, weed, burn land, spread manure . . . Transporting heavy things with a carry pole was the toughest work and was also used as punishment. Xiangzai and I hardened our shoulders every day until we were able to carry a hundred *jin*.*

---

*1 *jin* = 1.1 pounds.

Breakfast was a bowl of rice, and the midday meal, which we ate around eleven, was another bowl of rice. After that, we had to wait until after nightfall for "dinner"—a bowl of thin rice gruel made from two *liang** of rice.

We all wanted to buy our own food to supplement the meager rations, but Mao Kourong confiscated our cash, issued handwritten passbooks in return, and only allowed us to visit the local cooperative store once every two weeks to buy cigarettes, matches, sesame cakes, and other such small items. I learned how to smoke and discovered the strange ability of tobacco to suppress the howling pangs of hunger.

Starving, we wrote home asking for food. Because every letter was opened and read, we had to use coded language to tell our families about the atrocious conditions at the camp. My envelopes were double layered, with a thin blue paper inside the white envelope. One day, I had an idea. Carefully, I pried loose this thin blue paper, inserted a small letter with a truthful account of labor camp life, then reattached the thin blue paper and placed an ordinary family letter in the envelope.

My parents spent all their savings to help me, and about once a week I received a package with grain and canned foods. Xiangzai's father was far away in Xi'an, and his mother was a stepmother, so he received little support. I always offered to share my food with him, which made other people jealous, especially Xing Zhilian, who reported us to Mao Kourong.

Soon, the post office had to dispatch a special truck to deliver all the comfort parcels sent by our families. But the good times didn't last long. At the end of May, our camp suffered an outbreak of dysentery caused by poor management of the latrines. In truth, convicts defecated wherever they pleased. I was one of the first in our squadron to fall ill and had diarrhea more than thirty times per day. In the end, I shat thick red-white blood until I almost fainted.

Within three days, half of our brigade was ill. The camp command sent a telegram to the Shanghai Public Security Bureau, which dis-

---

*1 *liang* = 1.8 ounces.

patched a medical team to stem the epidemic. Among its members, there was a female doctor from the Department of Public Hygiene at my former college. I didn't know her, but she knew me. As she examined me, disheveled and in tattered clothes, she showed no sympathy, only contempt.

Every convict who didn't work hard enough or dared express dissatisfaction was punished harshly by Mao Kourong. His favorite torture was to double your work quota and cut your food rations in half at the same time. And if one person in our squadron committed the smallest offense, he would convene all of us after work and force us to listen to his lecturing and foul language, sometimes until after midnight.

It was always the same bunk: "You are the people's enemies!" "Your heinous crimes have caused great losses to the people!"

For all his crudeness, Mao Kourong chose his team leaders with great care, and they racked their brains to please him. Our leader, Xing Zhilian, reported everything we said and did. Even worse, he fabricated accusations. Mao Kourong never investigated these stories but accepted them at face value and dealt with them according to his mood until he had everyone walking on tiptoes in terror.

By mid-June, we had finished planting potatoes, peanuts, tobacco, rice, and other crops. The rice paddies were a ridiculous, sad sight. At the time, China was in the grips of a craze, conceived in the megalomaniac brain of Mao Zedong, for deep plowing and dense cultivation, and we had been ordered to replant the rice seedlings three times more densely than usual in order to triple the harvest. In the beginning, everything looked fine, but eventually all the plants died from suffocation.

The camp leadership also established a three-*mu* test paddy for deep plowing and ordered us to dig down ten feet and then shovel the earth back in reverse order. But instead of improving fertility, this method did not yield a single grain of rice. Xing Zhilian collected my sarcastic comments like small treasures, reporting every one of them to Mao Kourong, whose antipathy for me continued to grow.

"There is no time limit to *laojiao*," I said to Xiangzai. "How many years like this are we going to endure? One? Two? Three? The Communist Party will keep us here as long as it wants."

I wrote to my parents, asking them to go to the medical college and request that I be allowed to resume my studies. The party committee replied that my fate would be decided by the Public Security Bureau and that the college would take no further responsibility. On receiving this reply, I began making plans for an escape with Xiangzai.

In August 1958, Mao's Great Leap Forward shifted into high gear. In Anhui, Fanchang County falsely reported a harvest of 40,000 *jin* of rice per *mu*, followed by Tianjin, which boasted a harvest of 100,000 *jin* per *mu*. As proof of this, the newspapers published a photograph of a young girl sitting on top of the densely planted rice stalks. Xiangzai and I knew this was nonsense, but Xing Zhilian believed the papers.

The people's communes introduced the system of serving free food in huge canteens. Mao said that China would overtake Great Britain in fifteen years, and a people's commune in Zhengzhou of Henan Province proclaimed that true Communism would be achieved within three years. To keep pace with the rapid developments around the country, the camp leadership steadily increased our working hours, and by the beginning of October we were working nineteen hours per day, from three in the morning until ten at night.

Despite this, our food rations weren't increased. On the brink of starvation, everybody wanted the job of harvesting sweet potatoes and peanuts in order to eat while working. But our diet was lacking in oil, and no matter how much starch you ate, you never felt full. The raw sweet potatoes and peanuts were dirty and hard to digest, and a lot of people became sick with gastrointestinal inflammation.

The situation in the surrounding villages wasn't much better. I often saw long queues of more than a thousand peasants, including old people, women, and children, passing by with baskets of iron ore swinging from their carry poles and learned that they had been sent by their commune to Horse Saddle Mountain to carry back iron ore for the Great Steel-Making Campaign—a return journey of several hundred *li*.

I couldn't stop marveling at the madness of the Communist Party.

The peasants told me they had been forced to leave their ripe crops to rot in the fields in order to take part in the Great Steel-Making Campaign. Soon after, we saw the results. Many peasants tore down old houses, selling the wood as fuel to the commune's canteen for a few yuan, which they used to buy grain. Three months after Mao launched the people's communes and ordered free food to be served in the canteens, the famine struck.

The edema in my legs spread to my face, and my calves became thick as my thighs, making it difficult to walk. It took more than an hour to drag my bloated, heavy legs from the barracks to the fields, and when I finally got there, I could hardly stand straight, let alone work. The camp doctor told me to keep my legs high when sleeping to improve circulation and reduce the swelling. This worked, but as soon as I stood up, the swelling returned. Xiangzai also suffered from edema, although not as severe as mine. Despite this, the camp leadership insisted that we continue working nineteen hours per day.

One day when my heavy legs refused to budge, I suggested to the other convicts that we pitch camp by the fields so that we wouldn't have to walk an hour from our barracks. Adding his own inflammatory details, Xing Zhilian promptly reported this to Mao Kourong, claiming that I had criticized the Great Leap Forward. When this reached the ears of the camp commandant, Li, he flew into a rage and immediately convened the whole camp for a *douzhenghui* against me, at which I was accused of trying to foment a rebellion and relieved of my duties as deputy team leader.

But the convicts, on the verge of physical collapse, had nothing left to lose and protested by refusing to work. Everybody woke up with the bell at 3:00 a.m., but as soon as we got to the fields, we lay down and went back to sleep. The team leaders screamed at the top of their lungs, but we ignored them. At dawn, someone was dispatched to get food. After we had eaten some breakfast, we worked for a while, then sat down again. In this manner, we endured until nightfall. After dark, we lay down and slept in the fields, then returned to the camp at 10:00 p.m. and went to bed again.

When more and more convicts started trying to escape, the camp leadership decided to come down hard. In November 1958, eight prisoners were put on "trial" at the White Grass Ridge labor camp for attempted escape. The field was a dense, humming mass of human beings, the atmosphere thick with terror. Their hands tied behind their backs, the eight escapees were prodded onto a podium by the rifle butts of the policemen. Everybody was wondering whether they would be executed on the spot. As the verdicts were read, the policemen forced the men to kneel, striking them violently in the neck to make sure their heads were bowed. Each convict received an additional sentence of four to ten years.

"Whoever tries to escape will learn the law firsthand," the camp commandant warned us.

Following my removal as deputy team leader, Mao Kourong transferred Xiangzai to another team, moved his bed from beside mine to the upper bunk on the opposite side, and warned us to not engage in any secret plans. A few months earlier, Xiangzai had been the picture of an aviator: handsome and lithe. Now he had lost every trace of his old swagger. He was dark and emaciated, his eyelids swollen, and his spirits were in a state of utter dejection.

We were being destroyed, and our only hope of survival was to escape. By mid-November, the time was ripe. Mother wrote to me saying that Father had been sent to Qinghai Province to "take part in the construction of socialism." I realized he had run afoul of the authorities. I wrote back to Mother, asking her to explain in more detail. Concealing her letter in the hard cover of a book, she told me what had happened. Because Father had worked for the collaborator Wang Jingwei in Su County of Anhui Province in 1943, he had been branded a "historical counterrevolutionary" and sent to Qinghai for labor reform at the end of October. Mother also told me that her adopted brother Wang Bing had been sent to a labor camp in Fengbu, Anhui Province, for having served as a voluntary police officer in Shanghai's International Settlement before liberation.

Worried I would do something rash, she admonished me to stay calm and said she would come and see me at White Grass Ridge in December. I had lost all faith in my country, my society, my family, and my own life. I had no future to hope for, no past to remember. I showed Xiangzai the letter. He felt the same despair. From that moment, every time we had a chance, we secretly discussed plans to escape from the camp, return to Shanghai and see Mother, and then leave the country once and for all.

10

Escape

(December 1958–February 1959)

On December 14, 1958, before dawn, Xiangzai and I packed our knapsacks and dropped them through the small window behind his bunk, then washed ourselves and ate breakfast as usual. When the team leader blew his whistle for the morning assembly, we exited the barrack first, turned to the rear of it, picked up our knapsacks, and ran as fast as our legs would carry us.

It took us two minutes to reach the farm's tobacco-curing house. We continued sprinting toward the Ouyang Ford at Sand River. We crossed a bridge and came to a village where bent, famished peasants were queuing up for the day's work. Keeping our heads down, we walked toward the main road from Hangzhou to Wuhu.

This was a dangerous move, because we hadn't gotten far, and it would have been easy for the patrols dispatched by Mao Kourong to catch us. But they didn't, perhaps unable to imagine that we would take the easiest, straightest route.

According to our plan, we turned east on the main road and arrived at the county seat of Guangde, twenty miles southeast of the camp, by nightfall. There, we bought some food and rested for a while, before continuing our escape through the night by the light of the moon and stars, heading east over the border into Zhejiang Province.

Walking another twenty miles, we reached the town of Si'an at 5:00 a.m., took a bus to Jiaxing, and then boarded a train to Shanghai, arriving at the North Station in the evening. The escape had given us our strength back, and we felt no fatigue despite not having slept. From a general store on Baoshan Road, I made an operator-assisted telephone call to Mother and asked her to meet us at the North Station. She arrived there with my sister Hongming and took us to the Old Zhengxing restaurant on Zhejiang Middle Road.

"What are your plans?" she asked us.

I told her we had no future in China. Our only hope was to escape abroad. Mother and Hongming were worried. They wanted to tell us to give ourselves up but knew we wouldn't listen. On the other hand, if they helped us with money and we were captured, we would be severely punished, and they would be implicated. It was already late, and the restaurant was otherwise empty. We had to speak quietly and make our decisions quickly.

"What route will you take?" Mother asked.

"We plan to go to India via Tibet and then make our way to Hong Kong and find Uncle Lu," I replied.

Mother said it was a long journey, that our chances of success were slim, and hesitated whether or not to help us. Finally, she relented before our entreaties and gave me five hundred yuan, which in those days was a lot of money.

As we parted, she asked to see us one last time the next evening. Having said goodbye, we were suddenly overcome with fatigue. Because we didn't have any papers, we couldn't stay in a hostel and had no choice but to return to the train station, where we each found a bench to lie down on.

Before I had fallen asleep, a public security officer walked over and asked to see our documents. Unable to produce any, we were taken to the police office at the train station. There were many other people there, waiting to be questioned. Xiangzai and I were separated, but I could see him. The police had taken our knapsacks from us but not the money, which I had hidden in my pants. As soon as we were interrogated, the game would be over.

At this moment, I was filled with a powerful determination and, taking advantage of a short lapse in the attention of the police, stood up and fled the station out to the road, disappearing among the pedestrians. I crossed Sichuan Road and came to the Bund. By this time, it was around midnight, and there were no police in sight. I walked back and forth, feeling bad about leaving Xiangzai behind. There was no way I could return and rescue him.

Suddenly I ran into Xiangzai at the corner of the Bund and Nanjing Road. We hugged each other with joy.

"How did you escape?"

"The police didn't see you sneak out. I just followed you," he said.

"But how did you know I was on the Bund?"

"I don't know. I just had a feeling you would come here."

It was a miracle, one of the strangest things in my life. The winter night was damp and cold, and we had nowhere to go. All we could do was saunter about on the Bund. In 1958, with Shanghai engulfed in the Great Leap Forward, this famous, elegant boulevard looked like a construction site. In front of the municipal building, there was a row of small blast furnaces, and the sidewalk was cluttered with piles of ore, pig iron, coke, and slag.

Of course, we should have left Shanghai right away. But I was young and ignorant in the ways of the Public Security Bureau and wanted to see Mother one last time.

That morning, I telephoned Father's cousin Auntie Bai and asked her to go to my house and tell Mother to meet me at 6:00 p.m. at the Grand Theatre. At around 5:30 p.m., as dusk fell, Xiangzai and I sat down in the coffeehouse just west of the cinema and ordered some food. I told Xiangzai to stay put and went alone to meet Mother.

Because it was dark, I couldn't see that she was shooting warning glances to me and rushed to greet her. A big sturdy man popped out of a corner and grabbed me. Several other men stepped forward. I realized they were plainclothes policemen and that I had walked straight into a trap. I will never forget the torment on Mother's face. The policemen asked me where Xiangzai was.

"He won't make it by himself. Return to the camp together!" Mother shouted.

I was about to accuse Mother of betraying us there and then but, tempering myself, realized that the problem probably lay with our arrest the previous evening. Without money, Xiangzai wouldn't survive. Having decided to return to the camp and plan another escape, I brought the policemen with me to the coffeehouse.

"The game's over; we have to go back," I said to Xiangzai.

When he saw Mother surrounded by the plainclothes policemen, his face turned ashen white. The officers wanted to take us away immediately, but I protested, "We are hungry. Let us eat before we go."

Mother also insisted on eating first, and the policemen relented. I told the waiter to bring another bowl and pair of chopsticks and asked Mother to sit down with us. The policemen sat down at another table, keeping an eye on us. I quickly slipped the five hundred yuan back to Mother.

With her head lowered to the rice bowl, she whispered, "There was a letter from me in your knapsack. The police at the train station knew that you had escaped and returned home. This morning, officers from the Public Security Bureau came to ask for you. In the afternoon, Auntie Bai came over, and they forced her to tell them where you were."

A crowd had gathered at the entrance to the coffeehouse, and the waiters and guests thronged around our table, staring at us. It was chaotic. A few of the policemen stood up and dispersed the crowd and told us to finish our meal.

While the policemen were busy dealing with the onlookers, Mother gave me a few bills from the money I had returned to her and said in a low voice, "Take this. You'll need it."

I took the money and stuck it under the inner sole of my shoe. Xiangzai and I ate until we were stuffed. Mother followed us out of the coffeehouse and watched us as we boarded the police jeep.

"I'll come and see you soon!" she shouted.

The jeep drove off with screaming sirens and shortly arrived at the infamous Tilanqiao Prison. After being body searched, Xiangzai and I were separated. In my cell, there were some thirty people locked up in a space of 160 square feet, fitted with a flush toilet. The prisoners were of all descriptions, but they were friendly and made space by the wall for me to lie down. We slept lying on our sides, head to foot, packed like sardines, the foul, moldy air reeking of urine and sweat.

We were given two meals a day: a bowl with three *liang* of rice with a spoonful of vegetables on top. For New Year's Eve, everybody dreamed of a piece of meat—in vain. Our biggest problem were the fleas that hid in our underwear. The adult bugs were white and fat; the older ones turned black. When you squeezed them between your nails, there was a crisp popping sound as the blood squirted from their engorged bodies. With nothing else to do, we took off our clothes and scoured them for flea eggs, but you could never get rid of them.

Around New Year's Day 1959, we heard on the radio that Castro had led his guerrilla troops into Havana and that the Cuban Revolution had been won. I was glad, because I had always thought Latin America was the best place for a revolution. "As soon as I get out of China, that's where I'll go," I told myself. Looking back, I realize how unrealistic this idea was and how full of romantic illusions my head was in those days.

On January 6, a policeman arrived from the White Grass Ridge labor camp, shouted my name and Xiangzai's, and handcuffed us together. The night we arrived back at the camp, we were denounced at a big *douzhenghui*. The other convicts shouted slogans at us, cursed us with the foulest language, and rained their spittle upon us. All we could do was keep our heads down and endure the humiliation in silence.

The struggle meeting continued for more than two hours. To our surprise, Mao Kourong was gone, replaced by Commandant Song, who gave a speech demanding our confession in return for leniency. Afterward, we were locked up in the storehouse together with two other convicts, Leng Xiaohua and Wu Miaoxin, and guarded by four militiamen from a neighboring village. The men worked in pairs in twelve-hour shifts, each of them armed with a rifle.

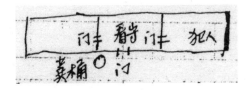

Used as a confinement cell for disciplinary punishment, the storehouse was made up of three rooms, with us convicts to the right and the guards in the middle. We slept on beds of hay, which were warm and comfortable, and used a latrine just beside the outer door.

We guessed that Mao Kourong had been blamed for our escape and transferred somewhere else. Commandant Song took a liking to Xiangzai; I had a feeling he would soon be let out of the storehouse. Sure enough, two days later, Xiangzai was sent back to work with our team. My fate was different. Considered the mastermind of our escape, I had to stay in the storehouse and was interrogated by a short, fat, dusky officer from Shandong.

"Tell me about your plans to escape abroad," he demanded.

When I refused to confess, he told me, "We will have to let you taste the iron fist of the proletariat."

By now, I was starving and never felt full no matter how much bulk I ate. In the evenings, we sat in the dark, eating from the mountain of raw peanuts in the storehouse. They tasted like raw fish in the beginning, but the more I ate, the better I liked them; however, as a result, all three of us suffered from chronic diarrhea. Night and day, we asked the guards for permission to go to the toilet, pestering them to the limit of their patience.

After two weeks, my case had still not been decided. I reckoned with four possibilities: arrest and a criminal conviction; transfer to another farm; transfer to another squadron; or confinement for three to six months, then further disciplinary action.

At midday on January 27, my cellmate Miaoxin returned from the kitchen and handed me a note from Xiangzai: "You go first. I'll come after you. Go to my aunt in Hangtou. I'll meet you there."

I discussed the matter with Miaoxin. He agreed it would be dangerous to try another escape. If things went wrong, I would be shot dead on the spot. Miaoxin told me to think carefully. I was afraid, but the fear evaporated before the thought of spending the rest of my life in prison.

That night I put everything I needed into my knapsack and went to bed in my clothes, without taking my shoes off. The duty guards were playing chess in the outer room by the light of a kerosene lamp. At around 4:00 a.m., I threw off my blanket, stood up, and asked to go to the toilet. Having received the guard's permission, I stepped out through the door, pulled down my pants, squatted over the latrine, and released my spluttering diarrhea. One minute later, I hastily cleaned myself, fastened my trousers, and then, under the cover of darkness, leaped down the terrace with long strides and ran toward the main road by the boiler room, darting from the cover of one manure pile to another. Luckily, there was no moon that night. Two minutes later, I was gone without a trace.

I followed the same route as in the previous escape, crossing the Ouyang Ford and continuing south. As the day broke, I walked toward a distant mountain in the southwest. Someone had told me I would find the town of Shijie in that direction, and to prevent the search patrols from intercepting me at Guangde, I decided to make a big detour fifty miles west to the river town of Wuhu and then catch a Yangtze ferry or a train to Shanghai.

I reached Shijie, twelve miles from the camp, at 8:00 a.m. This is a famous place, but at the time it was run-down, a scene of bleak desolation. I walked into a restaurant looking for breakfast. The attendant replied that he had nothing but Shaoxing rice wine and sugar. I was so hungry I could hardly move and asked for four *liang* of the wine and half a pound of sugar, washing the sugar down with the wine as the attendant looked on in disbelief.

I continued six miles west toward Shizipu, jumped on a bus, and arrived in Wuhu at five in the afternoon. The train to Shanghai had already left, and there were no more departures that day. At the pier, they told me the ferry to Shanghai would arrive at 2:00 a.m. I found a restaurant serving food, ate, and returned to the pier to wait for the ferry.

I was in a fourth-class cabin with eight other people. There was a restaurant at the stern of the ship, which actually served rice and hot dishes. I must have eaten too much and too fast, gulping the food down without even chewing, because when I went to the toilet, I shat undigested, discolored rice. The ferry chugged along the mighty Yangtze toward Shanghai, docking at Pier 16 at about midnight, January 30.

I walked north along the Bund toward my home on Xi'an Road. The iron gate in front of our house had been removed, probably to be melted down in one of the "backyard blast furnaces" for the Great Steel-Making Campaign. I entered the courtyard. The light in Mother's room was on. I moved close to the window, stood on tiptoe, looked in, and saw Mother knitting in bed, Wang Ou sleeping by her side. I wanted to knock on the window and ask her to let me in. But reason overcame my emotions, and I drew my hand back.

I needed documents. Suddenly I had an idea and headed straight toward the medical college. It took me almost three hours to get there. I snuck in through a hole in the bamboo fence by the soccer field and made my way toward the library. There was an open window, protected by an iron grille. I managed to squeeze myself between the bars and entered the familiar old reading room.

Quickly, I found the desk where the book borrowers' IDs were kept in a wooden box, put four of the IDs in my pocket, then left through the open window. Walking north, I passed the party committee office, jumped over the campus wall, and hurried along East Temple Bridge Road.

The first rays of dawn appeared on the horizon. Without stopping, I walked to Beijing West Road and knocked on the door of my uncle Wang Bing's mistress Xi Junfang. We didn't know each other very well, but she knew that Uncle Wang thought highly of me. She was surprised to see me and closed the door behind me quickly so that her sister's family next door wouldn't hear us talking. I asked her to go see Mother and get the five hundred yuan I'd returned to her; I told Xi Junfang I would come back the next day to pick up the money. Having heard the story of my escape, she said she admired my courage and agreed to help.

After leaving her apartment, I crossed the Huangpu River and boarded a bus to Hangtou Town in Nanhui County, where Xiangzai's aunt lived. A peasant, about fifty years old, she was cooking when I arrived at her house around noon. I told her I was Xiangzai's friend and that he had asked me to wait for him there. She examined me, didn't say anything, and gave me some food. The rice was steaming hot and fragrant, but there were no vegetables or meat.

She continued with her housework in silence. I sat by the table looking out through the door, hoping Xiangzai would arrive soon. I figured that if he didn't show up by nightfall, he would have either lost faith or been arrested, and I would have to return to Shanghai alone. But at 2:00 p.m., Xiangzai appeared. I jumped to my feet with joy and gave him a big hug. His auntie, however, was very cool, as if she had something on her mind.

"The camp leadership sent search patrols to look for you everywhere, with orders to shoot you on sight," Xiangzai said. "I escaped the same evening and took the same route as last time."

February 1 was New Year's Eve in the Chinese lunar calendar.* Early that morning, we returned to Shanghai. I asked Xiangzai to wait for me in the People's Park while I went to Xi Junfang to pick up the money.

"Your mother asked you to meet her at 9:00 tomorrow morning at the secondhand shop on Huaihai Middle Road," she said, handing me the five hundred yuan.

"It's too dangerous. Tell her we can't see each other this time."

To make the stolen IDs our own, Xiangzai and I had our pictures

---

*The Chinese New Year's Eve of 1959 was actually on February 7.

taken at a studio and asked to have them ready the next day. In the afternoon, we returned to Hangtou, where we helped Xiangzai's auntie harvest turnips.

"She knows we have run away and told me we should give ourselves up and return to the camp," Xiangzai said in a low voice.

"Do you think she'll report us?"

"No. I'll just tell her that we're going back to the camp."

There was no special food for New Year's Eve. Xiangzai's auntie simply asked him to catch a couple of fish in the river, and she prepared them for us. On the morning of February 2, we returned to Shanghai, picked up our photos, found a deserted room in a Western restaurant close to the Bund, and replaced the photos from the stolen IDs with our own.

The hardest part was to copy the seal embossed on the original photo. I showed Xiangzai how to create an embossment by pressing a blunt pencil against the back side of his photo. He was skillful and finished the job in a few minutes. When we had glued our photos to the IDs, you couldn't tell the difference from the original. We then faded the owners' names with bleach and replaced them with our new pseudonyms. In one of the student IDs, there was a special student discount travel card for the New Year's holiday, which we used to buy tickets at half price to Chengdu in Sichuan Province. On February 3, we left Shanghai and set out to seek a new life.

11

On the Brink of Freedom

(February-April 1959)

Having learned a lesson from our arrest at the Grand Theatre, I gave Xiangzai half of my money in case we were separated or caught. We helped and trusted each other like brothers and, inspired by the lines of the Hungarian revolutionary poet Sándor Petőfi,* prepared to risk our lives for freedom:

> All other things above
> Are liberty and love;
> Life I would gladly tender
> For love: yet joyfully
> Would love itself surrender
> For liberty

Ximeng had cast me aside. Zhou Xiaoying had left Xiangzai. Now our lives were on the line. Xiangzai probably never forgot the note I

---

*Sándor Petőfi (1823–1849) is considered one of Hungary's greatest poets. A key figure in the Hungarian Revolution of 1848, a struggle for independence from the Habsburg Austrian Empire, Petőfi joined the Hungarian revolutionary army and was last seen alive at the Battle of Segesvár, July 31, 1849.

had written to him in confinement: "For freedom, we must not let the 'law' intimidate us. We must scorn it and be ready to struggle until death. Life is nothing but a brief episode in the endless recycling of matter. WE are eternal!"

We talked a lot on the train, about our families, studies, love, friendship, dreams, setbacks, and uncertain futures. We railed at the darkness of Chinese politics and the people's ignorance and blindness and felt a great sadness regarding the future of our country. We criticized Mao harshly for his treachery, arrogance, and hypocrisy. Sometimes, when our discussions became particularly loud and heated, we left our seats and continued talking at the end of the wagon.

We arrived in Chengdu on February 5 and checked into the Shandong Hotel. The room was simple and clean. In a hurry to get to Tibet, I went straight to the bus station to make inquiries. There were no direct buses to Lhasa, and the route was divided into several sections, with a total price for the entire fourteen-hundred-mile journey of 110 yuan per person. With only a bit more than 400 yuan between us, we would have to be careful with our money and keep moving in order to minimize the cost of food and lodging.

But our two escapes in two months had taken their toll on Xiangzai, who said he needed a rest. He was like a little brother to me, and to make him feel better, I agreed to take it easy for a few days. We walked the streets of Chengdu, ate at restaurants, and went to several movies.

After three days, I told Xiangzai we had to get going, but he said he wanted to stay put a little bit longer. One week passed, and he still didn't want to move. Even worse, he kept going to expensive restaurants and seemed determined to spend his last penny. I grew nervous and angry and insisted that we leave right away, unable to see that Xiangzai had somehow lost his will to fight.

"Honestly, Hongci, you know we'll never make it. The Communist Party is everywhere, and the people are its eyes and ears. There are only three choices left for us: suicide, Xinjiang, or surrender."

"Have we come this far just to kill ourselves?" I said angrily. "Do you think we could find a place to hide in Xinjiang? You know Russian and want to escape to the Soviet Union, but do you know if the Soviets will take you in? And if we give ourselves up, the Public Security Bureau will send us straight back to White Grass Ridge. Do you think we can expect leniency from them?"

I was about to say that this escape had been his idea but bit my tongue. In any case, Xiangzai refused to move, and our separation became inevitable. I decided not to waste any more money on food and drink. I had already given him half of the five hundred yuan and didn't know if the money I had left would be enough to get me to Tibet and India. From now on, I would have to save every last penny.

Each time Xiangzai stumbled into our room in a stupor of gluttony and drunkenness, I would boil inside with fury, but the friendship we had established in these past few months of adversity held me back, and I clung to the hope that he would regain his senses.

After twelve days, Xiangzai was still eating and drinking as if there were no tomorrow. Finally, I made the painful decision to proceed alone. At noon on February 19, when Xiangzai was napping, I left a goodbye note for him on the table and bought a bus ticket to the town of Ya'an in western Sichuan.

The six-hundred-mile journey to the Golden Sand River,* traversing a majestic landscape of soaring peaks and deep valleys, opened a new world for me. Just out of Chengdu, the bus entered the West Sichuan Plains, which resembled the fertile, abundant Jiangnan region back home. After the Qionglai Mountains, the terrain grew steeper. By the time we reached the ancient town of Mingshan, dusk was falling. That fairy-tale scene, with smoke rising wistfully from rows of black brick houses, will always remain with me. Continuing west, we entered a range of colossal mountains, and the bus wound its way along perpen-

---

*The Golden Sand River, or Jinsha Jiang, originating on the Plateau of Tibet, is the name of the first stretch of the Yangtze River, which meanders 3,200 miles in a northeast direction through the Chinese heartland before reaching the sea at Shanghai.

dicular cliffs and emerald-green creeks to our destination for the evening: Ya'an, the capital of the Xikang.*

Once again, I used my fake ID to get a room at the People's Hostel. The streets of Ya'an were lined with bustling markets, and the people appeared to be simple and honest. The next day, I boarded a bus to Kangding. Chugging up the dirt road, the bus stopped for a break at the highest vantage point. In the southwest, we could see Mount Gongga, twenty-five thousand feet, awesome in its grandeur. As the bus descended into the Dadu River valley, the river at the valley floor grew from a fluttering silver ribbon to a tempestuous beast.

Standing on the famous Luding Chain Bridge,[†] I thought about the dreams and ideals of the Red Army in the early days of the revolution and the bleak, tyrannical country Mao had created. Having shed its blood to liberate the toiling, oppressed peasants of China, the Communist Party had immediately set about securing its grip on power and depriving its enemies, imaginary or not, of their freedom. Revolutions, it seems, are destined to devour themselves.

After Kangding, we climbed steadily to a vast, windswept high plateau, where the temperature fell far below freezing. Although I was wearing a cat-fur coat, I only had a pair of miserable PLA cloth shoes with no lining, and my feet were numb with cold. I had been told I would develop altitude sickness at thirteen thousand feet, but the Que'er mountain pass was eighteen thousand feet, and I was still feeling okay.

We made it to another plateau and shook our way to Garzê, the capital of the Garzê Tibetan Autonomous Region. The town itself was sparsely inhabited, but there were PLA camps everywhere, and the roads were filled with soldiers and army trucks.

---

*Xikang Province, encompassing the Kham region of eastern Tibet, the traditional land of the Khampa people, was an administrative region between 1939 and 1955.

†According to Communist lore, the site of one of the most famous battles of the Long March. On May 30, 1935, the Communists defeated a contingent of the KMT army and crossed the bridge, allowing them to continue their Long March to the north. Several accounts, however, refute the contention that a major battle took place.

I stayed in a hostel close to the bus station. An old man told me about the Tibetan uprising that had broken out recently and said it would be dangerous to proceed to Lhasa. This news both worried and encouraged me, because while the fighting posed a definite risk, the confusion would also provide cover and might improve my chances for a successful escape. Disregarding the old man's advice, I decided to press forward.

Out of Garzê, the endless, glum high plateau was covered in deep snow, with only a few forsaken yaks huddling about here and there. At noon, the bus arrived in Manigango, where we were stopped by a group of party cadres.

A leader boarded the bus: "Last night, we were attacked by Tibetan bandits, and lost two comrades. We want to transport them to Dege on the roof of the bus. Okay?"

Naturally, we said nothing. The cadres hoisted the two corpses onto the roof and then squeezed themselves in among us. The atmosphere of war grew heavy, and I began to fear that the bus would come under attack.

Dege lay by a creek between two high mountains, with a few scattered houses on their slopes. The population was probably not even a thousand. I stayed at a hostel together with the others. One of the travelers told me the fighting up ahead was fierce and that the roads were blocked. He said the only open approach to Lhasa was from the north and that I would have to go to Dunhuang and enter Tibet through Qinghai Province.

The food was much more expensive than in Chengdu. A bowl of soup with tofu and vegetables cost seven jiao.* I counted the money in my pocket and discovered that I only had a little bit more than one hundred yuan left. If things continued like this, I would soon be stone broke.

As I was deciding what to do, I met some people who had been stranded in Dege for a long time. They were getting ready to walk to Jomda on the other side of the Golden Sand River. I asked if I could

*Ten Chinese cents.

join them. Many of them were road workers and knew the area well, and they agreed to help me.

One day, a convoy of trucks loaded with Tibetan POWs drove into town. I went to the Public Security Bureau's detention center to see what was going on. Disheveled, haggard, and frightened, the POWs were brought down from the trucks and lined up. A policeman counted them. Two corpses were thrown down from a truck. I inspected the two young dead bodies carefully. Filing into their cells, the POWs bowed before them. In low spirits, I returned to the hostel to find out about our departure.

"The soldiers guarding the bridge say there is heavy fighting ahead and that we will be killed if we cross over. They won't let us do it," an older man said.

"Tomorrow, a truck carrying charcoal will return to Garzê together with the POW convoy," a man from the hostel announced. "Anybody who wishes to go with them may do so."

I had been stuck in Dege for a week and was running out of money. With no hope of making it to Lhasa, I decided to return to Chengdu, take stock of the situation, and make new plans. I took a seat on the charcoal truck, leaving Dege with the POW convoy. The Tibetan fighters were disciplined and seemed to have good relations with their captors. Some of the lamas even offered cigarettes to the guards, who accepted them gladly.

The PLA protected all Han Chinese, even the hoodlums and scoundrels. As long as you were a Han, you were a good person in their eyes, and they never asked you for any documents. I didn't have to pay for the ride and sat inside the cabin protected from the wind, which was a lot better than what the POWs had to endure.

"These men are all murderers and will be severely punished," a policeman said. "We are establishing a labor camp in Dawu and will send them to be reformed there."

We passed through Garzê and returned to Kangding. There, I ran into Pan Changsheng, a student I had befriended on my last visit to the town. He took me to his friend Zhou Tianzhu, who gave me a place to sleep. Changsheng hadn't been able to find work in Kangding and wanted to return to Chengdu but didn't have money for the bus ticket. I thought that if I paid for his ticket, perhaps he would let me stay in his house in Chengdu.

At Zhou Tianzhu's house, I drank Tibetan butter tea for the first time. After boiling pieces of brick tea in water for a long time, he poured the strong reddish-brown infusion into a bamboo churn, added butter and salt, pumped the handle rapidly until the butter had melted and been mixed with the tea, and poured us the milky white drink, which tasted delicious. They also treated me to *tsampa*, or roasted barley, the Tibetan staple food.

Because I needed to cut my expenses as much as possible, I said I wanted to take some butter and *tsampa* with me back home to Shanghai. They helped me buy fifteen *jin* of *tsampa* and five *jin* of butter and wrapped them into an oilcloth backpack.

Around March 10, Changsheng and I returned to his house in Chengdu. Changsheng told his parents I was a university student from Shanghai traveling around China and would be staying in their house for a while. I had only sixty yuan left. I considered several options but couldn't make up my mind and spent my days walking around the city, killing time. Passing the Shandong Hotel, I had to peek through the entrance at the room where Xiangzai and I had stayed, even though I knew he was gone.

The fleas I had caught at the Tilanqiao Prison began breeding like crazy, and I had to clean my underwear in boiling water at Changsheng's house. Although his family saw there was something amiss, they didn't report me to the police. I realized I had to get going again and sent a telegram to Xi Junfang, asking her to tell Mother to telegram a hundred yuan to me at Changsheng's address.

The money arrived the following day. To keep one step ahead of the Public Security Bureau, I bought a bus ticket to Kunming and then took Changsheng for a farewell meal at a Western restaurant in the Guanshengyuan Hotel. I was carrying Father's pocket atlas of China.

Although small, it was detailed, and during my time at Changsheng's house I studied it time and again, trying to find a new escape route.

Remembering the verdict I had seen posted in Si'an, Zhejiang Province, sentencing a man to twenty years of hard labor for attempting to escape to Hong Kong across the land border, I knew that route would be dangerous. The population in southern Yunnan Province was dense, and it would be easy to catch me there, too. The only alternative, it seemed, was to cross over the border into Burma from western Yunnan.

The journey from Chengdu to Zhanyi in Yunnan took three days. We spent the first night in Heishitou Township of Guizhou Province. Standing there at dusk, gazing at the distant peaks on the horizon, I was seized by a delusion that beyond these mountains lay a foreign land and that if only I could reach it, I would be free.

In Kunming, I bought a bus ticket to Xiaguan, two days' journey west along the Burma Road. The lush, mountainous landscape was beautiful, and everything seemed at peace. When we reached Xiaguan, I counted my money and realized that I must have lost some of it along the way. I decided to walk, heading north along the western shore of Erhai Lake, enjoying the scenery. When I got hungry, I ate *tsampa* and butter, washing it down with springwater from the mountains.

My goal was Gongshan County, in the sparsely populated northwestern corner of Yunnan, where I planned to cross over the border into Burma. But when I reached the village of Shaxi, I was told there was no road leading where I wanted to go and that I would have to return to Xiaguan.

Once I was back there, I headed west. The road climbed sharply. Up ahead, I could see Black Dragon Mountain, its winding ridge covered in snow and ice. In Yangbi County, I walked into the local hostel. The receptionist, who was nursing a baby, put down her child, and as she raised her head, I saw the most beautiful woman I have ever met. I thought of Ximeng and wondered how she was. By now, Bao Yougen had returned from East Germany. Perhaps they were already married. That night, I lay awake a long time, unable to fall asleep, my mind clouded with bitter memories.

The next day, I came to the famous Yaquan, "Dumb Spring," which Zhuge Liang had drunk from in *Romance of the Three Kingdoms*.* Dying of thirst, I didn't have time to worry whether the water would make me lose my voice. I was young and strong and could walk forty miles from dawn to dusk. After Yongping, the road descended into the Lancang River valley,† where the imposing Gongguo Chain Bridge appeared up ahead. As I passed the sentries, my heart pounded madly from fear that I would be stopped and questioned, but luckily they ignored me.

At Wayao, the road split, with the wider Burma Road continuing in a southwesterly direction and the other, narrower road heading northwest. There were many small blast furnaces around Wayao, and the place was busy. I continued on the narrow road. That night, I found a dry, flat place to lie down, but the shrieks of owls in the forest kept me awake. In the distance, I could hear other mysterious sounds, which unsettled me even more.

At the first glimpse of dawn, I got back on the road. That baffling sound kept growing until it was as loud as thunder. I felt a strange fear but pressed forward. After a sharp turn in the road, I stood before a wide, roaring, mighty, foaming, swirling river: the Nujiang, "Angry River."‡

I washed my face in the ice-cold water. The road ran north along the river. After the village of Liuku, I reached a suspension bridge at about 9:00 a.m. It was even larger than the Gongguo Bridge, with sentry guards at both ends. Emboldened by my previous success, I passed them

---

*Zhuge Liang was a famous statesman during the Three Kingdoms period (A.D. 220–265) and a hero of *Romance of the Three Kingdoms*, one of China's most beloved historical novels. In Yunnan to catch Meng Huo, the southern king, he became dumb after drinking water from Yaquan and only regained his voice after a wise man instructed him to drink water from the Anle spring as an antidote.

†Lancang is the Chinese name of the Mekong River, which, flowing south, traverses Laos and Cambodia before reaching the sea at Saigon in Vietnam.

‡Nujiang is the Chinese name of the Salween River, which flows south through Burma to the Andaman Sea.

without batting an eye and continued north on the western side of the river.

The landscape grew menacing. The mountains here run in transversal ridges, with perpendicular cliffs thousands of feet high. I took out the atlas and studied it carefully. Gongshan County was 300 miles to the north, and the China-Burma border 125 miles to the west. If I continued north along the Angry River, I would be entering the Himalayas and have to start mountain climbing.

I decided to cross the border at Lushui instead and took a risk by asking some people I met along the road for directions. They told me I had walked too far and would have to head back toward the bridge. There, I found the mountain path leading to Lushui.

After walking uphill for about an hour, I came to a stretch of open land on the side of a mountain. There were some government buildings on the slope above the road. In the distance, I could see a path disappearing into the mountains. I said to myself, "That must be the way to Burma."

According to Father's pocket atlas, Lushui lay outside the restricted border zone, and I felt quite safe. Casually, I walked into the county government's canteen and asked a cook if I could buy a meal. A brisk fellow, he gave me a big bowl of rice and a bowl of soup with salted meat for only two jiao. When I had eaten my fill and was leaving, I passed a wall pasted with verdicts from the local court but, having seen many such notices along the way, ignored them.

From the canteen, I walked toward the walled compound on the slope below the road, saw a barbershop, and, stroking my hair and beard, decided to have a haircut. I stepped inside and put down my knapsack. While one of the barbers seated me in his chair, the other one left the shop. Just as we were finishing up, he returned with a group of men, who stood round me and asked to see my documents.

I showed them my fake ID and a forged certificate from my college, stamped with a chop I had carved from a bar of soap, which said that I was in western Yunnan to do epidemiological research. After examining my documents, they told me to come with them.

I was taken to a white two-story building. They asked me to sit down in an office, keeping a close eye on me. There were two cadres among them. The first one was thin and tall, in his twenties, dressed in a blue khaki Mao suit. His insidious smile unsettled me. The other cadre was shorter, about thirty, and dressed in a bleached gray Mao suit. After about half an hour, a leader entered the room.

"This is Secretary Shi of the Lushui County party committee, who has come to speak with you in person," the shorter cadre introduced him.

Secretary Shi sat down in front of me, looked at my fake ID and forged certificate, and examined me from top to toe with suspicion.

"What is your real reason for coming to Lushui?" he asked.

I stuck to my story and requested his assistance in carrying out my scientific research. An old hand, Secretary Shi didn't believe a word of my pretty lies. He insisted on detaining me in order to make further inquiries and said I would not be released until all matters had been clarified.

I was taken to the county prison. Except for an enamel mug and a steel spoon, all my possessions were confiscated, and I was locked into cell number ten at the northern end of the prison, with another prisoner assigned to guard me temporarily.

Later, I learned that Lushui actually lay inside the restricted border zone. Ever since the British army's occupation of Pianma* in 1900, the de facto border between China and Burma had been the Gaoligong Mountains, parallel to and just west of the Angry River. But because neither the Qing nor the KMT nor the Communist government had recognized this demarcation officially, all Chinese atlases drew the line at the Kachin Hills a hundred miles farther west. Unaware, I had walked into a restricted border town in broad daylight. It was April 10, nine weeks since I'd left Shanghai.

---

*Pianma is the Chinese rendition of Hpimaw, a settlement traditionally inhabited by the Lachid people of Kachin State in northern Burma.

12

Fiddlehead Congee

(1959-1960)

Within one year, the Great Leap Forward had become the Great Famine—the deadliest man-made catastrophe in history. As the country's peasants were worked to the bone, firing backyard steel furnaces, building dams, and tilling fields, their harvest was hoarded in state granaries, shipped to the cities, exported to the Soviet Union and Eastern Europe in exchange for weapons and technology, or transformed into high-grade fuel for China's nuclear program. When the malnourished peasants failed to meet production targets, they were accused of hiding grain. Inflated figures, a pyramid of party yes-men, and schemes such as "dense planting" and "deep plowing" exacerbated the situation. The lone voice of reason and sanity, Defense Minister Peng Dehuai,* was denounced as a Rightist and purged. After all the domestic animals had been slaughtered, only starvation remained. The young and old died first,

---

*Peng Dehuai (1898–1974) was a veteran revolutionary, commander of the Chinese troops in the Korean War, and defense minister from 1954 to 1959. Following his purge, he was imprisoned from 1966 until his death.

and population experts estimate that when the famine subsided in 1962, more than 30 million people had paid with their lives for the callous folly and unbridled utopian megalomania.

A s the old saying goes, "A gambler who has lost his shirt will continue gambling, even if he has to bankrupt his whole family." Risking my life, I had traversed half of China and made it to the Burmese border, only to be caught on the brink of freedom. How could I give up now? As the turnkey locked my cell, I was already making plans for another escape.

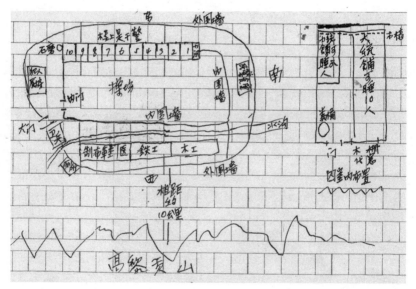

The Lushui prison

The Lushui prison sat on a terrace hewn out of the mountainside. On the ground floor, there were ten cells, with offices, dormitories, and storerooms on the floor above. In front of the building, there was a dirt soccer field.

My cell had two communal plank bunks. I was told to sleep on the smaller bunk and thrown a big blue police overcoat to use as a blanket. The prisoner assigned to guard me slept on the larger bunk.

The next morning, I had my first good look at this person. He was about forty, of medium height, withered and frail, with an introverted expression. Speaking in a low voice, he introduced himself as Ai Lun.

We were lined up on the soccer field for roll call. The group leader shouted his orders and took us for a jog around the field. As soon as he opened his mouth, I knew he was a northerner and had been a soldier.

The prisoners came in every shape and hue, from all walks of life: Han, Lisu,* cadres, peasants . . . In all, there were seventy to eighty inmates, of whom about ten were women.

The other prisoners were marched out to work in single file with bamboo carrying frames fitted to their backs. Ai Lun was one of them. Some of the shackled inmates went to the prison factory to make cloth shoes. I stayed in my cell, where the guards brought me food—rice with some meat and vegetables—at 10:00 a.m. and 4:00 p.m.

Toward the evening, the laborers returned. Ai Lun told me it had taken him four hours to carry a hundred-pound sack of rice from the Leap Forward Bridge up the mountain to Lushui. All the rice carried by the prisoners was for the local party cadres and their families. The prisoners were also sent out to collect firewood from distant forests.

"The work is heavy, but at least we have enough to eat," he said.

Ai Lun and I soon became friends. He had been a local cadre and was serving a sentence for economic crimes. He asked me what I had done. Of course I had to lie. I told him I had come to Yunnan to conduct medical research and had entered the restricted border area by mistake.

"That's the Gaoligong Mountain," he said, pointing at the high mountain visible through the window. "Burma is right on the other side. Usually, people are not allowed to cross the bridge without a border area permit. I don't understand why the guards let you pass."

---

*A Tibeto-Burman ethnic group and one of China's fifty-six official minorities, with a population of 730,000.

"But according to the map, the Burmese border is still far away," I said.

"You must have an old map," he said with a laugh.

If, on that day, I had continued walking, not asked anybody for directions, not eaten in the government canteen or gone to the barber but headed straight up into the mountains, I might have made it to Burma.

Cursing my carelessness, determined to make another escape, I inspected the cell. In front of the rammed earth wall, a row of wooden stakes had been driven into the ground to prevent prisoners from digging tunnels, but the gap between the second and third stake was large enough for me to squeeze my head through.

"If I can get my head through, I can get my body through," I thought.

My greatest fear was that the local Public Security Bureau would send a telegram to the medical college and inquire if a student by the name of Li Zhuodan, the name I had used for my forged ID, had been dispatched to Yunnan to conduct research. To keep one step ahead, I began digging a hole.

As soon as Ai Lun was out of the cell, using my stainless steel spoon as a tool and the blue overcoat as a cover, I dug like a marmot, hiding the earth between the planks of my bunk. At night, Ai Lun slept like a log and didn't hear me digging. Every half hour, at the guard's approaching steps, I feigned sleep while he indifferently pointed his flashlight at my bunk.

The rammed earth wall was thick, and after digging for three days and three nights, I had still not reached the other side. There was no going back: escape was my only option. Neither Ai Lun nor the guards discovered what I was up to. The space beneath the bunk was filling up, and I had to keep pushing the planks farther and farther apart. My fingers were torn and bleeding, but the thought of freedom made me senseless to the pain.

On the morning of the fourth day, I finally reached the other side. My plan was to crawl out through the hole after dark, choose a section of the perimeter wall where the prison building blocked the guards' line of vision, make a ladder by sticking pieces of firewood found on the ground into the cracks in the earthen wall created during the ramming, scale the wall, and head up into the Gaoligong Mountains.

Excited, nervous, I widened the hole. Suddenly I felt sharp pain between the thumb and index finger of my right hand and withdrew it. It was covered with blood, stabbed straight through by a knife. The cell door was thrown open. Several guards stormed in and dragged me out, showering me with kicks and punches.

Within a couple of minutes, I was surrounded by people. My hand was bleeding profusely, my ribs were throbbing, and my head was reeling. All I could hear was angry, incomprehensible shouting. The police stripped off my clothes and tied my hands behind my back, stepping on it to tighten the rope as hard as possible, just like how they tie a man about to face the firing squad.

The blood circulation in my upper arms was cut off, and my veins swelled to the bursting point. I rolled on the ground, writhing in excruciating pain. But nobody was taking any pity on me, and the guards kept pummeling me with their heavy boots.

"Explain yourself, and we will loosen the rope!" Xu Shuhou, the local judge, shouted.

In a daze, I nodded my head. Judge Xu signaled to the guards to loosen the rope, ordered the blacksmith to rivet shackles onto my ankles, handcuffed me behind my back, and then pushed me into the cell. The chain between the ankle shackles was quite long, making it possible to walk, but the heavy, sharp shackles cut straight through the skin.

"How were you supposed to escape through this hole?" Judge Xu snorted sarcastically.

Perhaps he was right. Even if I had finished the hole, it would've been difficult to squeeze my body between the two stakes, especially the hips.

The guards ordered some prisoners to fill in the hole with rocks and earth and told me to sleep beside Ai Lun on the larger bunk. When Ai Lun returned in the afternoon, he was shocked at the sight of what I had done, but nobody criticized him. I became an ordinary prisoner, no longer received individual meals from the guards, and ate with the other inmates.

I lay sleepless through the night, contemplating my situation. Forced to admit another failure, I couldn't afford to be foolhardy any longer. I decided to reveal my true identity and start from scratch.

The following day, Judge Xu interrogated me. I told him all about the Anti-Rightist Campaign and my two escapes from the White Grass Ridge labor camp.

"You shouldn't have been in such a hurry to dig that hole," he said sympathetically. "We have a severe lack of doctors and would have been able to find work for you. Now that you have committed a crime here, things will be much more difficult."

Ai Lun showed me how to protect my ankles with rags. Later, I picked up a trick from another prisoner and hung the shackle chain from a rope fastened to my belt, which made it easier for me to move around.

The handcuffs were also very painful. It was almost impossible to sleep with both hands fastened behind my back. One day, on my way to the toilet to empty the latrine bucket, I picked up an old nail from the ground. At night, I stuck the nail into the lock of the handcuffs and fiddled about, poking it here and there. Suddenly they fell open. I was mad with happiness and slept well that night.

At dawn, I locked the handcuffs again and waited for the group leader Wang Zhangcan to come and open them so that I could go to the toilet. Every night, I opened my handcuffs before going to sleep and then locked them again in the morning. Ai Lun didn't notice. Sometimes, I even took them off for a while during the day to feel a bit more comfortable.

I had worn every thought, idea, memory, and feeling threadbare. What more was there to think about? Freedom? My future was ruined. I could have despaired, considered suicide, but somehow I was still full of the will to live. Recalling the perplexing events of my life since meeting Ximeng, I began to invent fictional characters and construct the outline for a play. Only twenty-five years old, I had already experienced the ups and downs of a lifetime.

The Lushui Public Security Bureau soon received a reply from Shanghai confirming my identity. No longer suspected of being a KMT agent, I was treated somewhat better. At the beginning of May, Ai Lun was released. I was sad to see him leave. Even though he had been keeping an eye on me for the leadership, he was a good man and had never used this opportunity to hurt me and curry favor. On the contrary, he had helped me and given me much valuable information about the local situation.

The prison guards removed my handcuffs and transferred me to cell number two. I slept on the bunk beside a young Bai* by the name of Cha Wei, whose father had been the tribal headman in Lushui. Right after liberation, the Communist Party had treated the Lisu, Bai, and other ethnic groups in the region well, but during the political upheavals of the Anti-Rightist Campaign and the Great Leap Forward everybody in Cha Wei's family had been arrested, and he himself, a cadre in the county government, had been jailed simply because his father was considered a reactionary element. I gleaned a lot of useful information from Cha Wei. Lushui County, with a population of some forty thousand people, ran like a strip along the Angry River valley. The PLA maintained a fortified camp at the Pianma Pass and patrolled the border, making it extremely difficult to escape to Burma. After sentencing, everybody in the Lushui prison was eventually sent to the Lijiang labor camp in northwestern Yunnan.

Three inmates were awaiting execution. One, a militia leader named He Zhanxu, had fled across the border to Burma but had been sent back by the Burmese and sentenced to death. Naifang, a Lisu, had killed a man, while a man by the name of Make, also Lisu, was on death row for being an imperialist Christian preacher. All three were in shackles.

"It was Naifang who saw you digging the hole and reported you to the guards," Cha Wei told me.

One day, the prison guards suddenly stormed our cell, screamed my name, handcuffed me again, and reduced my ration to two bowls of

---

*One of China's fifty-six official minorities, with a population of 1.8 million.

rice per day. Cha Wei was not punished but interrogated several times and whispered to me that Zhao Mingzhu had told the prison leadership I was trying to organize a prison breakout. A Bai youth who slept on the opposite bunk, Zhao Mingzhu was awaiting his sentence for accidently shooting and killing a man. Desperate to ingratiate himself with the authorities, he had been eavesdropping on our conversations and snitched everything we said to the prison leadership, peppering his reports with speculations.

The kitchen worker Yang Mou strictly enforced my reduced ration and only gave me a bowl of thin gruel made from one *liang*, about two ounces, of rice two times a day. I was so starved my eyes turned black. But because I had done nothing wrong, I refused to beg for mercy and endured in silence for a month. Finally, the prison leadership took off the handcuffs and allowed me to eat with the other prisoners but kept the ankle shackles on.

For the first time since my arrest, I was allowed to wash my clothes. A fellow prisoner showed me how to remove my pants while shackled.

One day, two Public Security Bureau officers came to see me and asked me to design a new office building for them. I was a medical student! But I understood their mentality. First, they thought a university student knew everything. Second, if I told them I couldn't do it, they would be convinced I was simply unwilling to help. I decided to give it a try. After asking them about their requirements for the building, I went to work and actually managed to produce a few design drawings that they seemed satisfied with.

A few days later, Judge Xu brought Pu Fushi, a fifty-year-old Lisu prisoner, to my cell, together with some maps of Lushui County.

"These maps are old and full of errors. I want you to draw a new, detailed map according to Pu Fushi's description and include every village. Pu Fushi has been all over the county as a caravan driver and is very knowledgeable. He will tell you everything. I want you to finish the job in one month," Judge Xu said to me.

I couldn't believe my ears. Why would he serve the geography of the whole region on a silver plate to an escape artist like me? Were they testing me? I knew as little about mapmaking as I did about architectural drawings, but for the same reason as before I couldn't refuse this strange request.

Every day, I met with Fushi to work on the map, asked him about villages, mountains, and rivers, distances and directions, and also drew the passes and roads to the villages on the Burmese side. Because the map contained hundreds of place-names, it was a complicated job, even more difficult than I had anticipated. In draft after draft, we revised and improved the map.

This was Yunnan's rainy season, which made life even more miserable for the prisoners who had to labor outdoors. Fushi was glad not to have to carry firewood from the forest in pouring rain and stretched our mapmaking assignment as long as possible. He was a horse caravan driver by profession, had been to many places, knew many people, spoke good Chinese, and was a virtual encyclopedia for local history and politics.

After one month's work, we managed to produce a reasonably accurate, detailed map of Lushui County. Studying it carefully, Judge Xu pointed out a few mistakes and asked us to make another revision. When he was finally satisfied, he took away the new map but inexplicably allowed me to keep the old ones.

It was six months since I had left Shanghai. Mother did not know where I was and was sure to be worried, but the shame of my repeated failures kept me from writing. Finally, I managed to write a short letter informing her of my imprisonment. Shortly after, I received a big comfort package from her with a blanket, clothes, and canned food, which caused a lot of whispering among the guards and other prisoners. It was the fifth blanket Mother had sent me since my first incarceration. I had left the others behind at White Grass Ridge, together with my most precious memory—the photographs of Ximeng. The parcel lifted my spirits, and I settled in to prison life.

Slowly but surely, the disastrous effects of the Great Leap Forward spread to Lushui. At the time of my arrest, the kitchen staff had simply placed a big wooden barrel filled with rice in the middle of the soccer field and allowed the prisoners to help themselves. But after the rainy season, the rice was mixed in equal parts with corn flour, and everybody received only one scoop.

When I had been in the Lushui prison for five months, Judge Xu came to see me.

"Your behavior recently has been quite good. The government has decided to remove your ankle shackles," he said, calling for the blacksmith Chufu Siba, who drilled out the rivets and took the shackles off my feet.

To my surprise, I found that I could hardly walk. Having dragged those twenty-pound shackles around for such a long time, I had become so used to them that when they were suddenly removed, I felt as if I were walking on the moon. I thanked Judge Xu and mumbled something about being willing to reform myself.

He brought me to a small room by the prison's shoe factory, where he handed me some medicines and instruments.

"From now on, you will be responsible for the prisoners' medical care. Do a good job, and don't cause any problems," he said.

I promised to do my best, although, to be honest, I was not a fully trained doctor. I wrote to Mother and asked her to send my old textbooks. I had one diagnosis tool—a stethoscope—and made great progress in the art of auscultation.

Lu Hanying, the prison head, often asked me to come to his dormitory room on the second floor to administer his injections. He subscribed to the *People's Daily*, *Yunnan Daily*, and *Eastern Daily*, which he kindly allowed me to read. Having been cut off from the outside world for six months, I was starving for news and learned of three major events.

First, China and Burma had signed a border agreement, according to which the Burmese would hand over the three villages Pianma, Gulang, and Gangfang to China in exchange for a large swath of disputed land. Second, there had been fighting on the border between China and India, with the Soviet Union's supporting India. Finally, the National People's Congress had decreed a special amnesty for

KMT POWs from the civil war to coincide with the tenth anniversary of the People's Republic of China.

There were very few local Han in Lushui. Most of them were cadres transferred from other places. The majority of the native inhabitants were Lisu, with a smaller number of Bai. The scattering of Han born and bred in Lushui all said that their ancestors had come to the region as soldiers from the north four hundred years earlier, during the Ming dynasty.

The Bai were more advanced than the Lisu and usually occupied the small, fertile plateaus known as *bazi*, where they cultivated rice. The Lisu lived up in the mountains, engaged in slash-and-burn cultivation, planted corn as their staple food, and raised pigs and chickens. While the Bai dressed more or less like Han Chinese, the Lisu wore colorful linen clothes woven and sewn by their women, wound a piece of black cloth around their heads, and walked barefoot. Their soles were unbelievably hard, and they were able to carry heavy loads on stony paths as if walking on paved roads.

All the Lisu, both men and women, smoked dried tobacco leaves, some of which still carried a tint of green. I tried this tobacco but found it hard on the lungs. Nobody in Yunnan, whether Han, Bai, or Lisu, ate meat every day. Instead, they feasted on meat every two weeks or so, sometimes more than a *jin* per person. Ham and cured meat were especially popular, and people loved to eat the fat.

Before liberation, the Lisu had been oppressed and exploited by the chieftains, who maintained their own armies, levied arbitrary taxes, and held powers of life and death over the common people. During World War II, the Japanese had occupied the area, and there were many reminders of their presence in the region, as well as stories of heroic resistance against the invaders.

Christianity had a long history in the Angry River valley, and most of the Lisu were Christians.* After liberation, all the foreign mission-

---

*In the decades preceding 1949, the Morse family from Missouri was the mainstay of missionary work in the upper Mekong and Salween river valleys. The family's

aries had left, but the Lisu preachers had continued to spread their religion. During the Great Leap Forward, the Christian congregations had opposed the communization of the villages and helped people escape to Burma, thereby incurring the wrath of the Communists, who had killed a Christian by the name of Yuehan Naba, sentenced the preacher Make to death, and given others heavy sentences.

After Wang Zhangcan was released at the end of 1959, to my surprise, the prison head asked me to be the new group leader. I accepted the job. Having received military training in middle school, I knew how to line up, assemble, run, and count off and could shout orders with as much authority as Zhangcan. The prison leadership was happy with me, and I became a leader among the prisoners.

Just before the Chinese New Year of 1960, a large contingent of prisoners awaiting sentencing was transferred from Lijiang to Lushui, swelling the population of the latter to more than 200. The catastrophic effects of the Great Leap Forward had fueled resentment against the government, and the Communist Party had clamped down hard, arresting its opponents in droves.

Built to hold a maximum of 120 prisoners, the prison became overcrowded, and because many of the new prisoners were sick, my workload was greatly increased. My diagnosis for the majority of them was tuberculosis, with many concurrently suffering from heart disease.

I wrote a report to Lu Hanying, asking the government to improve the prisoners' living conditions and provide sufficient quantities of medicine, warning of the dire consequences if the situation was not improved. But the government ignored me completely. On the contrary, our rations were reduced, and sick prisoners were forced to work.

Our grain rations were cut from one *jin* per day to seven *liang*— a starvation ration for the prisoners who had to do hard labor. As the person in charge of doling out the food, I felt sorry for them. Previously,

---

life, work, and adventures have been retold in two books, *The Dogs May Bark, but the Caravan Moves On* and *Exodus to a Hidden Valley*.

I had been able to give everybody one heaping ladle of rice. Now I could only give a flat ladle. Having devoured their minuscule portions, the prisoners gazed at me with imploring eyes, their stomachs screaming with hunger. I looked down at the bottom of the empty bucket and could only shake my head.

Chronically starved, the prisoners were easy prey for the omnipresent TB bacillus, and one after another they succumbed to this terrible disease. In his health, Zhang Xiangyin had been as strong as an ox, able to carry two sacks of rice at a time. Now, with tuberculosis eating away at his lungs, he became pale, drawn, and thin as a stick of firewood, walked with heavy steps, and had to stop every other second to catch his breath.

The number of sick prisoners grew until half of the inmates lay ill. Finally, Lu Hanying decided to do something and ordered the convicts to go up into the mountains and collect *juecai*, "fiddlehead," a species of fern with large leaves. I also picked the plant, which was very abundant in the spring.

We boiled it, then chopped it and mixed it with rice to make fiddlehead congee. This removed the raw taste and made it edible, but the fibers were still long and hard to chew. Fiddlehead contains few carbohydrates and is basically a stomach filler, like the husks and chaff we had mixed with our rice at White Grass Ridge, the only difference being that it didn't make defecating quite as painful.

Following this "reform" in our diet, each prisoner received three ladles of fiddlehead congee per day, which appeared to be sufficient. But according to traditional Chinese medical theory, fiddlehead is "cold food" that absorbs the oil in the intestines, so the more people eat of it, the hungrier they become. Therefore, using this vegetable to combat hunger was like trying to put out a fire with gasoline.

To make things worse, to cover the plant's foul taste, too much salt was added, so everybody was consuming about one *liang* per day. But when salt accumulates in the bodies of sick, malnourished people, they are often afflicted with edema, which is exactly what happened. More than half of the inmates experienced swelling of the limbs and other body parts, leaving a "barefoot doctor"* like me at a loss for what to do.

Around March 1960, a Public Security Bureau officer secretively dropped a folded piece of paper to me from the second floor. I picked up the note and read it. It was the Lushui County Procuratorate's indictment. I was a Rightist who opposed the party and socialism, who had absconded from labor education, and who had planned to escape abroad, betray my country, and join the enemy. These heinous crimes were further aggravated by the fact that I had refused to express any remorse for my wrongful deeds. On the contrary, I had attempted another escape and therefore deserved a severe sentence.

The harsh tone frightened me. For these crimes, even the death penalty was possible. I had no close friends in the prison, and there was nobody I could confide in. All I could do was stuff the piece of paper into my pocket and wait for my sentence.

Two weeks later, the guards brought me to the brick kiln below the prison for my "trial." With my head held down, I was led into a small, dim hut, where Judge Xu sat behind a low table with a middle-aged woman to his right and a Public Security Bureau officer to his left, and was seated on a low stool facing them.

Judge Xu informed me that the man sitting beside him was the people's juror and pronounced the court proceedings open. He asked me some questions, which I answered without arguing. Because my attempted escapes were facts and the evidence of my hole in the wall irrefutable, I wasn't in a position to dispute anything. Basic questions such as how I had become classified as a Rightist and whether it was right to "oppose Rightists" all seemed distant and insignificant.

According to the rules, the procurator should have been present to read the indictment, but this formality was dispensed with. The people's

---

*A common term during the Cultural Revolution, "barefoot doctor" was used to describe the medical personnel with basic training and simple equipment who provided medical care in China's impoverished rural regions.

juror, for his part, was just a furnishing and didn't say a word. Judge Xu told me to stand up and pronounced the verdict of the Lushui County People's Court: "You are a counterrevolutionary who has attempted to flee the country and defect to the enemy and are hereby sentenced to six years in prison. If you are dissatisfied with this sentence, you may appeal."

I received the verdict with mixed feelings. On the one hand, my sentence was light compared with those of other escapees. But I was still disappointed, because Judge Xu had hinted that I would be treated with leniency. What worried me most were the current living conditions in the prison. If I had to eat fiddlehead congee every day for six years, I wouldn't survive. As a word of comfort, Judge Xu told me my sentence was not written in stone and that if I behaved well, I would be eligible for early release.

With the arrival of the rainy season, the crops grew quickly, and several new vegetables, such as bok choy, squash, and sweet potato leaves, appeared in our congee. As our stomachs swelled, so did the servings, until each person received a big pot of congee. These pots were a specialty of Yunnan, made of tin, and held about eight to ten *jin* of food. Looking back, I can hardly believe I was able to eat such a quantity of stew in one meal.

Bok choy and squash were ordinary vegetables, but the sweet potato leaves tasted terrible. One day, there were ordinary potato leaves in our congee. No sooner had I ladled up the new congee mixture to the prisoners than they began to vomit. Many became dizzy, their hands and feet grew numb, and some of them collapsed.

I realized that they had been eating poisoned food. From my books on internal medicine, I learned that the stems, leaves, and flowers of the potato plant contain the toxin solanine, which can kill people. I ran up the stairs to tell Lu Hanying of my discovery. Seeing me enter through the door, the Lushui County procurator screamed at me, "Who are you? What are you doing here? Get out of here right away!"

"I have come to make a report on the cause of the disease," I replied, bracing myself.

This only made him angrier, and he screamed at the top of his lungs, "This is none of your business. Get out of here!"

Seeing that the poisoning had caused them to lose face, I left the room and walked down the stairs. I hadn't eaten the congee. And because the procurator had screamed at me to mind my own business, I washed my hands of the matter. The most severe cases were taken to the county clinic, while Dr. Huang was called in to treat the other prisoners poisoned by the solanine.

At the end of 1958, I had experienced the madness of starvation for the first time at White Grass Ridge and learned that when you've been starving long enough, you will never feel full, no matter the quantity of stomach filler. In the late spring and early summer of 1960, I experienced starvation for the second time. Every day, I ate two huge pots of mixed congee but didn't feel the least bit full. The prisoners who had to labor were going crazy, stuffing everything they could find up in the mountains into their mouths.

The most severe kind of edema was tubercular peritonitis. During their sleep, prisoners with TB swallowed phlegm containing the TB bacillus, which entered the stomach, penetrated the intestinal walls, and finally spread through the lymph nodes to the peritoneum, eventually causing tubercular peritonitis. Patients with this condition suffered from extremely high blood pressure, which often led to heart failure. Their skin turned black and lost its elasticity. A horrendous odor emanated from their pores.

One of the prisoners with tubercular peritonitis was Bo A Naiba. Although he was severely ill, the prison leadership still required him to cook feed for the pigs. He sat by the wok, a human skeleton with a huge, bloated belly, exuding a foul smell. A few days later, he was gone.

Other people died even faster. I remember a Lisu youth by the name of A Nuonai who looked okay going out to work in the morning, even joking with his fellow inmates. Suddenly, with no warning, he dropped dead on the spot. And then there was Tang Mou. Ordered to carry firewood, he walked and walked until he collapsed on the road. The other inmates carried him back to the prison. But as soon as his feet had been lifted up on the bed, he breathed his last breath.

As the prison doctor, I was helpless. The only cure for malnutrition is of course wholesome food, of which there was virtually none. Second, there was a severe shortage of medicine, making it impossible for me to control the situation. But as always, the Communist Party had to find a scapegoat, and I became its first target.

The Lushui Public Security Bureau requested two doctors from the local health authorities to inspect the situation at the prison and determine if there were any problems with my work. After examining the patients carefully, they could only concur with my opinion that the most severe cases were suffering from a combination of tuberculosis and heart failure, and they compiled a list of recommendations for these patients.

Sick prisoners must be allowed complete rest, with food rations increased and medicine made available. The most seriously ill prisoners must be released and allowed to return home in order to receive medical care. Because both doctors defended me, the Public Security Bureau could not in decency punish me, but neither did it pay the doctors' recommendations any heed, and it continued to force the prisoners to work as before.

A week passed. With prisoners dying like flies, the Public Security Bureau finally sent the most severe cases to the local clinic, which put up a few tents to receive them. I will never forget Duan Chengding, who was forced to work despite his severe edema. One day he collapsed. I took him to the clinic. The next day, I brought him the dextrose and other medicines his family had sent.

"Old Xu, I am finished," he said to me, his eyes filled with tears.

On the third day, I was informed by the clinic that Chengding was dead. As far as I recall, every sick prisoner sent to the clinic died there.

By now, the Public Security Bureau had no choice but to stop forcing sick prisoners to work. Except for the shoe factory, all production was halted. The prisoners begged me for medicine. The Lisu, in particular, had a superstitious belief in injections. With only enough medicine for a few full treatment courses, I chose to divide the pitiful amount of drugs evenly and gave a medically useless dose to each patient, hoping for the placebo effect. Sometimes, I had no medicine at all for a specific indication, and if the patient kept pestering me for an injection, I simply administered a solution of pure water to keep him quiet.

Because the prison leadership could not afford to buy modern drugs, it struck upon the idea of using Chinese herbal remedies instead. One day, they brought in a local herbal doctor who administered his own secret panacea. Using a 10-cubic-centimeter syringe, without any sterilization procedures, he injected a brownish solution into the arm of the patient, who often suffered a severe infection at the injection site. Some of the prisoners' arms swelled to the size of a honey melon, and they fell ill with fever and vomiting.

I had no right to say anything and could only look on helplessly as he wreaked havoc, before attempting to control the infections with sulfa and penicillin. The leadership's stupidity, indifference, and cruelty astounded me. I could hardly believe we were living in the twentieth century.

As the TB epidemic continued to reap its victims, some of the female prisoners also fell ill with the disease.

One of the female prisoners was a woman from Kunming by the name of Lei Lianfang. About twenty-five years old, she had been working as a cadre in the propaganda department of the Lushui party committee. I never found out why she was in prison. She had a handsome face but appeared drained and dispirited. Having grown up in Kunming, she carried herself like a city girl. She worked in the prison's shoe factory binding soles. But the leadership seemed intent on making life sour for her and often ordered her to do heavy physical labor. One day, Lei Lianfang barged into my "consultation room," a dark and humid thatched hut, and informed me with tears in her eyes that she had been coughing up blood. Before I had time to say a word, she pulled off her jacket and shirt, baring her breasts.

"Hurry up. Listen!"

Examining her with my stethoscope, I detected an obstruction in her lungs, nodded my head, and asked her to put on her clothes again. The wave of death had struck fear in her heart, and she begged me to save her life.

"There is not enough medicine. I can only give you one injection of Rimifon per day, but don't tell anybody," I said.

Sure enough, He Zhanxu, the death row convict who worked with Lianfang in the shoe factory, snitched to the prison leadership that I was giving all the good medicine to her. A Public Security Bureau officer came to see me and warned me to stay away from Lianfang, saying that she specialized in playing with men.

"I do not like Lei Lianfang. There has been nothing improper between us," I told the officer. "She is ill, and it is my duty to treat her. If you suspect us of having any kind of illicit relationship, I will not treat her anymore, and you can take her to see a doctor at the local clinic."

Soon after, Lianfang was released, lifting a burden from my shoulders. In August 1960, I received a letter from her, saying that she was laboring at the Seven Tree Farm by the Angry River in the southern part of Lushui County and thanking me for saving her. I didn't write back.

Finally, the Lushui County government was forced to adopt serious measures to stem the torrent of death. An ox was slaughtered, and soybeans were purchased to make tofu.

The authorities also allowed prisoners to buy dog meat with their own money. There were a lot of dogs in the Angry River region, and the price for a big dog was only about two yuan. A group of prisoners would pitch in a few jiao each, slaughter a dog, and have enough meat to last a few days.

I became an expert at hanging dogs. This method leaves blood coagulated in the meat, giving it a foul smell that has to be allayed with spices. Fortunately, Yunnan produces every imaginable spice, and the cooked dog meat was tasty.

There is no medicine like food. After a month of better treatment, our health improved, and the death rate dropped. By that time, my list of dead prisoners ran to seventy—one-third of the Lushui prison population. Strangely, there was not a single female prisoner among the dead. I was glad for Zhang Xiangyin, who had looked marked for death but miraculously managed to pull through.

Slowly, things returned to normal. I wrote to Mother, informing her of my six-year sentence. She wrote back admonishing me to exercise self-restraint and sent me a steady stream of money, books, and daily necessities. Although there was also a lack of goods in Shanghai at that time, she even managed to send me food, which helped me survive through those most difficult days. I kept asking her for news of Father, but she would only say that he was in Qinghai and that everything was fine.

On the evening of September 25, 1960, the new Lushui prison leadership informed us that a number of prisoners would be transferred to the Liuku detention center down in the valley on the eastern side of the Angry River. I was on the list, together with Li Wenyu, Duan Peng, He Zhanxu, Make, Naifang, and others.

The next morning, we carried our belongings down to the suspension bridge, where the guards told us to wait. A truck came chugging along the river from the north. Looking under its canopy, I saw a large group of convicts. One of them told us that they were from Jade River County and that they were on their way to the Lijiang labor camp. I wondered why the prison leadership had lied to us, saying that we were being sent to Liuku. We spent one night in Eternal Peace County's detention center and continued on the winding road toward Lijiang, a picturesque historic town some one hundred miles northeast of Lushui as the crow flies.

13

Angel of Death

(1960–1961)

As we traveled north, two towering snow-draped mountains appeared in the distance: Haba to the west, with a flat top; Jade Dragon to the east, sharp and jagged. Between them, the Golden Sand River tumbled down from the Himalayas through the famous Tiger Leaping Gorge. Humbled by the beauty of our motherland, I was filled with a powerful longing to return to this place as a free man.

On the evening of September 28, we arrived at the Lijiang prison—a small, old, glum prison with a high perimeter wall—and were brought to a dim, overcrowded cell. At mealtime, a large number of Tibetan convicts lumbered forth in shackles, their heavy chains rattling the ground with an infernal sound.

On the third day, all prisoners with sentences less than ten years were escorted to the Dayan Farm labor camp more than a mile northwest of Lijiang. Carrying my heavy bundle, most of it books, I passed the office of the Lijiang party committee as I trudged along the dirt road toward Jade Dragon Mountain until we arrived at a large courtyard compound.

After an inspection by the guards, we were locked into a cell with a dirt floor and a two-story communal plank bunk running along the length of one wall. The ceiling and walls were blackened with soot from the bonfires lit to keep warm in winter. I made my bed beside the carpenter Duan Peng, hoping that we could stick together and help each other.

The evening meal was everybody's first concern. We were starving, and our greatest fear was that there would be nothing to eat in this new place. At food time, we were brought into the courtyard in groups of ten until it was packed with prisoners. The meal was one small cup of steamed corn flour and rice, but there were a lot of vegetables and extra helpings. Duan Peng and I nodded to each other; with some luck, we might be able to scrape through. Nobody was celebrating, though, because we knew we were in for hard labor.

A prison officer blew the whistle for assembly. As newcomers, we were lined up in the middle, surrounded by the old prisoners. A tall, swarthy cadre appeared before us. He had a flattop haircut, a low forehead, a face full of deep creases, a flat nose, a wide mouth, thick lips, a stubble beard, and an arrogant smile.

"That's Mu Shiqin, the political commissar. A mean fellow!" an old convict whispered to me.

From his surname, I guessed he was Naxi,* and his accent confirmed my conjecture. His voice was deep and resonant, savage in its authority. He spoke about the upcoming National Day celebrations, ideological reform, and the fall harvest.

Suddenly his face contorted: "We have some new arrivals today. Some of them might be under the illusion that our security is lax, and

---

*One of China's fifty-six official minorities, with a population of 300,000.

be dreaming of making an escape. Now stand up and make yourselves known!" he thundered.

I heard Duan Peng's name called out. The next one was mine. Unable to believe my ears, I hesitated. Commissar Mu shouted my name again. Terrified, I walked over and stood beside the other seven men.

"Put these men in shackles," Commissar Mu ordered with a cold sneer.

Four blacksmiths riveted the shackles around our ankles as the other prisoners looked on in petrified silence. The shackles were lighter than those in the Lushui prison, but the chains had only four links, making it almost impossible to walk. My heart felt as if somebody had poured lead into it. Looking extremely pleased with himself, Commissar Mu dismissed the assembly.

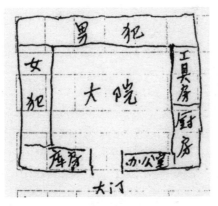

The courtyard at the Dayan Farm
labor camp

After dark, the guards placed one row of latrine buckets in the court-yard in front of the male prisoners' cells and one row in front of the female prisoners' cells. Anybody who needed to go to the toilet during the night had to step out of the cell, report to the guards in a loud voice, and discharge his or her bladder and bowels right there in front of them. Every morning, the area around the buckets was a disgusting cesspool of piss and shit. Some prisoners on duty would clean up the worst mess, but the foul stench had seeped into the ground, and the courtyard reeked permanently of human excrement.

For the National Day, we were allowed three days' rest and given a bit of meat. Shackled, Duan Peng and I had nothing to celebrate. On October 4, I went with the others to work in the vegetable fields, where the guards, feeling sorry for me, allowed me to sit alone in a far corner of the field and do some simple weeding and then helped me back to our cell in the evening.

The next day, I was told to chop firewood in the courtyard. A female cadre threw me an ax, a big hammer, and some chisels, pointed to a pile of thick tree trunks, and ordered me to split them open. I had no idea where to start. There were no saws in western Yunnan. People there simply hit chisels into the trunk at even distances and struck them with a sledgehammer until the trunk fell open, then chopped the wood into smaller pieces. After half a day of futile attempts, I had still not managed to split a single trunk.

In the afternoon, I was summoned to Commissar Mu's office.

"I have read your file," he said. "You are a traitor to the Communist Party and our country. And for all this, you have received a mere six years. You might just as well have been sentenced to twenty years, even life. The party has treated you with extreme leniency. Now you must show your gratitude, atone for your crimes, and reform yourself. I warn you. If you persist in your opposition and try to escape, I will destroy you."

As he spoke, I had the opportunity to examine his face at close range. Every aspect of it exuded arrogance, conceit, and contempt. Of all the public security officers I have ever met, none was as detestable as Mu Shiqin. To me, he was nothing but a fascist, and fate had dictated that we would be sworn enemies.

After two weeks, my shackles were taken off, and I was moved to a prison compound in a village two miles down the road. A cadre brought me to a stone quarry on a mountain slope ten minutes' walk south of

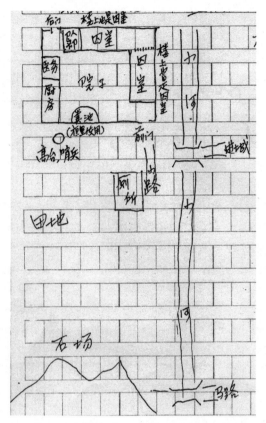

Prison compound and road to stone quarry, Lijiang

the prison, where the convicts were busy blasting, breaking, and transporting stones.

This was the third detachment of the Lijiang Prefecture's construction brigade, made up of about one thousand convicts. I was assigned to work with a man by the name of Zhang Bingsong. We carried chunks of blasted boulders and rocks split by the stonemasons up to the road, where we piled them into cubes so that the surveyor could calculate the volume and then lifted the rocks onto horse carts for transportation to the construction site of the Public Security Bureau's new offices.

Some of the boulders were huge. It was easy to injure your back, and you had to take great care not to have your fingers and hands crushed. Gloves wore out in no time. It was the most primitive work, and every evening, after carrying several tons of rocks, we returned to our barrack washed out with fatigue.

One day, Wang Jinru, the leader of our detachment, sought me out at the quarry.

"Xu Hongci, I hear you are a university student. Even had plans to study abroad," he said. "Your problem is minor. Work hard, and you will still have a bright future!"

I examined his face, and to my surprise I could see that his smile was sincere, free from malice. Every time I saw him, he smiled like this, and I gradually let my guard drop. In this harsh environment, the smallest kindness and politeness from anybody in authority was a comfort and made me feel a little bit safer.

Min Guozheng, the inmate who slept next to me, was a Bai from Lanping County. Small but strong, he was skillful at manipulating heavy boulders. One night, I was awakened by his rapid breathing and violent convulsions. Thinking that he had fallen ill, I was about to get up from bed and call for the doctor, when Bingsong held me back.

"He is masturbating," he said in a low voice.

Sure enough, after a little while, Guozheng's breathing calmed down, and he lay still. But as the food situation grew worse and our health deteriorated, Guozheng lost his sex drive and no longer stirred at night.

By the end of 1960, our prison fare contained no corn flour, potatoes, or green peas. Instead, we were given "chicken beans," a specialty of Lijiang the size of a rice kernel, oblate and brown, which were boiled and then steamed. Our rations consisted of one ladle of chicken beans and one bowl of pickled cabbage soup, which everybody finished to the last drop, although it was as sour as vinegar.

The chicken bean's husk was hard to digest and, in combination with the strongly acidic cabbage soup, made many prisoners sick with chronic gastrointestinal inflammation, including me. Every morning around 3:00, I would wake up with a terrible stomachache and have to go to the latrine, sometimes squatting over the stinking bucket for more than half an hour. Sick with malnutrition and diarrhea, I lost weight rapidly and then developed edema, which spread upward from my ankles all the way to my eyelids.

Li Zhenghong, a Bai youth from Heqing County, knew a lot about wild plants and was always able to find edible leaves and roots. Learning from him, I too brought back plants to cook in the evening. The soup from these plants was usually bitter, but no matter how bad the taste we were lucky to have this food. To prepare them, you needed firewood and salt, which were in great demand among the convicts. Everybody looked for twigs, branches, and pieces of wood on the way to and from the quarry. Some people asked the kitchen for salt; others told their families to send it.

One day at the end of 1960, Wang Jinru shouted my name: "Xu Hongci. You have a package from your mother!"

The parcel contained canned meat, Corning's milk powder, ice cream powder, Japanese pork fat, and other delicacies. In her letter, Mother wrote that there was a severe food shortage in Shanghai and that everything in the package came from Uncle Lu in Hong Kong. She hadn't eaten anything herself but saved it all for me. Tears filled my eyes.

I ate these treasures carefully but realized that such a small amount, however nutritious, would not restore my health. It was calories we needed more than anything else. To still my hunger pangs, I started smoking again, not rolled tobacco leaves like in Lushui, but the Golden Elephant brand, a mild, first-class cigarette that cost three jiao a pack.

One day in January 1961, our whole detachment was marched to Baisha, about thirteen miles to the north, to dig sand. A bitter wind swept down from Jade Dragon Mountain. The only way to stay warm was to work without stopping. As soon as you took the shortest break, the freezing cold cut straight to your bones.

Without a single bite of food or drop of water, we worked for eleven straight hours until 6:00 p.m. Guo Wenzhang, our team leader, ordered us to keep going. Some of the men simply ignored his orders and sat down to rest in depressions shielded from the wind. Suddenly,

Dai Chaogang, a convict whom I knew from the Lushui prison, collapsed to the ground, unconscious.

Taking turns, exhausted, cold, and starving, I and three other convicts carried him on our backs as fast as we could to the clinic in Lijiang, squeezing the last drop of strength from our bodies. The clinic sat on a mountain slope, its single dimly lit ward crowded with severely ill patients. After receiving an injection of glucose, Chaogang slowly awoke from his coma.

"I'm afraid it's all over for me," he said.

"You'll be all right. Stay here and have a good rest," I replied.

"Hurry up!" the guards shouted.

I took leave of Chaogang and staggered back through the pitch-black night to our barrack, praying for him, hoping he would pull through. Three days later, we were informed of his death. I knew that he had died of hypoglycemia and that Guo Wenzhang was directly responsible for making us work that long without any food. But who was going to hold him accountable? Chaogang died no better than a dog, one of the countless convicts driven to their deaths by disease, malnutrition, and forced labor. Among the survivors, terror and discontent reduced productivity to virtually nil.

In the quarry, I worked with Zhou Ruzhang. His eyelids were swollen with edema, his strength sapped. Unable to move larger boulders, we fiddled about, carrying smaller rocks and trying to look busy. Lijiang is seven thousand feet above sea level, and the winters are freezing cold. Often, we would just curl up in some shielded place and try to catch some warm rays from the sun.

Ruzhang was a Naxi, had accompanied his father on trading trips to Deqin in Tibet and to Calcutta in India, and was familiar with these routes.

"If we stay here, we'll die like everybody else. Let's escape," he said one day.

He was right, but I reminded him that our prison was small and that the guards had a clear view from their tower.

"The rear gate is the weak point. In the evenings, people come and go, and there is a bit of confusion. We could escape that way," Ruzhang replied.

"The mountain passes are buried in snow. Even if we make it to Deqin, we'll never be able to cross the Himalayas. We'll freeze to death."

"We'll hide out in the mountains, steal a yak, slaughter it, gather strength, and bide our time, then make the crossing when the weather gets better."

I realized that his plan was nothing but the wishful dreaming of a young peasant, and I told him I would not go along.

On death's doorstep, man can become an animal and abandon every moral principle he has established in the course of his life. In our prison, convicts stole like kleptomaniacs, defecated where they pleased, fought, squealed, and were capable of every other hideous and despicable act.

I saw prisoners rub their faces with their own urine in the morning as a kind of self-inflicted punishment. Personal hygiene was almost nonexistent, clean clothes even rarer. I too became a savage. During those months, I didn't wash myself or my clothes one single time. As soon as there was a sunny day, the prisoners threw off all their garments and picked fleas from their scrawny, naked bodies.

I wanted to make one last stand and get out of this foul dungeon. But I realized it was too late: I was too weak to trek any longer distance, and an escape would spell certain death.

One evening at the end of January 1961, Wang Jinru summoned me in a loud voice. I walked down the stairs and reported to him. He pointed to a stool and told me to sit down. He and Guo Wenzhang were sitting on their respective beds. Having been in prison for three years, I had learned to read the faces of tyrants. "Trouble," I said to myself. Wang Jinru came straight to the point.

"Why have you been making plans to escape with Zhou Ruzhang?"

I wondered how Wang Jinru had learned of my conversations with

Ruzhang. Concealing the matter would serve no purpose. I told them about our discussions.

"Why didn't you report his proposal immediately?" Wang Jinru asked. "You know we have treated you well."

"If I had reported him to you, you would have put him in shackles," I replied.

"You're the one whom we should put in shackles," Wang Jinru said severely. "He has already confessed, but you are still trying to protect him."

That evening, Wang and Guo assembled all the convicts for a big meeting, ordered me and He Weiquan to stand up in front of everybody, and announced that we were being punished with shackles for not reporting Ruzhang's escape plan. Unbeknownst to me, Ruzhang had also talked with Weiquan about escaping, and just like me Weiquan had not reported the matter to Wang Jinru.

It is almost impossible to describe the despair and anger I felt at being put in shackles for the third time. I wanted the whole world to go up in flames together with me. Once again, I had been branded the bad egg, and all the other prisoners were ordered to discuss their own ideological shortcomings with me as the glaring, stinking negative example.

The following day, despite the shackles, I was sent out to work as usual. Carrying an iron drill rod on my shoulder, I shuffled through the main gate with the rest of the team, dragging my chains with heavy steps toward the quarry. When I had gotten about fifty yards, Wang Jinru called my name and told me to come back. I made my way to him over by the gate.

He looked at me and said, "You are in bad health and in shackles. You don't have to work. Stay in the camp. I'll put you on the sick list, and you can read newspapers."

I couldn't fathom his motive for this unexpected kindness. Subsequently, every morning, I sat in the courtyard and read the newspaper aloud for about ten convicts on the sick list, not even bothering to see if they were listening.

Wang Jinru asked Kuang Zhong to treat me. But Kuang Zhong didn't have enough medical knowledge even to cure a cold.

"Just give me food, and I'll be all right," I told Wang Jinru.

"How much do you need?" he asked.

"Double rations," I replied.

That same afternoon, Wang Jinru asked the kitchen to double my rations. Suffering from chronic gastrointestinal inflammation, I was so ill I could've dropped dead on the spot at any time like Chaogang and so many others. If I had been forced to labor in the quarry, I don't think I would have lasted another week.

On my tenth day in shackles, at mid-afternoon Wang Jinru returned to the camp in a good mood. He called me to his room and said, "Xu Hongci, I'm convening a meeting at the brick kiln tonight and removing your shackles. Tomorrow, you will be transferred to the infirmary to work. You will have better food there and be able to work and regain your health at the same time. But there are no guards in the infirmary, so don't you dare take advantage of the situation and try to escape. I've vouched for you to the production brigade. You have to do me right. If you try to escape again, you will be severely punished."

I finally realized that Wang Jinru was a good man. He had actually done everything possible to help me. He had put me in shackles not to punish me but for show and as a warning and then made arrangements for me to work in the infirmary, thereby saving my life.

Moved, I didn't say anything for a long time. I promised him I would not try to escape and would reform myself and work well at the infirmary. Wang Jinru nodded his head. From that day on, he and I established a special kind of friendship, which was rare in the labor camps.

In the evening, all the convicts were escorted by the prison guards to the brick kiln for the meeting. Still shackled, Weiquan and I walked slowly. We crossed a bridge and followed the horse cart road toward the brick kiln, situated on a hillside at a couple of miles' distance.

I had never walked that far with shackles and was exhausted, walking and resting, then walking some more. The road passed through fields. At the foot of the hill, we turned onto a larger road, where people stared at us with startled, hostile eyes. A group of children pelted us with stones, shouting at and taunting us. Luckily, we were wearing cotton-padded clothes; otherwise, we would have been hurt. They followed us all the way to the brick kiln. I endured the humiliation in silence, not thinking, not feeling.

By the time Weiquan and I arrived, the meeting had already been under way for quite some time. The guards seated us in the first row.

Wang Han, a big northerner, was kneeling in front of everybody. A former bandit, he had joined the PLA, fought well against the KMT, and been promoted to senior captain. During the Anti-Rightist Campaign, a murder he had committed during his years as an outlaw had been brought to light, and he had been sentenced to twenty years. But Wang Han insisted he had given his life to the revolution and had never accepted his verdict. On this evening, Commissar Liu had chosen him as the negative example in order to reestablish discipline among the convicts and raise productivity.

Acting as Liu's hatchet men, Chen Rupin and two other convicts beat Wang Han until his face was covered with blood. When Wang Han still refused to kowtow, they stripped off his padded jacket, undershirt, and pants and continued to beat him, forcing him to kneel on broken bricks, as the other convicts shouted earsplitting slogans. Rupin was a butcher by profession and, if Commissar Liu had ordered him to, would have executed Wang Han on the spot.

I admired Wang Han's stubborn stoicism. It grew dark. Finally, Commissar Liu announced that Wang Han would be punished with shackles, while Weiquan and I, having confessed and reformed our ways, would be shown leniency and relieved of ours.

It was the cruelest *douzhenghui* I had ever attended. Wang Han was fitted with a pair of shackles that must have weighed thirty pounds, making it impossible for him to walk. In the darkness, the blacksmith injured my ankles as he was drilling out the rivets, but the pain was nothing compared with these torture instruments, and I told him to hurry up.

The next evening, I was escorted to the infirmary by Qiao Zuoli, a *liuchang renyuan*, or "post-sentence detainee."* Too weak to carry my belongings, exerting my last drop of strength, I struggled for almost two hours, collapsing on the infirmary's doorstep. Seeing how sick I was, the head physician immediately put me in a single, real bed by a stove in the number one ward for severely ill patients.

I fell into the sleep of the dead. For the first time during these ruinous months, I was given a chance to rest, real food, and medical care. My nerves, taut as piano strings, began to relax. It was almost like coming home. My only thought was sleep, and having lain down, I was like a paralytic, unable to move, lacking even the strength to go to the toilet.

On the first day, I managed to exchange a couple of words with the doctors and nurses. On the second day, I slept in a half coma. I could hear the doctor Yu Kaixu calling on me to eat but was too tired even to open my eyes. I lay in my bed as memories mingled with dreams, and scenes from Shanghai, Kunshan, Beijing, Hangzhou, Fujian, and White Grass Ridge played in my head. I saw my mother and father, grandmother, younger brother and sisters, Ximeng, Derun, old comrades from the underground party . . . relatives, friends, now clearly, now in a haze. Sometimes, I could even hear their voices.

The most beautiful moments in my life reappeared before me. I felt a peace of mind and a happiness I had never previously experienced. Now and then, I could feel somebody moving me, a doctor giving me an injection, voices, but remained immersed in my dreams and memories. It was a near-death experience, and if I had continued to sleep in this blissful state, I am sure I would have passed away.

But the doctors did everything they could to save my life and injected me with a steady stream of cardiotonics and glucose. When I

---

*During the Maoist years, convicts were, as a rule, not released after having served their sentences but were kept in their original prison, under slightly better circumstances and with a small salary, for as long as the authorities saw fit. The official euphemism for this extrajudicial practice was *jiuye*, "taking up employment." In prison parlance, it was called "moving from the small courtyard to the big courtyard."

awoke from my coma after three days, everybody drew a sigh of relief. Dr. Cao, the head physician, focused his efforts on treating the chronic inflammation of my intestinal tract, and through his skillful care the inflammation slowly receded. But my edema, caused by a long period of malnutrition, couldn't be cured as quickly.

About ten days later, Dr. Cao asked me to go to the light ward to help take care of the patients there. I set out with Dr. Yu for the three thatched huts in the pine forest up on the mountain slope but was so weak that it took me half an hour to walk three hundred yards. I forced myself to keep going, because my experiences during my three-day coma had made me realize that the will to struggle was the only way to keep death at bay.

I carried the medicine box into the ward. The patients were of all different ethnic groups—Han, Bai, Tibetans, Yi, Naxi, Lisu—dressed in their respective ethnic clothes. Some of them were lying on reed mats spread out on the dirt floor; others were sitting around bonfires, warming themselves, boiling water, and cooking gruel. Dr. Yu gave them injections, while I administered the drugs. Returning downhill to the infirmary was much easier. After that, I walked up to the light ward two times a day and assumed responsibility for the patients there.

The herbalist doctor Zhao Yuxian was serving a five-year sentence. A big man with a rough appearance and little culture, he spoke Chinese with a heavy Bai accent, set great store in friendship, and liked to help other people. He often invited me to eat steamed meat with aconite root—a popular tonic among people in western Yunnan. Yuxian was an expert at finding the beautiful aconite plant, which is extremely poisonous raw and used by hunters on arrowheads to kill prey swiftly. Its toxins are removed by decocting the root with pork for twenty-four hours, and the infusion is a nutritious, strong restorative for people weakened by disease.

Nobody suffered more than the Tibetan convicts, who were accustomed to daily meals of milk and meat and deeply attached to freedom. Locked up like this on a diet of chicken beans and sour cabbage soup, they quickly deteriorated both mentally and physically. Almost all of the several hundred Tibetan prisoners transferred from Deqin and Zhongdian to Lijiang perished in the camps. Behind them were left their *puluo* felt overcoats, which were made into clothes for the other convicts, and as late as 1970 prisoners in Lijiang were issued overalls made of *puluo*—a grim indication of the number of Tibetan convicts who succumbed in the *laogai*.

Under heavy pressure to reduce mortality among *laogai* convicts, the party still refused to touch its grain reserve. Instead, the leadership devised even more (or less) ingenious ways to fill our stomachs. Eggshells were mixed with bone powder and bran and distributed as *lingaibing*, "calcium cakes." Tree leaves were crushed and pressed, the dregs filtered out, and the green juice served as *yedanbai*, "leaf protein," which had a terrible, raw taste and was hard to drink.

Outside the infirmary, we built large cement basins and filled them with water to cultivate *marimo*, "ball seaweed." After gathering *marimo* from a nearby river, we added buckets of urine as fertilizer, and in one day and one night the water in the basin turned green. Without the equipment to evaporate and dry the seaweed, we simply ladled up the muddy green slush mixed with urine and gave it to the patients to drink, with good results.

Pine needle juice from Masson pine was effective in treating edema. At the time, my whole body was swollen with the disease. After drinking this concoction, I urinated throughout the night, and by dawn the latrine bucket was half-full with my piss. When the edema had disappeared, I was shocked to see what remained of me—a shriveled bag of bones.

I wanted to stay at the infirmary for a long time. I could have learned a lot about medicine from the other doctors, and I enjoyed the companionship. But nothing worried the *laogai* leadership more than seeing convicts become friends, and as soon as they identified a prisoner with a tendency to socialize, he was promptly transferred. So after only a bit more than a month in the infirmary, on the instigation of Li Yuanlin, the cadre in charge of discipline, I was sent back to the third detachment, where Wang Jinru was still the leader.

By then, the detachment had been moved to some shacks by Democracy Square on the western side of Lijiang and assigned to make door and window frames. Wang Jinru gave me a small hut to use as a clinic and put me in charge of the health care of some seventy convicts.

Our food situation improved somewhat, and we received a ration of one *jin* of corn flour per person per day. Although the quantity was limited, corn is at least a proper food agreeable to the digestive system. This had a positive effect on the convicts' health, and gradually work attendance and morale improved. But TB still cast its shadow over the brigade, and from the infirmary there was a steady stream of news of fellow prisoners who had died of the disease.

The death of a convict named Zhen was applauded. As a group leader, he had extorted food from the members by threatening to make false reports about them to the leadership. Fed up, they agreed to spit in the rice they gave to him, kneading it into *fantuan*, "sticky rice cakes," laced with their TB bacillus. After eating these ill-gotten cakes without misgivings, Zhen contracted the disease and died.

One day, a guard asked me to help him mount a painting. I followed him into the storehouse, where paper, scissors, glue, and the other necessary materials were laid out on a table. Lifting my head, I was overjoyed to see rows of cured hams hanging from the ceiling. The guard was in his room doing paperwork, ignoring me.

"I haven't had meat for a long time. Today, I'll have a little feast," I said to myself and cut down two fat hams with the scissors, wrapped the meat in paper, hid the package in the waist of my trousers, and returned to the camp. That night, Old Yu and I ate our fill.

The more I got to know Wang Jinru, the more I appreciated his generosity and open mind. Having observed that my reading was omnivorous and scattered—medicine, mathematics, physics, chemistry, literature, and Marxism—he asked me, "Why don't you concentrate on medicine?"

"In the future, I want to be a researcher and need a broad foundation of knowledge," I replied.

"Study hard," he said approvingly. "Knowledge is the only thing people can't steal from you."

The summer and fall of 1961 were rather uneventful. I was hoping to pass the remaining three years of my sentence peacefully. I studied and began dreaming of starting a new life after my release. But in October, the tranquillity was broken, and we were sent back to the Baisha village to reclaim land for a new farm.

The shovels struck sparks against the hard earth—pebbles and gravel covered with an inch of soil. It took the leadership a month to realize nothing could be cultivated. We were transferred again, first to the pine forests of Jade Dragon Mountain, then to the Lashiba Farm south of Lijiang, and finally, soon after the Chinese New Year of 1962, to Pianjiao, some six miles south of the third bend in the Golden Sand River, where a farm was being set up to receive the region's convicts after the completion of the Lijiang Public Security Bureau's new headquarters.

14

How to Bore a Blast Hole

(1963–1965)

In 1959, Liu Shaoqi, China's No. 2, had supported Mao's Great Leap Forward. But in 1961, he returned to his home village of Huaminglou in Hunan Province for the first time in nearly forty years and was devastated by the suffering he encountered. At the Conference of the Seven Thousand, the largest meeting in the party's history, held in January 1962, Liu Shaoqi, departing from his scripted keynote text, debunked the claims of the Great Leap Forward's success, and for the first and only time Mao himself was forced to make a "self-criticism." Liu's speech marked the beginning of an end to the famine, as well as the final estrangement between the two leaders.

During his year at Pianjiao, Xu Hongci worked as a land surveyor and camp doctor, with special charge of Lijiang's forty-nine surviving Tibetan convicts. The local peasants were friendly and the fall harvest plentiful, allowing the prisoners to recover from the worst ravages of the previous years' starvation. Then, in early 1963, the Pianjiao Farm was suddenly disbanded, and all the convicts were transferred to the Lijiang Copper Mine—the fief of Xu Hongci's nemesis Li Yuanlin.

In the spring of 1963, I was transferred to the Lijiang Copper Mine Brigade, twenty miles northeast of Lijiang. The truck drove past a brick kiln and, winding down the serpentine road toward the Golden Sand River for more than an hour, arrived at the brigade's main camp in Shudi, situated on a hill above the Yuejin Bridge.

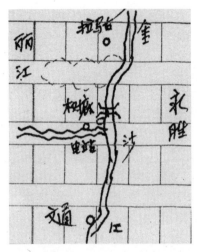

Map of Shudi, Lamagu, and Wentong

There were two mines. The *laogai* convicts worked the Lamagu mine, one day's march north on the other side of a high mountain, while the post-sentence detainees labored in the Wentong mine, one mile down the road south of Shudi. There were also a 300-kilowatt hydropower plant, a vehicle repair shop, a horse cart team, and other facilities.

Although the valley's ore vein held a rich reserve of copper, the remote location, rugged terrain, and poor communications made it impossible to mine on an industrial scale. Instead, the copper was hand mined by *laogai* convicts and post-sentence detainees using the simplest tools and most primitive methods.

After two days in Wentong, we were reorganized into new teams and driven to the hydropower plant by the Yuejin Bridge, where the other convicts were locked up in a wooden barrack near a small tributary to the Golden Sand River. There were some eighty men in our team, led by Guo Xiangyi, a thirty-year-old prisoner from Huaping County with a frog-like face who was usually taciturn but prone to violence whenever he got angry.

I continued my work as a doctor and shared a tent beside the prison barrack with the statistician Yi Zexun. The climate was pleasant. Yi Zexun had served as an intelligence officer in the KMT's Seventy-First Army, been taken prisoner of war during the Jinzhou campaign in Manchuria, then escaped back to Yunnan before being arrested during the Campaign to Eliminate Counterrevolutionaries in 1955 and sentenced to ten years.

The convicts' work was simple and hard: to dig sand from the riverbank and carry it in bamboo baskets to the construction site of a new canal for the hydropower plant. An ordinary basket held 150 pounds of sand, and it took one man an hour and a half to carry a basket from the riverbank up to the construction site, with four return trips per day. There was no road, and the convicts had to climb awkwardly up a narrow footpath, which caused a lot of bad falls.

Twice a day, I brought my medicine chest to the construction site to treat injuries and minor complaints. Severe cases were sent to the infirmary, which stood on the top of a hill an hour away by foot. The head of the infirmary was a post-sentence detainee named Wang Yonghua. Unlike the doctors in Lijiang, he didn't welcome me and never said a kind word.

Standing by the Golden Sand River—the first stretch of the Yangtze—I wanted to become a fish and swim all the way back to Shanghai. The river was about three hundred feet wide, and the current was swift, with rolling, swirling eddies. Its majestic roar filled my heart with awe. Few people dared to swim in the freezing-cold water.

There were sentries at both ends of the bridge, and nobody was allowed to stand on it. Contemplating the hostile mountains and harsh conditions, I wondered if I would be able to survive the two remaining

Xu Hongci

第一部分　在战争中度过童年

我于1933年9月10日出生在上海北四川路鑫庆坊。我还有两个姐姐，他们在一、二八淞沪抗日战争时全家逃难先后得急病死去，于是我成了老大。我父亲叫徐之萦，生于1907年。祖母曾作战，祖父是安徽休宁人，曾在上海一家当铺里做朝奉，父亲在他五岁时，他竟去世了，以后祖母就回娘家，和哥哥吴萃五在一起生活。吴萃五这人很有本事，做过端典之类行的买办，后来自己开厂开矿，做到发城火柴矿公司经理，成为中国第一代民族资本家。他对我父亲非常好，竟把他自己的儿子一样，一直培养他读到商业专科学校毕业，后来还帮他找到高薪工作。因为我父亲是孤儿，从小寄人篱下，所以生性懦弱，优柔寡断，在家庭的重大决策方面，往往缺少主见，听从母亲的摆布。我母亲叫王亚梅，生于1910年，她是大资本家的女儿，从小娇生惯养，非常的任性。我的外祖父叫王子林，江苏扬州人，在上海做丝茧生意发了财，后来又做房地多投机生意，成极大资本家。此人不识字，专门拿手于玩弄权术，做生意门槛精要极了，特别善于应付复杂的社会关系，我看他和国民党、汪精卫伪政府、英国人、日本人、青红帮的关系都不错，解放以后，共产党时他也不错，没办法弄平，所以活到八十九岁才去世。他亲生的母没有儿子，领养了一个儿子，比我母亲小五岁，叫王纪丙。此人很无聊，成了纨袴子弟，一生落拓，现在老婆孩子在美国都不认他，但他跟我的关系倒一直不错。外祖父后来娶了一个和我母亲年纪一样大的小老婆，生了一

The first page of Xu Hongci's original memoir, which runs to 380,000 Chinese characters, the equivalent of about 240,000 English words

Fires in Shanghai's Zhabei district during the Japanese attack on October 27, 1937

The People's Liberation Army enters Shanghai in May 1949

The Grand Theatre, where Xu Hongci gave his first speech, in 1952, and was arrested during his first escape, in December 1958. Photograph taken in 2015

Xu Hongci with his classmates at the Shanghai No. 1 Medical College. He is the third student from the right in the back row

Lintong Street, where Tang Ximeng lived. Photograph taken in 2015

For six weeks in the spring of 1957, the Chinese people were encouraged by the country's leadership to speak their minds. Then, on June 8, Mao sprung his trap. The "hundred flowers" period was transformed into the Anti-Rightist Campaign, and those who had dared criticize the party became the targets of its wrath. Shown here, a wall of *dazibao*, the popular method of public criticism

The gate of the Courtyard of Four Lights, originally a guild hall for merchants from the city of Ningbo. Xu Hongci was held here upon his arrest on April 8, 1958, before his transfer to the White Grass Ridge labor camp. Photograph taken in 2015

Lijiang's Democracy Square, where Xu Hongci was sentenced to twenty years in prison at a verdict rally on January 17, 1969, and where his close friend Zhang Manjie was executed. Photograph taken in 2015

The Leap Forward Bridge across the Angry River (Salween River) at Liuku, in western Yunnan. Xu Hongci crossed this bridge on April 10, 1959, the day his second escape ended in failure. Photograph taken in 2015

During denunciations at an afternoon rally in Red Guard Square, Provincial Party Secretary Wang Yilun is accused of being a "black gang element," a term referring to denounced party officials and academics. Harbin, Heilongjiang Province, August 29, 1966. Xu Hongci underwent several public denunciations similar to this one. (Photograph by Li Zhensheng, courtesy of Contact Press Images)

Another public denunciation. Here, a peasant criticized as a class enemy is forced to bow in the traditional acknowledgment of guilt. Liaodian commune, Acheng County, February 27, 1965. (Photograph by Li Zhensheng, courtesy of Contact Press Images)

This jacket, similar to the one Xu Hongci writes about, is displayed at the Laogai Museum in Washington, D.C., and belonged to the convict Liu Zhuanghuan. Like Xu Hongci, Liu was incarcerated in the White Grass Ridge labor camp. There, he committed suicide. (Photograph by Dermot Tatlow, courtesy of the Laogai Research Foundation)

A stretch of Xu Hongci's final escape route, a few miles from the town of Duomei in the mountains south of Lijiang. Photograph taken in 2015

Xu Hongci and his wife, Oyunbileg, in Mongolia

Xu Hongci and Oyunbileg with their two sons, Anjir and Buyant

Xu Hongci and Oyunbileg during a return trip to Mongolia

years of my sentence. Although I had never been in a mine, I knew that mining was the hardest work and that the death rate was extremely high. If the leadership sent me down into the pit, would I make it?

One day during work, all convicts were suddenly ordered back to the camp and locked up in a prison barrack by the roadside. Everybody found it odd. This barrack was in serious disrepair, and under the weight of the convicts stomping around inside, it collapsed without warning. Hearing the crash and screams for help, I rushed out of my tent to a scene of bedlam and began taking care of the injured. Luckily, nobody had been seriously hurt.

The leadership immediately ordered the convicts to be locked up in the vehicle repair shop instead. A heavy atmosphere of martial law settled on the brigade. About this time, a high-ranking cadre arrived with his entourage in a black car from Lijiang.

Later in the afternoon, Commissar Liu asked me to give this bigwig an injection and told me to do a good job. Nervous, I walked over to the brigade headquarters and saw Liu sitting with the high-ranking cadre at a stone table by the entrance. He was about forty-five years old, with a piercing, haughty expression. His secretary handed me the syringe and instructed me to administer an intravenous injection.

The cadre rolled up the sleeve of his white shirt, revealing a plump arm.

"Do you know what you are doing?" he asked me harshly in his northern accent.

I nodded my head. This cadre was so fat I couldn't even see his vein, but finally, carefully, I inserted the needle and administered the injection as Commissar Liu looked on breathless with anxiety. The procedure concluded, I gathered my instruments, bowed to the leaders, and hurried back to my tent, where I told Zexun what had happened.

"He came here to eat fish," Zexun explained.

I finally realized what was going on. There is a rare, delicious fish in the Golden Sand River, and sometimes high-level cadres would come to Shudi to have a feast.

"A high price for a single meal," I said to myself. "Several hundred men kept away from work for a whole day. Scores injured."

There was a small commercial center by the brigade headquarters, with a shop, a hostel, and a restaurant. The restaurant served one dish—a few thin slices of cured meat—for five jiao. Following Zexun's example, I went there to buy some meat but was reported to the team head, who called me to his office.

"I hear you have been to the restaurant," he said.

"Twice," I replied.

"Whom did you ask for permission?"

"Nobody."

"You have forgotten your place," he shouted. "You have absolutely no right to go to the restaurant. Go back and write a self-criticism!"

At this time, a Lisu convict carrying sand was seriously injured by falling rocks. Because I was out at the time, the guards sent the man to the infirmary, but he died on the way, and the disciplinary cadre Li Ruqing accused me of dereliction for not having been at my post. Like most other *laogai* cadres, he was narrow-minded, intolerant, and unforgiving and, compounding this error with my having been to the restaurant without permission, decided to punish me by sending me down into the Lamagu mine.

Xu Hongci's carrying rack

One day in June, I set off with my heavy bundle of belongings and books up into the mountains, climbing one reluctant step at a time. Fortunately, my old friend Duan Peng had made a carrying rack for me, and its curvature and line fitted my shoulders perfectly, which saved me a lot of pain and effort. To this day, I still have fond memories of that carrying rack.

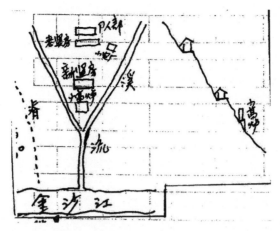

Overview of the Lamagu mine camp

It took me four hours to reach the top of the mountain, where, to my surprise, there was a stretch of flat land, with a primary school built on it. The road descended. At the bottom of the valley, I could see a few houses—the prison barracks of the Lamagu copper mine.

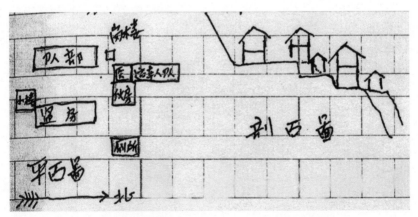

Detailed drawing of the mine camp

Upon my arrival, my belongings were inspected by none other than my old enemy Li Yuanlin, the disciplinary cadre from the Lijiang infirmary.

"So here you are again!" he said in a mocking voice.

His pale, sharp face disgusted me. I turned away, unable to look at him.

Leafing through my books, he shook his head. "You'll have no use for these here," he said, throwing them to the ground one by one. "You must focus on work and on reforming yourself."

There were about two hundred convicts at the mine. Our team leader was a Naxi by the name of He Yaozong. One look at his obsequious bearing and you knew he was a zealous snitch.

As soon as I had put down my belongings in my barrack, the squadron leader Liang Manqi brought me to a large rock by the brigade office and seated himself above me. He had probably heard bad things about me from the brigade headquarters, because his words were venomous.

"You are a traitor to the party and the nation," he told me. "Now you will go down into the mine shaft and labor with your two bare hands like the other convicts."

He told me to prepare a basket. The next day, I followed my team to the southern mountain, halfway back toward Shudi. The low, narrow, dark mine shaft was a shock. Because I am rather tall, I kept knocking my head into the ceiling. Initially, I didn't even realize we weren't mining but prospecting, searching for the ore layer and trying to determine its direction, thickness, and quality.

Each tunnel face was worked by two leadmen and one carrier, also called a *maweizi*, "horse tail." Taking turns, one leadman held the borer while the other swung the sledgehammer, putting down four or five blast holes to a depth of twenty-five to thirty inches. After that, the explosives were arranged by the team leader or the prop setter, both of whom were trusted by the authorities and allowed to handle the blast caps, explosives, and lead wire.

I was assigned to work as a horse tail. When the dust had settled after the explosion, I made my way to the tunnel face with the bamboo basket tied to my rack, loaded the basket with rocks, and carried them out of the shaft. Ore was collected at the entrance and brought back to the small melting furnaces at the end of the day. Debris was emptied over the cliff. This had to be done in one clean movement; otherwise, you would accompany the rocks more than a thousand feet down into the Golden Sand River.

Inside the shaft, there was an electric bulb every thirty feet or so. Gradually, I got used to the darkness. It was incredibly humid, with water dripping everywhere. You had to wade through knee-deep puddles, and your back was constantly soaking wet from the rocks.

The shafts were crooked and winding: high, low, wide, narrow. I couldn't walk straight with my heavy load, but when I leaned forward, the rim of the basket scraped the shaft ceiling, and the basket was worn out in a day. So instead, I had to tie a rope to the basket, let it rest on my butt, and more or less crawl.

I made friends with a couple of the other horse tails, Chen Wanshou and Ma Dengyun from Yongsheng County, who taught me the tricks of the trade. Dengyun gave me a cushion that I tied to my waist with a leather strap to keep the heavy basket from scraping the skin off my lower back. They also showed me how to pour the rocks over the cliff by pulling a rope tied to the bottom of my basket and told me to put big rocks on the ground and roll them over the edge one at a time, because if a big rock got stuck in the basket, it could throw you over the cliff.

After a while, I started to like going down into the mine. Because there was only one entrance, with no possibility of escape, the guards never entered the pit, making it a free world where we could find ourselves a relatively dry, secluded place to sit down and have a smoke and chat.

Dengyun and Wanshou were members of the Great Harmony Party, a local political party opposed to the Communists.

"The Great Harmony Party has many groups in Yongsheng County. When one group is arrested, another one pops up. We don't communicate with each other, but we share the same guiding principles. For example, we're all opposed to the Great Leap Forward and the Soviet Union," Dengyun explained.

Because of the heavy labor, we received three meals a day. After breakfast, each convict was given a big maize bun to bring to work. At lunch, the electric bulbs blinked three times, and we would gather at the mine entrance to roast our buns over a bonfire. By *laogai* standards, our grain ration of fifty *jin* per month was plentiful, but the backbreaking work still left us hungry. Fortunately, whenever the cooperative store in Shudi had food, we were allowed to send one man there to buy some.

I worked as a horse tail for more than two months and managed to make a good impression on our squadron leader, Liang Manqi. He wasn't an ordinary party cadre but a geologist who had done prospecting work on the copper vein and had stayed on to help the leadership set up the mine.

"How is work?" he asked me in a friendly voice, his anger from our first meeting gone.

"I can carry as much as anybody else," I replied. "But I'm six feet, and in some places the tunnel is only four, so I have to crawl. If you can let me be a leadman, I promise to do a good job."

After considering my request for a while, he replied, "Okay. You can work together with Wang Wenhe."

Wenhe was a Han from Lushui serving eight years for trading in opium. Short and sallow, he smoked like a fiend but was a good worker. We practiced by the mine entrance, and in the beginning we made a spectacle of ourselves. Sometimes we hit the other man's hands black and blue. Sometimes the bore rod got stuck in the hole, and we weren't able to finish one blast hole in a whole day. But after a month of trial and error, we finally got the hang of it and were sent into the mine to work as leadmen.

After each explosion, we removed loose rocks with pickaxes and cleaned the area thoroughly. The new tunnel face always presented a different challenge, protruding here, sunken there, never flat and smooth, and the key to efficient tunneling lay in the ability to, in accordance with the contours of the face and the distribution and direction of the rock layers, determine the optimal position and depth of the blast holes for the next day's explosions, as well as the best order of the blasts.

The rock strata were complicated, and we often found basalt or red bed layers behind limestone strata. In red bed, we could tunnel 60 to 150 feet a month; in basalt, only 10 to 15 or even less. The copper ore was all in the limestone layer. Limestone with pink red spots was called *hongzijin*, "red purple gold," while bright silver spots were *baixila*, "white tin meat," and green spots were *kongqueshi*, "sparrow stone." The copper contents varied from 0.01 to 5 percent, and the mining threshold was 0.1 percent—that is, two pounds of copper in a ton of rock was considered economically worth mining.

If we hit an ore stratum when tunneling horizontally, we had to dig a shaft both upward and downward to determine the layer's thickness. While tunneling upward was difficult, going downward was even harder. Water was constantly accumulating at the bottom of the shaft, and because we didn't have electric pumps, we had to pump it manually one bucket at a time. Sometimes we were in such a hurry that we entered the tunnel before the smoke had cleared, were knocked unconscious by the fumes, and had to be carried out.

The work was an eye-opener. Seeing my fellow convicts create a labyrinth of tunnels one sledgehammer strike at a time, I admired their ability to *chi ku*, "eat bitter," and felt proud of having been able to adapt to this harsh environment. I might not have had any future to speak of, but at least I had seen, experienced, and toiled in the deepest, darkest guts of human industry.

In the summer of 1963, the rift between China and the Soviet Union became official. During such upheavals, the labor camps habitually singled out the *zhishifenzi*, "intellectuals," as the main enemy. If there was a row between China and the United States, the *zhishifenzi* would stand accused of being U.S. agents. If Beijing had a conflict with Taiwan, the intellectuals would be Taiwanese *zougou*, "running dogs." So in the present split with the Soviet Union, we were called Soviet spies.

Without hesitation, the labor camp leadership designated me the most dangerous enemy. Having never either opposed or supported the Soviet Union, I couldn't understand their reasoning. I had always taken a pragmatic attitude toward the Russians, trying to learn from their strengths but also criticizing their faults and mistakes. During the brief "hundred flowers" period at the medical college, I had criticized the Soviet Union and been denounced as anti-Soviet. Now, following the Sino-Soviet split, having decided to keep my mouth shut, I became suspect for my silence instead.

Mining work wore out shoes in no time, and because the labor camp didn't issue these, Mother sent me a steady supply. Footwear was no small matter. Many convicts did not own a single pair of shoes and had to make their own. The horse tails went through a pair of home-made straw sandals in a day.

Even more important was Mother's moral support. She always found the books I asked for and sent me every issue of *Science Journal* to keep me up to date on the latest scientific discoveries. An article in that publication by my old classmate Tang Yao awoke painful memories and regrets. In every letter, I asked Mother how Father was doing, but she would only reply that he was fine and tell me not to worry. Never having received a letter written in his own hand, I had an ominous feeling but was unable to guess the worst.

In the winter of 1963, a strange thing happened at the mine. By then, Yunnan had recovered from the worst ravages of the Great Leap Forward, and the markets were brimming with cured meat and white sugar. The leadership allowed the convicts to go over the mountain to Shudi to buy these commodities, and every one of us had some cured meat hanging above his bunk and a few bags of sugar under his pillow.

I had a good friend on the horse cart team, Zhao Kuan, who helped me buy all the meat and sugar I wanted. The first thing we did after work was to light a bonfire to boil the meat. Sometimes, late at night, when everybody else was sleeping, I would sit on my bed and eat a pound of plain sugar one spoon at a time. The least bit of improvement in our living conditions had a positive effect on our productivity. Most of us preferred to work overtime rather than return to our barracks for a round of mind-numbing political studies. As our diet and lives improved, there was less illness, and the doctors had less work to do.

On holidays, the convicts had the energy to organize cultural activities. Some sang Peking or Huadeng opera, others played the *huqin*, a two-stringed Chinese violin. Chen Zongzhao's magician show was the most popular event. He had worked in an acrobatic troupe and was especially good at card tricks. Once, the Public Security Bureau sent a team to our labor camp to show movies three nights in a row, which was appreciated by the convicts.

For the Chinese New Year of 1964, Wang Xilin, the head of the mine, told the kitchen to prepare ten dishes—a real feast. I still remember the delicious Yunnan sweet meat, which I had never eaten before. Once, we trapped monkeys in a shallow pit and cooked them. Monkey meat is bright red and sweet. Li Zhong, a KMT soldier who had eaten human flesh during the war against Japan, said that monkey meat reminded him of it.

In May 1964, I was transferred to the No. 1 team to work as a leadman with Zi Zhongyun, a big, lazy, good-natured fellow from Yongsheng County who never brushed his teeth. The other members on my team were the statistician Gou Dingpeng, who was doing five years for bigamy; the blacksmith Zhang Manjie, a KMT lieutenant colonel serving a ten-year sentence; and the security officer Wang Shaozhou, who loved to gossip and sow discord.

Once, Zhongyun and I had finished a blast hole and handed it over to Shaozhou for blasting. When we returned the next day, we discovered that the explosives hadn't been detonated, and because we couldn't find Shaozhou, we had to take care of the matter ourselves. Many convicts had been blown to pieces checking misfires. I was extremely careful, adding water as I groped for the explosives. I pulled out the lead wire: no blast cap. It wasn't a misfire but an empty shot.

We immediately informed Dingpeng. For a long time, he had suspected Shaozhou of stealing explosives, lead wires, and blast caps, and the two had argued over this. Now that Dingpeng had solid proof, the leadership conducted a search and discovered Shaozhou's hidden cache. He was locked up in solitary and, after holding out for several days, finally confessed: the Great Harmony Party had bribed him with food and money to steal blast caps, explosives, and lead wires for a plot to blow up the brigade headquarters and stage a breakout.

Every member of the Great Harmony Party was locked up in solitary. Their leader at Lamagu was Tan Chongling. About twenty years old, he was an avid reader and often borrowed books from me and sought me out for conversations. But as soon as I exchanged two words with him, I was reported to the leadership and had to be on my guard. Fortunately, I wasn't implicated in his conspiracy. In any case, their plan was childish. The brigade headquarters was guarded, and ammonium nitrate is only effective in a blast hole. In air, its explosive force is weak, and they would never have been able to blow up the building.

With Shaozhou gone, Zhongyun and I were put in charge of blasting—a real science. Usually, we used Korean ammonium nitrate, wrapped into sticks with wax paper. After connecting the lead wire to the blast cap, I pressed the cap into the explosive and fastened it tightly with a string, then stuffed the stick into the blast hole with a wood rod and sealed the hole with mud.

During my time at Lamagu, I set off countless explosions and always found the work stimulating. To be sure, blasting killed a lot of people. Lethal accidents were mainly caused by groping for misfires without using water or by miscalculating the length of the lead wire. But if you knew what you were doing, it was quite fun. The other convicts looked up to the blasters, and because we were trusted by the government, for once the leadership left me alone.

By the fall of 1964, only six months remained of my six-year sentence, and I was looking forward to returning home.

Just before the National Day, all convicts were moved to a new prison complex farther down the mountainside, built on three terraces, with six prison barracks on the upper two, and the kitchen, sports field, toilets, and washing rooms on the lowest, all surrounded by a high perimeter wall.

Shortly after the move, Liang Manqi sought me out for a talk.

"I had heard a lot of bad things about you and thought you were a rotten egg. But I can tell now you're not a bad man. You even have a bit of talent. The leadership wants to transfer you to the geological team. Would you like to join us?"

"I don't know geology, so what can I do?"

"You are good at mathematics. You can do calculations," he said.

My first task on the geology team was to measure the altitude of several hundred points in the mining area. This was difficult, painstaking work. Every day, with the help of two assistants, I had to carry the instruments to distant mountaintops, starting with the national altitude points and working my way down toward the mine. The whole job took us three months to complete. After this, I helped my team member Zhang Linzhen arrange the data and do the calculations so that he could produce a comprehensive geological map for the region.

I worked well with Linzhen, who was a dedicated young man. I wondered what he had done to deserve five years in prison. China desperately needed young geologists with his kinds of skills. Probably he had simply spoken his mind.

One morning in January 1965, I stepped into our office.

"Xu Hongci," Linzhen called out with his peculiar voice. "Zhao Shiyi has been blown to pieces!"

I couldn't believe such a good man would die so horribly. Returning into the tunnel to check a misfire, Shiyi had just turned a corner when the explosion ripped through his lower body and killed him on the spot. If he had arrived even a second later, he might have survived. I grieved for him and for his family. But he was buried hastily, without a funeral.

15

No Way Home

(1965-1966)

O n April 10, 1965, I had served my six-year sentence in full. But
after pronouncing me officially "released," Li Yuanlin informed
me that I would not be allowed to return to Shanghai and would have
to remain at Lamagu as a *liuchang renyuan*, "post-sentence detainee."

Despondent, I moved my belongings down the hill to the dormitory for *liuchang renyuan*, which in any case was an old prison block.
I knew there would be little difference between life as a post-sentence
detainee and that of a convict. At least I was allowed to make myself a
proper bed out of a few wooden planks and didn't have to report to the
guards when I needed to take a piss at night.

The thought of spending the rest of my life in this remote mountain valley was unbearable. On the other hand, any rebellion by me
would be sure to incur the wrath of the Communist dictatorship, with
unforeseeable consequences. Faced with this agonizing choice, I decided to bide my time and settled into life as a *liuchang renyuan*.

The Communist Party takes a peculiar view of justice. Once it has
deprived you of your freedom, it will never restore it completely.
Detainees are only marginally freer than convicts and are definitely not

considered full citizens. If you behave well as a detainee, you might have your *maozi*, "cap," the official stigma in your dossier, removed, but no matter how hard you work, the party will never let you out of its sight, and you will always be a second-class citizen barred from better positions, sometimes even prohibited from studying.

Soon after, Li Yuanlin asked me to be the prison doctor at the mine. Initially, I hesitated, well aware there would be conflicts with the leadership, but after his repeated requests I accepted the job. For the sake of convenience, I was allowed to live by myself in a room in the old prison block and cared for the detainees who lived above me.

The economy that year was rather good, especially in Yunnan, where policies such as the free trade of pork had brought the markets back to life. With better food, the number of patients suffering from TB and edema dropped dramatically, and our workload was reduced. The most common complaints were external injuries, arthritis, and stonecutter's lung.

I often stayed in my room reading books on medicine, science, Marxism, and literature. Li Yuanlin wanted me to study Chinese medicine and gave me a few books on the subject, but having leafed through them, I found myself unable to stomach the unscientific approach. This annoyed Li Yuanlin, who made it into a political issue and accused me of being a *yangnu*, "slave to the West."

After my "release," I received several letters from Mother with news about our family. My paternal grandmother had died of gastrointestinal inflammation during the Great Leap Forward. My younger brother, Hongnian, having served three years in a labor reform camp, had gone way out west to Yining in Xinjiang, on the border with Kazakhstan, to live with the younger of my two sisters, Yunqing. Mother said she needed me to take care of her. As my homesickness grew, I became less and less able to conceal my discontent.

To strengthen their control over the post-sentence detainees, the authorities assigned Mu Shiqin, my old adversary from the Dayan Farm, as the new political commissar at Lamagu. He hadn't forgotten me and measured me up with a look of hate.

One day, he commandeered more than thirty post-sentence detainees, including me, to move a transformer from Wenhua to Shudi, a distance of twelve miles. It was a four-thousand-pound monster, boarded up in a wooden crate. I had no idea how we were supposed to move it. Some of the old hands chopped down two trees, lashed them to the transformer with thick ropes, then fastened poles perpendicularly across the two mainstays and divided us on both sides. On the given signal, we actually managed to lift it from the ground on our shoulders and made our way up the mountain road one small step at a time. When the leader shouted "Rest!" we lowered our poles onto wooden forks, rested for a moment, and switched shoulders, before hoisting the transformer again.

In the beginning, I stood at the back, but because the men up front kept injuring themselves, I moved forward. My shoulders swelled up terribly. It took us three full days to reach the Lijiang Plateau. On the fourth day, the road descended, which made our job even more difficult, because the pull of gravity put an enormous weight on the men up front.

Approaching the mine, we had put down the transformer for a short rest when it suddenly tilted forward and was on the verge of falling over the side into a deep gully. At the last moment, a detainee by the name of Mu Changbao jumped up and pushed back the transformer with all his strength, narrowly averting a disaster. "Long live Mu Changbao!" I said to myself. But Mu Shiqin pretended as if nothing had happened and simply ordered us to continue.

Li gong shu zui, "atone for crimes through meritorious services," was one of the most hackneyed slogans of the labor camps. Changbao had just performed a good deed by saving the transformer with that timely, crucial shove. Why did Commissar Mu act as if he hadn't noticed? It was just one more proof that the labor camp cadres only saw the bad things, never the good. After five days of backbreaking hardship, we put down the transformer at its final destination: the construction site of a new ore dressing plant.

I got to know some engineers and technicians working on the plant: Fu Gang from Kunming, Cai Wei from Hebei, and Zhou Ronggun from northern Jiangsu. Fu Gang, a short man with a big head, was an excellent engineer. Old Cai looked like a typical northerner, with bushy eyebrows, big eyes, and bearded cheeks, and was able to use the abacus with lightning speed. Zhou Ronggun was the oldest, weak, and sickly. They sympathized with me and told me that the only alternative to a graveless death was to get out of this hell as soon as possible.

Commissar Mu, who reserved a special loathing for *zhishifenzi*, suspected us of bad-mouthing the Communist Party and hatching counterrevolutionary plots and deployed informants who reported our every word and action. More experienced detainees had learned to mind their own business, do nothing but work and sleep, and never utter an extraneous word, muddling through their days with the sole aim of getting out of the camps alive. New to life as a post-sentence detainee, I continued to make friends: the most taboo thing in the labor camps.

At the end of 1965, a new salary system was introduced for the *liu-chang renyuan*, and each of us was classified into one of eight grades according to education and skills. Commissar Mu designated me "technical secondary school graduate," with a salary of forty-two and a half yuan per month. I didn't argue with him, but I knew he wanted to keep his heel on my neck and shared my thoughts in a letter to Mother. At this time, I posted my mail in a letter box in Shudi and didn't realize that the labor camp leadership was reading all of it. In any case, forty-two and a half yuan was better than my previous salary of twenty-seven yuan, and from then on I was able to send fifty yuan to Mother every three months.

In preparation for a visit by the prefectural hospital's mobile X-ray team, the leadership asked me to draw up a list of convicts potentially suffering from stonecutter's lung. Naturally, I had to be truthful, but I must have put too many patients on the list, because the leadership was furious and suspected me of exaggerating the medical situation in order to make them look bad.

A week later, I was relieved of my duties as a doctor and transferred to heavy labor in the Wentong mine. I didn't mind. I hated Lamagu, and I was willing to do any kind of work as long as I got out of that abominable place.

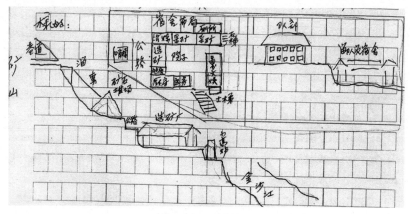

The Wentong mine

There were about one hundred detainees working at the Wentong mine, divided into mining, milling, smelting, and geological teams. I asked to work in the mine but was assigned to carry leftover ore back from a small abandoned mine five miles up the road on the other side of the Yuejin Bridge.

In my state of health, carrying 150 pounds that distance was about as much as I could take. The ore was scattered all over the place, and it took a long time simply to fill a basket. By the time we started back, it was already noon. Although it was January, the valley was hot and humid, and the sun beat down on our necks until we were soaked with sweat. At Wentong, I put down my basket, completely exhausted, unable to move another step.

One day, on the way back from the mine, I walked into the house of a Lisu family and asked for water. To my astonishment, I learned that the head of the family was 108 years old, his wife 102, and the son and his wife already more than 80—a genuine, happy five-generation family. Their storage chest was full of corn, and although their life was simple, to me it seemed a small paradise of domestic bliss. The sight of the old man and his wife smoking leaf tobacco, carefree and content, filled me with sadness and envy.

After one week as a coolie, I had had enough and went to see Liang Manqi, who was now in charge of the geological team at Wentong.

"I can't take it anymore," I told him. "How many grams of copper will you be able to extract from this basket? It's not worth it. Can you please ask the leadership to allow me to return home?"

"Frankly, we don't trust you, and we will not let you return to Shanghai. It would only be asking for more trouble from you," Liang Manqi replied. "You haven't reformed your thinking. For you, this will be a protracted task, and you must be prepared to remain here for a long time. Hard labor is the only way to purge your mind of all those reactionary ideas. Look at you. You are not even willing to carry ore."

Although Liang Manqi maintained a stern facade with me and often criticized me with pompous party hogwash, I knew that he actually liked me.

"Why do I have to carry ore? Can't I do something else?" I replied.

"We don't need any more workers in the mine," he said, hesitating. "Okay then, you can chop wood."

I recalled the pile of thick logs on the road above the kitchen and my failed attempts as woodchopper at the Dayan Farm. At least it would be better than carrying ore. The next day, I set off to work with an ax, sledgehammer, and chisel. Having used the sledgehammer a lot as a leadman, I was rather strong and able to chop wood quickly. The kitchen was happy with my work, and I became the woodchopper at Wentong.

Yang Yumin, Yang Wencan, Ran Youwen, and the other members of the geological team at Wentong were weak in mathematics and asked me to teach them the subject. With Liang Manqi's permission, I gave them two classes a week and corrected their homework.

Wencan came from a Bai family of scholars in Jianchuan, fifty miles southwest of Lijiang, was about thirty years old, and had a degree from a secondary medical school. His father, a historian, had passed on his interest in classical literature to Wencan, who wrote a beautiful hand of calligraphy. Having completed his three-year sentence, he had already been held as a post-sentence detainee for seven or eight years.

My students worked diligently, and after we were finished with algebra, I also taught them geometry. At this time, the regime was calling on everybody to study the works of Mao Zedong, and some of the students were worried that they would be criticized for preferring mathematics to the profound thoughts of the chairman.

"We cannot develop our country simply by studying the works of Mao Zedong. We have to study mathematics too," I said to encourage them, unable to foresee that this single utterance would be used by the party to incriminate me during the Cultural Revolution.

At the beginning of 1966, the domestic scene was stable. Everything appeared at peace. The leadership invited Yongsheng's Huadeng opera troupe—an unprecedented grand occasion in our labor camp. Although it was a simple, county-level troupe, it put on a moving show, and I still remember some of the songs they performed. The female actors were pretty in their makeup and costumes, and because almost all of us, both detainees and cadres, were bachelors craving for the opposite sex, we watched the performance with great pleasure.

"Look," said Wencan, poking me in the side and pointing to the cadres in the front row. "They're in seventh heaven."

Turning my head, I saw Qiao Zhonglin and the other cadres sitting with their mouths ajar, practically drooling.

One day, I saw Liang Manqi jump into the Golden Sand River and swim with confident strokes through the swirling eddies to the other side, where he climbed up on a rock and rested in the sun for a while before swimming back again. I also tried swimming in the river, but the current was too fierce, and I was forced to turn back. Wencan teased me for being a *hanyazi*, "dry goose." "Let me be a dry goose," I said to myself, not the least offended. Water and fire do not coddle foolhardy heroes.

Later, I was transferred to the job of carrying rocks for the construction of a perimeter wall around the mine's storage yard. Our team leader was He Zijing, a Bai from Jianchuan who, having cast off the shadow of death from the Great Famine, had once again become a strong, sturdy fellow. At this time, his father was visiting with him, and Zijing was in high spirits. One day, he challenged me to carry with him a boulder weighing more than four hundred pounds. Gritting my teeth, I was able to hold my own. Zijing's enthusiasm proved contagious, and for a while our whole team was swept up in a wave of labor competition, with all of us vying to carry the heaviest, most impossible stones.

Sometimes, we were sent to carry sand, used to make the fire-resistant wall of the small blast furnace, from a quarry that sat on top of an eleven-thousand-foot mountain above the Lamagu mine. Setting out at dawn, we reached the quarry at dusk. At the top, it was like a different world. When you gazed north toward the Himalayas, all you could see was mountain upon mountain, shrouded in wistful clouds. The most distant peak visible was Daliang, which lay in Sichuan Province at a distance of several hundred miles. The next morning, we returned down the mountainside with our baskets full of sand. Passing Lamagu, I couldn't help taking an extra look at the place, wondering who had died and who was still alive.

One day, I read in the newspaper that Prime Minister Zhou Enlai only slept four to five hours per night, rising in the small hours to conduct state affairs. This gave me the idea to reduce my sleep in order to find time to study. Every evening after our political study session had finished at 9:30, I brought my books with me to a streetlamp by the rail tracks above the ore milling factory, where I sat down and studied, sometimes until 2:00 a.m.

I continued like this for a few months, but the lack of sleep had a long-lasting negative effect on me, and for more than ten years I was afflicted with a terrible neck pain. My health problems were worsened by overwork, especially carrying heavy loads, and I was suffering from severe edema in the right side of my scrotum. Although there was no inflammation or pain, the edema hindered my movements. I asked Dr. Yan to treat me, but he couldn't think of any good method. This problem also plagued me for many years.

On the afternoon of May 22, we received tragic news from Shudi: Liang Manqi had drowned while swimming in the Golden Sand River. According to eyewitnesses, he had jumped into the water as usual, swum to the middle of the river with strong strokes, but then suddenly sunk, reemerged once and cried for help, then disappeared beneath the churning waves forever. I grieved his death, not yet realizing the consequences it would have for me personally. We often saw corpses floating down the river, men facedown, women faceup. Believing it would be possible to retrieve Liang Manqi's dead body, the leadership dispatched two guards to intercept it downstream, but after waiting for a full month, they gave up. In truth, their chances for success had been slim, because he could just as well have floated by at night. Later, Liang Manqi's wife, a peasant woman from Yongsheng, came to Shudi to receive some financial compensation for her bereavement. They didn't have any children.

Following Liang Manqi's death, the leadership transferred Mu Shiqin to Wentong, while a cadre by the name of Wang Diankui assumed responsibility for discipline. A tall fellow with sunburned skin and a strict demeanor, Wang Diankui never revealed an inkling of a smile under any circumstances, and although he kept his temper under control and spoke with a low voice, I knew he hated our guts.

"Squadron leader Liang was a young man at the peak of his strength who wanted to flaunt his skills and met his fate in this manner. You should learn a lesson from that," Commissar Mu said, mocking him at a meeting.

At our first study session, I seated myself by the Ping-Pong table to take notes as usual but was told by Wang Diankui that he was replacing me with Duan Yuliang. Wang Diankui also collected counterrevolutionary things I had said and done from the other post-sentence detainees who, seeing that I had lost my benefactor, racked their brains to smear me. Suddenly I was in all kinds of trouble. I could feel the heat but didn't panic and carried on as if nothing had happened.

I received a letter from Mother, saying that Father had returned to Shanghai aged, weak, and in bad health. I wrote back immediately to comfort her. Two weeks later, I received a second letter from Mother: Father was dead. I was shocked and heartbroken at the news. I had always been doubtful regarding Father's true circumstances. As I wrote to Mother, I cried and had to keep wiping my cheeks with a handkerchief. Even this little sign of emotion was reported by Duan Yuliang to Wang Diankui. Although Father and I had held many different viewpoints, I had always felt his love for me, and my biggest regret in life is that I never had a chance to reciprocate it.

Around that time, Yao Wenyuan's article "On Three-Family Village: The Reactionary Nature of Evening Chats at Yenshan and Notes from Three-Family Village"* appeared in the newspapers, heralding Mao Zedong's "Great Proletarian Cultural Revolution." I thought it was a squabble within the cultural world, and failed to see that it would have implications for me.

In June, the leadership gave me a technical assignment: find a new way of drying the concentrated copper ore mud, which at the time was simply left out to dry in the sun.

"The mud contains twenty-six percent copper. Several tons are being blown away by the wind each year," Li Ruqing said to me. "Try to solve that problem."

After I studied some books on the topic, my first thought was to dry the mud with electricity. But having calculated output versus power consumption, I realized it wouldn't be economical. Li Ruqing proposed using capillary action to extract the water from the ore mud. I thought it sounded like a good idea and said that we should give it a try.

I designed an experimental facility to be made of wooden planks and asked Li Yanfang for a pound of nails.

---

*Yao Wenyuan (1931–2005) was a literary critic from Shanghai and a staunch Maoist. Rather than "On Three-Family Village," it was his article "On the New Historical Play *Hai Rui Dismissed from Office*," published on the instigation of Mao on November 10, 1965, that set the Cultural Revolution in motion. A member of the infamous Gang of Four, Yao Wenyuan was sentenced to twenty years in prison in 1976.

"There are none," he replied.

Angry, determined to conduct the experiment, I pulled out old nails wherever I could find them and constructed the contraption to help my country economize with its resources. But just as I was racking my brain, doing everything I could to improve our technology, on July 6 I received an order from the leadership, transferring me to Lijiang for *xuexi*, "study."

16

The Price of Truth
(1966)

The Cultural Revolution was the final paroxysm of the Maoist era, fueled by the chairman's basic instinct—to stay king of the hill, 700 million lives be damned. First, he unleashed the country's restless youths, dubbing them Red Guards and instructing them to "be violent." The young zealots tortured their teachers, looted homes, and boarded free trains to Beijing, where they attended mammoth mass rallies, marching through Tiananmen Square waving the Little Red Book and shouting, "Long live Chairman Mao!" All over China, peasants and workers began their day by bowing to Mao's portrait and asking it for instructions. His main target, President Liu Shaoqi, was deposed, and the reclusive defense minister, Lin Biao, elevated to second-in-command. Next, party cadres, called "rebels," were set upon their leaders, who were denounced as "capitalist roaders," purged, and replaced by army officers. As faction spawned faction, the infighting, chaos, and violence spread to every nook of society. In many factories, production ground to a halt, and for the next ten years the country's schools and universities remained in a state of complete dysfunction, leaving China's lost generation to find its own way through a nightmare that destroyed countless lives, families, and friendships.

Seated on a horse cart and escorted by Wang Diankui, we shook and bumped our way to Lijiang. Looking back down at Shudi, I never wanted to see the place again. Up on the wide expanse of the Lijiang Plateau, our horse picked up the pace, and around 3:00 p.m. it trotted into a forbidding prison, Lijiang's infamous *jiagongchang*, "the processing factory," one *li* south of the Dayan Farm.

The four of us, Wencan, Zhang Manjie, Zhang Qinghua, and I, were brought into a large block by the northern courtyard and assigned to the upper bunks. The cell was already full, about thirty men in all. Wencan recognized a friend, Chen Huaixin.

"What will we be studying here?" he asked.

"This is a *jixundui*, 'collective study camp,' for the most reactionary post-sentence detainees. We are here to study and resolve our ideological problems," Huaixin replied sardonically, shrugging his shoulders.

I could hardly believe my ears. Even last night, hadn't I been busy at work for the benefit of our motherland, conducting tests for a new method to dry the copper ore mud? Wencan was also upset. Manjie, however, appeared at ease, arranging his belongings. I saw him stick a wad of money inside his shirt.

"How much have you got?" I asked.

Smiling secretively, Manjie put one thumb in the air, meaning a hundred yuan.

"You've been able to save that much in less than one year as a post-sentence detainee?"

Manjie nodded his head.

Among the four of us, Qinghua had the most to fear. Having seduced the wife of the convict Huang Yigan during her visit at Lamagu and been caught sleeping with her, he knew he was a prime target for the dictatorship's iron fist. Soon, none other than Li Yuanlin stepped into our block. Like a ghostly apparition, he seemed to follow me wherever I went. His appearance filled me with revulsion.

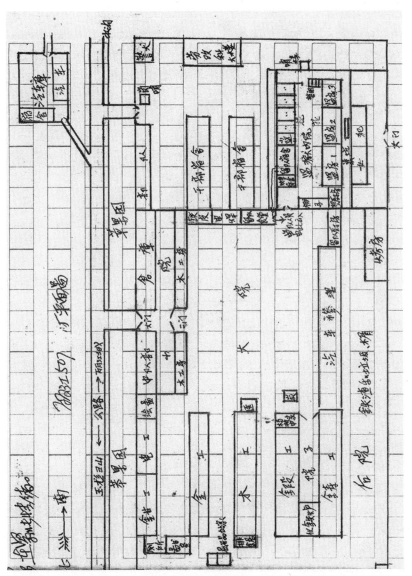

The processing factory (later renamed the 507 Agro-machinery Factory)

The men in our block, rounded up from the various labor camps in the Lijiang region, had been singled out by the authorities as the most recalcitrant post-sentence detainees, and all of us were at risk of coming to grief in this dismal place. Among the men, I recognized Wang Zheng, a bricklayer from the construction brigade who was as domineering and haughty as ever. There was also a young detainee by the name of Fan Pu, who smiled and laughed all the time, attracting people's attention with his carefree attitude. Exhausted and depressed, I slept like a log through the night.

The next morning, Commandant Yang, the prison head, walked into our block and looked over every detainee harshly.

"The Cultural Revolution has started," he declared, "and all class enemies and bad elements must be uprooted and swept away. You have opposed the party and socialism and are guilty of the most heinous crimes. Now, having served your sentences, you are taking part in production as *liuchang renyuan*, and the government is giving you a generous salary that is much higher than the earnings of a peasant. But you are still not content and continue to engage in counterrevolutionary activities."

His eyes stopped on me. "Here we have this tall man from Shanghai, who planned to betray our nation and join the enemy. Treating him with utmost leniency, the government only sentenced him to six years' labor. Now he is stirring up a fuss about returning to Shanghai. Rest assured, Xu Hongci. Shanghai does not miss you, and we will never let you return there to breed more calamity for the future. You will remain here and atone for your crimes. This is the place where all of you will atone for your crimes!"

With the Cultural Revolution in full swing, the local Public Security Bureau had actually rounded us up in order to prove its fidelity to Chairman Mao, taking aim at detainees who displayed the least bit of independence and ability to think critically. If Li Yuanlin, Commandant Yang, and the others had failed to ferret out an appropriate number of class enemies and bad elements, they would have appeared lacking in the zeal to make revolution and would themselves have been crushed beneath its wheels.

On the third day after our arrival, the theatrical piece directed by Commandant Yang began in earnest. At 8:00 a.m., all the convicts and detainees from the processing factory and nearby Dayan Farm were lined up on the basketball court outside our block and seated in rows facing a table and a microphone. The atmosphere was tense. Everybody looked anxious. You could tell a major event was about to take place.

I chatted quietly with Wencan. We agreed it was probably a *douzhenghui*, but had no idea who would be denounced. Presiding over the meeting in person, Commandant Yang accused us of refusing to reform ourselves, engaging in counterrevolutionary conspiracies, attempting to settle old scores, and vainly dreaming of restoring reactionary rule. He praised the wisdom of Chairman Mao in launching the Cultural Revolution and said the time had come to sweep out every single class enemy and bad element once and for all.

His eyes bulging, thumping the table with a clenched fist, Commandant Yang ordered a convict by the name of Yang Shukang to stand up.

Slowly, Shukang, sitting in the first row, stood up and walked over to the table. He was a robust fellow, about thirty years old, with a wide face and flat nose, thick eyebrows and small eyes, and a bit of stubble on his upper lip. Shukang looked down at the ground, his body trembling slightly.

Commandant Yang explained the heinous nature of Shukang's "crime": As a local cadre in Jiuhe Township southwest of Lijiang, Shukang had written a letter to the central leadership in Beijing, informing it that two thousand people had starved to death in Jiuhe during the Great Leap Forward. The central leadership had redirected this letter back to Lijiang, where the local authorities, enraged, had promptly sentenced Shukang to fifteen years in prison for "counterrevolutionary" activity.

Incarcerated in the processing factory, Shukang insisted he had spoken the truth and had written a letter to the Lijiang Procuratorate demanding a retrial of his case. Commandant Yang read the letter aloud. It was completely reasonable: Shukang simply requested a field investigation to determine how many people had starved to death in Jiuhe Township during the Great Leap Forward. If the number two thousand proved accurate, then he had told the truth and was innocent. If nobody had starved to death in Jiuhe, then he had written a false report and should be punished.

Shukang was naive to believe that the Communist Party would tolerate, even welcome, anybody who spoke the truth. It would never conduct such a field investigation. On the contrary, it annihilated people like Shukang who bore witness to history. Commandant Yang declared his letter an open challenge to the Communist Party and a counterrevolutionary call to restore the old order and said his arrogance must be punished severely.

But Shukang, having quickly regained his composure, was confident and obstinate. He refused to confess to any "crime," defended his actions, demanded a retrial in front of the five hundred convicts and detainees, and reiterated that he, through his own research, could confirm that two thousand people in Jiuhe Township had starved to death during the Great Leap Forward.

At this temerity, Commandant Yang blew his top, slammed the table, and ordered Shukang to be put in shackles and handcuffs. I admired Shukang's uprightness and stubbornness from the bottom of my heart but was puzzled by his futile attempt to smash a rock with an egg. I wanted to rush up and straighten this brave man out. But what could I do?

A group of zealots strode into action, screamed at Shukang, spat on him, and slapped his face. Emboldened by Commandant Yang's tacit approval, they proceeded to beat and kick him, pressing him to the ground and forcing him to kneel. But Shukang, bleeding from his nose and mouth, refused to be broken, straightened his back, and held up his head.

The pummeling continued until eleven in the morning, when a Public Security Bureau officer appeared and posted an execution notice on the wall of the metal workshop. Seeing the poster with its large characters written in red, everybody thought Shukang would be executed on the spot. Chaos erupted. I was shocked. If a man could be executed this easily, there would be no end to the terror of this place.

Commandant Yang stood up and, speaking through the microphone, told everybody to calm down.

"Shukang's heinous crimes deserve the harshest punishment, but this announcement concerns He Lican, who murdered the attendants of a cooperative store during a failed burglary. Although He Lican is young, the people's wrath is great, and he will suffer the capital penalty this morning at Democracy Square. Let him be a warning to you!"

After a break for lunch, the *douzhenghui* continued, with Shukang kneeling in front of the zealots who, eager to ingratiate themselves with the leadership, roughed him up with increasing brutality. I had seen Wang Han being beaten, but this was much worse, too horrible to watch. Shukang was tortured until 5:00 p.m., before being dragged off into solitary confinement in a small charcoal storage room by the forging workshop.

That evening, a small group gathered in the reading room under Li Yuanlin's supervision to discuss the day's *douzhenghui*. Scared stiff by the violence, everybody expressed his approval of the government's treatment of Shukang, cursed his heinous crimes, vowed to make a clean break with him, and pledged allegiance to the Communist Party. I too said these things, well aware that if I revealed the least bit of sympathy for Shukang, the next day I would be kneeling there right beside him.

The savage torturing of Shukang continued for three days. He was beaten to the ground, dragged up, and forced to kneel, then beaten to the ground, again and again and again. In the end, no longer able to sustain the horrific violence directed against his body, he fell over and lay curled up like a shrimp on the ground. His face, bereft of any expression, was swollen and covered in blood. But he was still alive. Perhaps he was thinking about those two thousand Chinese citizens who had starved to death during the Great Leap Forward.

On the morning of the fourth day, I had just gotten out of bed when I heard people whispering, "Shukang has hanged himself."

I was shocked but not surprised. Sooner or later, this kind of violence was bound to break even the strongest man. It was drizzling outside. I drew a deep sigh.

China's tragedy, I said to myself, is that it will never allow people to speak the truth. For speaking the truth, I have lost my freedom and my future. For speaking the truth, Shukang has paid with his life. And countless more will suffer for speaking the truth.

With Shukang dead, I thought the theater would be dispensed with for the day. Instead, another meeting was called. Because it was raining, the meeting was held in the vehicle repair workshop, a large space with room for more than ten vehicles, able to fit the five hundred prisoners.

Commandant Yang spoke: "Shukang insisted on fighting against the people as his enemy until the bitter end and has broken with the people by his own free will. Before hanging himself, he wrote several counterrevolutionary slogans with charcoal on his cell's wall. In order for you to gain a thorough understanding of his true reactionary nature, one person from each group shall participate in an inspection of his cell."

The charcoal storage room where Shukang had been kept in solitary confinement lay between the vehicle repair shop and the forging workshop. Led by Commandant Yang, some forty to fifty prisoners were lined up to view the cell in turn. I entered. Charcoal pieces were scattered on the ground. Shukang's body had been removed, but the cloth strip he had used to hang himself was still slung over the beam. Estimating the height from the floor to the cloth strip, I realized that he must have lifted his feet. I couldn't imagine the willpower and determination required to do this. On the wall, he had written slogans with charcoal. "Down with Mao Zedong!" "Long live the Communist Party of the Soviet Union!" "The victims of the Great Leap Forward will live forever in the hearts of the people!" The characters are etched into my memory.

Commandant Yang announced an allotment of four *liang* of kerosene and eighty *jin* of firewood for Shukang's cremation and said that anybody who chose to emulate him would be given the same "preferential treatment." That afternoon, passing through the forging work-shop, I heard a group of prisoners joking about the cremation of Shukang, poking fun at the solidity of his flesh and bones. Eighty *jin* of firewood hadn't been enough, and far from being cremated, Shu-kang's corpse had merely been charred.

Having driven Shukang to his death, Commandant Yang continued the struggle meetings for three more days. Wang Zheng was savagely beaten for the crime of *fandong xueshu quanwei*, "reactionary academic skills"—in other words, simply because he was a skilled bricklayer. We were all terrified. But by behaving like Hitler, Commandant Yang was actually the political loser, because even the convicts who still believed in the party grew doubtful of its policies for labor reform.

Li Yuanlin listened in on our group's study meetings almost every evening. Once, he ordered each of us to write a self-criticism. My topic was *baizhuan*, "white-collar specialism," a term used during the Cul-tural Revolution to criticize anybody who cared more for his own pro-fession than for politics: I wanted to return to Shanghai and had neglected my study of Mao Zedong's thought in favor of science and technology.

Manjie was told to write about his fear that the Communist Party would execute him and other former KMT officers if World War III erupted. Severely injured in the battle to wrest Pianma from the Japa-nese in 1945, he had fought against the Communists in Manchuria during the subsequent civil war and been taken POW, but managed to escape back to Yunnan, where he had traded along the old tea and horse caravan trail before being ferreted out in 1955. A brave soldier, he was extremely immature in political matters, blind to the Communist Party's real nature, and while he often worried that he would be exe-cuted if World War III erupted, he did nothing to protect himself, unable to fathom the party's twisted logic: "If you are afraid that we will kill you, then we will kill you."

17

Hell's Gate

(1966-1968)

On August 6, with no advance notice, the four of us were transferred back to the copper mine. When we arrived in Wentong at dusk, a group of labor camp cadres surrounded us, their faces ashen and vengeful. That day, Yang Fugui, the "smiling tiger," wasn't smiling. Even his pockmarks were livid.

We were herded into the courtyard. None of the other post-sentence detainees dared to approach us. He Zhengze, the detainee in charge of general affairs, had made advance preparations. Manjie was packed off to the infirmary, while Qinghua and I were locked up in the geology office. Only Wencan was sent back to his original team.

All the furniture in the geology office had been moved out, and the room stripped bare. I realized that our problems, far from being over, had just begun. Qinghua spread out his bedroll on the floor. After the evening meal, we were given a latrine bucket and handcuffed for the night.

Despite our distance from Beijing, every new shift in our misfortunes was directly related to Mao Zedong and the factional battles raging there. Following Mao's order to "bombard the headquarters,"* the Cultural Revolution had entered a new stage, and with every unit in the land under pressure to ferret out skulking class enemies and bad elements, the mine leadership was not about to let its prime targets slip away and forgo this opportunity to demonstrate its fealty to the Great Helmsman.

The next day, Manjie was dragged off to a *douzhenghui*. With heavy hearts, Qinghua and I pondered the party's next move. As targets of the Cultural Revolution, in addition to having to attend struggle meetings, we were at real risk of being resentenced as convicts. Although life as a detainee differed little from that of a convict, at least we didn't have to report each time we needed to relieve ourselves. If we were resentenced, we would once again lose even the right to piss and shit freely.

At 4:00 p.m., I saw Manjie being brought back from the struggle meeting and locked up in the infirmary. Well aware it would be my turn next, I prepared myself for the worst. Three days later, I was brought to the vehicle repair shop, where two hundred post-sentence detainees were waiting to denounce me.

Li Ruqing ordered me to be seated on a stool on the podium. Handcuffed, I looked out over the sea of familiar faces. Li Ruqing spoke first, listing my crimes: I opposed the great leader Chairman Mao. I supported imperialism and the Soviet Union. I had taken the road of *baizhuan*, "white-collar specialism." I was against socialism, the dictatorship of the proletariat, had attacked the labor camp leadership, sabotaged ideological reform, and so forth.

He mocked me as the model of a bourgeois intellectual and called on everybody to denounce and expose the "traitor" Xu Hongci. Finally, he reminded the detainees of Chairman Mao's new directive to fight with words and prohibited them from beating me. This, at least, was a sign of progress, and compared with Shukang, I was lucky. At the same

---

*The title of a *dazibao* written by Mao on August 5, 1966, signaling the purge of Liu Shaoqi.

time, Li Ruqing warned me to keep my mouth shut; any resistance would be severely punished.

The first person to denounce me was my math student Yang Yumin. I was taken aback. He accused me of having sabotaged the geology group's study of Mao Zedong's thought by teaching mathematics instead, misleading him and the others onto the path of white-collar specialism: "Xu Hongci told us we can't build our nation with Mao Zedong's thought and that we must use technology! He is a counterrevolutionary revisionist who opposes Chairman Mao! He should be beaten to the ground, kept underfoot, and never be allowed to stand up again!"

The next man in line was Peng Qixin: "Xu Hongci said that if there is a nuclear war, China's big cities will be annihilated."

Wang Yonghua accused me of prescribing medicines at random and criticized me for worshipping Western medicine and despising our motherland's rich medical heritage.

The meeting was lively. The detainees vied with one another to expose and denounce me. I spotted Wencan in one of the front rows. A few times, he seemed on the verge of standing up to speak but restrained himself and in the end said nothing.

Li Ruqing summed up the meeting: "Xu Hongci, you are a target of the Cultural Revolution. Raving reactionaries like you are extremely rare in the labor camps. Now accounts must be settled once and for all. You have been inciting the convicts and insidiously sabotaged their ideological reform. You are studying English because you are planning another escape. You must confess to your crimes and make a clean breast of your reactionary thoughts. Nobody can save you."

The struggle meeting lasted about four hours. Back in my cell, I lay down on my bed and contemplated the meeting's implications. Infuriated by Yang Yumin's ingratitude and betrayal, I had at least gained a clear grasp of my situation: all the accusations leveled against me had been ideological in nature, and none of them constituted a "crime" per se, which provided me some comfort.

My cellmate Qinghua, a former KMT soldier, came from nearby Yongsheng County. Suffering from chronic lung disease, he was always coughing. He took great delight in talking about his illicit sexual affairs, and his praise for Huang Yigan's wife knew no end. As a soldier in Kunming, he had participated in a military review by Chiang Kai-shek, and revered the generalissimo for his martial bearing, calling Mao Zedong an old lady in comparison. During our months together in confinement, we got along well enough, but later, in July 1968, we had a trivial argument that turned him into a mortal enemy, and the evidence he would concoct would almost kill me.

The turnkey He Zhengze was a native of Guangdong Province, about forty years old, short, square-faced, with thick eyebrows and big eyes. Although he never said an unnecessary word while carrying out his regular duties—putting on and taking off our handcuffs, bringing us our meals, and letting us out for some fresh air and exercise—he sympathized with us and gave us newspapers to read every day. When I asked him if we could have some books, he replied that we were not allowed to read novels, only political books, and brought us the collected works of Marx and Engels from the library.

Leafing through each volume in turn, I read the chapters I could follow. I found Engels's articles on the Franco-Prussian War particularly interesting. The revolutionary passion and profound ideas of these two German thinkers made a deep impression on me. The more I read, the more I realized the complete disjunction between our present reality and the socialism they had propounded. Whether this chasm was due to a misunderstanding of Marxism on the part of our Chinese revolutionaries or to the fact that they were actually pursuing their own brand of it is a question worth exploring. In a certain sense, Mao was right when he said, "The more books you read, the more reactionary you become." Indeed, I had read too many books.

After the three of us had been struggled with and denounced, the labor camp leadership left us to ourselves and ignored us. Strangely, we received our salaries as usual. The quieter things became, the more nervous we grew. Qinghua and I passed our days in speculation and conjecture, trying to glean the latest political winds hidden in the innuendos and oblique language of the daily newspapers.

All sharp objects had been removed from our cell to prevent us from committing suicide. Ordinarily, I have to shave every two or three days, and without a razor I grew a full beard. Seeing Qinghua pick his beard with his nails, one whisker at a time, I decided to give it a try. It was painful in the beginning, but I got used to it, and with a great effort I managed to pick my whole face clean. Ten days later, I repeated the process.

Because the electric light was kept on all night, we often had problems sleeping and killed time trying to catch the hundreds of flies buzzing around our cell, feeding them to a little spider that had woven its web in a corner. As the fly struggled to free itself, the spider charged forth, eating the fly's innards and leaving its shell. In those few months, I must have fed that spider thousands of flies. It became my companion, one who offered me a speck of pleasure. Unfortunately, I didn't react fast enough to save it from a spray of pesticide by a guard.

One evening, Commissar Mu gave a political lecture in the courtyard to all post-sentence detainees, using the Sino-Soviet split to launch another attack on me. Although Khrushchev had been removed from power in 1964, he was still being blamed for betraying Communism with his moderate reforms. Mao was Stalin's real successor—the torchbearer of the true Communist creed. Commissar Mu cursed Khrushchev, calling him the arch-criminal of modern revisionism, and used the occasion to praise Beria for his loyalty to Stalin. One day, according to Commissar Mu, Khrushchev had barged into Beria's office, pulled out a gun, and killed him. The newspaper reports stating that Beria had been put on trial, found guilty, and executed were all false.* I realized that Mu was lying through his teeth, and was saddened by the ignorance of the detainees, who seemed to believe every word he said.

---

*Lavrentiy Beria (1899–1953) was Stalin's secret police chief. Following Stalin's death in 1953, Beria was deposed in a coup led by Khrushchev and executed.

Commissar Mu driveled on about the present state of the Soviet Union, calling its leaders revisionist intellectuals, saying that the revolutionary achievements of the proletariat had been usurped by class enemies within the party and that the workers and peasants there had once again become slaves, just like in tsarist Russia. Finally, he came to his point: "If you want to study revisionism, you don't have to go to the Soviet Union! All you have to do is observe Xu Hongci, the perfect model of a bourgeois counterrevolutionary revisionist!"

If only Commissar Mu had known that, ten years earlier, the Communist Party had accused me of *opposing* the Soviet Union. To make those chameleons squirm, I decided to own up to that skeleton in my closet in future self-criticisms.

On December 2, I, Qinghua, and Manjie were handcuffed, taken to a meeting, and placed before the assembled post-sentence detainees. The cadre Yang Jielong read out Manjie's arrest order and told him to sign it. Manjie was dragged off to the Lijiang Prison to await his resentencing.

"The investigation of Xu Hongci and Zhang Qinghua will continue," Li Yuanlin told the assembly, before Qinghua and I were brought back to our cell and relieved of our handcuffs.

Three weeks later, we were released from our prison and returned to our original teams. As usual, no explanations were given. During these five and a half months of imprisonment, I had experienced the system's cruelty and suffered all kinds of indignities with a submissiveness that was new to me. Too many failures had blunted my spirit. I had lost the will to make a clean break and decided to seek temporary peace at the expense of pride and principles. In the end, however, when events proved this policy wrong, I had no choice but to muster the guts to free myself from this dictatorship once and for all.

I returned to team number three, where I was assigned to work as a leadman with He Zenggui. The Wentong mine ran three shifts. Occasionally, I worked the middle shift and was able to spend some free time in Shudi during the day.

One day, I was in a small restaurant to have a meal when Wencan sat down at my table and wanted to talk. The others watched us closely. Without a word, I pushed aside my rice bowl, stood up, and left. I had learned my lesson, and decided to be friends with nobody. Wasn't it all those old "buddies" who became your worst enemies during the denunciation meetings?

As soon as I was let out of my prison cell, I wrote a letter to Mother, telling her about my experiences during the previous six months and sending her one hundred yuan. She had already guessed my troubles and hinted in her letter that she too had encountered difficulties. Later, I learned that she had been subjected to several house searches by the Red Guards and that many of our family's valuable possessions had been lost, including all of the several thousand photographs Father had taken.

I worked together with He Zenggui for three months. Finally, I couldn't stand his insolence any longer and asked Li Yanfang to separate us. My new partner was Lei Yingyuan, a mild-mannered, hare-lipped convict from Yongsheng County who was absolutely loyal to the regime in all political matters and who reported every little thing he heard and saw to the leadership. One of the few grade-four leadmen at the mine, he was skilled, and we worked together for a long time.

Our team's task was to mine for ore, which I had never done before. Because all of the copper ore was contained in soft limestone, boring the blast holes was quite easy, but collecting the ore was much more dangerous than tunneling, and you had to erect new pit props for every yard of progress. Sometimes, the mining cavern grew to a height of twelve to fifteen feet. When all the ore had been excavated, the props were removed one by one from the inside toward the entrance, allowing the ceiling to collapse. This job was the most dangerous of all.

Once, I was boring a blast hole with another detainee when a huge rock came crashing down from the ceiling.

"Let's get out of here!" I shouted.

Ten minutes later, a massive boulder fell right onto the spot where we had been squatting.

During that period, the question of what to study occupied my mind. In the current austere political environment, studying medicine or science would serve no purpose. Considering the matter, I thought a foreign language might be useful in the future. In my book collection, I found an English grammar and an English-Chinese dictionary and asked Mother to send me the English edition of the *Beijing Review*. With study, my English improved greatly, and all the knowledge of the language I have now was basically acquired during those two years. But the labor camp leadership viewed my English studies as opposition to the works of Mao Zedong and preparation to join the enemy.

In the summer of 1967, as the Cultural Revolution shifted into high gear, President Liu Shaoqi was singled out as China's Khrushchev. The loudspeakers at the Wentong mine screeched propaganda and newscasts from early morning until midnight. One day, I had finished my morning shift and returned to the dormitory, but the loudspeakers kept me awake until ten o'clock in the evening. I don't know where I got the courage, but I rushed over to the mine office and asked Commissar Mu, who was sitting by a window on the second floor, to turn off the loudspeaker so that we could sleep. His face was contorted with anger. I turned around and returned to my bed. After five minutes, Commissar Mu actually did turn off the loudspeaker, but the incident was chalked up on my bill for later settlement.

Around that time, the labor camp leadership decided to build four permanent solitary confinement cells along the hydropower plant's tributary in Shudi. To my surprise, the first person locked up in one of these cells was Wencan.

Not until two years later did I learn of the reason for his solitary confinement. It seems that Li Guojun, the wife of the geology team's leader, Long Xianhua, had visited Wencan's workshop, become infatuated with him at first sight, and initiated a correspondence of secret love letters. One day, Li Guojun's wet nurse had discovered a letter from Wencan lying on the table and reported it to Commissar Mu.

A love affair between a high-level party cadre and a lowly post-sentence detainee was more than the labor camp leadership could stomach. Wencan had committed the unpardonable crime of seducing a female cadre, and to stop the scandalous news from spreading among the convicts and detainees, he was locked up in solitary for more than a year, without any of us able to guess the reason.

Throughout the winter of 1967–1968, the chaos of the Cultural Revolution continued to spread and deepen. All over China, "revolutionary committees" took power from the old party committees. Ordinary cadres organized "battle teams," attacked their leaders, and denounced them as capitalist roaders. At the copper mine, Mu Shiqin, Li Yuanlin, and the others all hastened to dub themselves "rebels." We often saw trucks loaded with Red Guards waving banners and placards driving through the mining area. Production was disrupted. Sometimes, the explosives and coke required for the mining work couldn't be transported in. Sometimes, the semirefined copper produced at the mine couldn't be sent to the Kunming Copper Works for further processing.

Following the establishment of a revolutionary committee in Lijiang, the army took power, and a PLA representative was stationed at the copper mine. Everybody was afraid of him. Even Mu Shiqin stuck his tail between his legs. Kang Zhengcheng, Lijiang's party secretary, was denounced at a *douzhenghui* held at the Lijiang Middle School. After the rebels had assembled two tons of confiscated "black material," they ordered Kang Zhengcheng to set the pile of books on fire and then pushed him onto it. He died on the way to the military hospital in Dali.

Having purged the old leadership, the revolutionary committee restored order at the copper mine and extended its antennas to the detainees and convicts. In early May, a meeting for all detainees convened in Shudi. Yang Guang, a seasoned executioner, gave a report attacking the evil trend of Rightists who were trying to reverse correct verdicts. He didn't name me, but I was clearly his main target. The other detainees shot me furtive, knowing glances, and I could feel the ominous wind preceding a storm.

Back in February 1961, I had promised Wang Jinru never to attempt another escape, but he was no longer with me, and I felt no obligation to keep that vow. I considered the possible escape routes. The western passage to Burma seemed doomed to failure. But I reckoned that if I made a big detour from Yunnan up to Xinjiang or Manchuria I might be able to escape to the Soviet Union.

As soon as I had the opportunity, I visited the detainees' reading room in Shudi to study the big map of China hanging on the wall there.

I could find two alternative routes to the Soviet Union: either through Yining in Xinjiang to Kazakhstan, or via Hailar in Manchuria into eastern Siberia. And then there was a third route to freedom: cross over from Erenhot in Inner Mongolia to Zamyn-Üüd in the People's Republic of Mongolia.

My chances of success were slim. I would be on foot, and as I'd learned from previous escapes, I knew the map didn't reflect the whole picture when it came to the topography. All I knew for sure was that the route from Erenhot to Mongolia passed through desert.

Wentong was surrounded by high mountains and a hostile landscape. If things went wrong during the first few days of an escape, it would be hard to move even a few *li*. I considered hiding out in an old mine shaft for a week before attempting to leave the area but was afraid the army might employ search dogs. My greatest concern was identity papers: any escape would be pointless without them. I began to ponder how to forge the necessary documents.

Following Commissar Mu's public criticism of me and Yang Guang's indirect attack, I was put under increased surveillance by the labor camp leadership.

One day in June, Li Yuanlin came to see me.

"I have heard that you have a small knife. Can I see it?"

"Okay," I said, struggling to conceal my fear.

I returned to my dormitory and showed him the small knife—a razor blade tied to a piece of wood. He inspected it carefully.

"What do you use this for?"

"To sharpen my pencils."

"Why do you use pencils?"

"To make notes when I am studying English."

Li Yuanlin returned the knife to me and let me go. Actually, I was using it to practice carving wooden blocks of type to be used to create my fake papers. Lei Yingyuan, who slept next to me, had seen this and reported the matter to Li Yuanlin. Although I appeared forthcoming, I had not dispelled Li Yuanlin's suspicion that I was planning an escape.

Feeling the heat from the leadership, I accelerated my preparations. Usually, I worked the middle and night shifts in the mine and used my free time during the day to carve type. To carve an official seal would be quite easy. The hard part was to forge an official document with the letterhead printed in red characters. Having pondered the problem for a long time, I had the idea to carve a block for each individual character stroke, outline the character lightly with a pencil on the paper, and then create each character one stroke at a time, making the letterhead look neat and clear, just as if it had been printed with an ordinary press.

To reduce the job's complexity, I chose the name Sichuan Province Wan County Revolutionary Committee (四川省万县革命委员会), because the characters for "Si" (四) in "Sichuan" and "Wan" (万) contain relatively few strokes. The most difficult part of the official Song typeface* to make was the horizontal stroke (一) and I had to carve an individual block just for the little triangle at its right end. Finally, I succeeded in carving blocks for all the required strokes, wrapped them in a piece of cloth, and hid them in the crack between the bunk frame and the wall.

Next, I needed to carve an official seal. This was dangerous, and I had to be extremely careful. Searching for a safe place to carve the seal, I hesitated for a long time.

Cash was another constraint on my escape plans. I had sent almost all my money to Mother. At the time, my monthly salary, including an extra allowance of twenty-seven fen per shift for working inside the

---

*A typeface used for official documents, developed with the advent of movable type during the Northern Song dynasty (A.D. 960–1127).

mine, was about fifty yuan. I was aiming to have two hundred yuan in my pocket when I made my escape. Because it would take about six months to save this amount, I wouldn't be able to execute my breakout until the end of 1968.

The enemy beat me to it.

In the middle of July that year, a chance event upset my plan. Large amounts of ore had accumulated at the mine, and the detainees were ordered to clean up the area. Zhang Qinghua, my cellmate from those five and a half months in confinement in 1966–1967, and whom I had not seen for a long time, also showed up.

One man shoveled the ore onto a bamboo scoop, and the next man poured the scoop into the basket on the back of a third, seated man. Usually, three scoops were required to fill the basket. The third man then stood up, carried the ore to the chute, and poured it out.

But Qinghua was different. First, he would only carry two scoops of ore in his basket. Second, he was extremely slow and took a long time to carry the ore to the chute and return. As the man in the middle pouring the scoops, I grew impatient and told him to stop slacking. This was a small matter, but Qinghua was a malicious man who nourished his grudges. Well aware that I was a thorn in the party's side, he decided to take his revenge on me for uttering this single reprimand.

After work, he went to see Li Tingfang for a talk. The next morning, Li Tingfang told him to write a report. Qinghua stayed in his room for three straight days, writing a report that, as I later learned, exposed my counterrevolutionary words during our confinement together. Having finished writing, he could hardly contain his glee and even challenged me to a game of chess. As I faced defeat, he slapped a piece onto the board. "I'll bury you," he said.

Li Tingfang was beside himself with joy at Qinghua's report. Here was the evidence he needed to send me to the execution grounds. Because we had spent five and a half months together in solitary confinement, Qinghua's report against me carried particular weight, although there was nobody to verify its truthfulness.

On August 12, at about ten o'clock in the morning, I was working down in the mine when I received a notice from the labor camp office ordering me to return. I went back to my dormitory and took off my work clothes. The kitchen worker He Guoqu looked at me sadly and knowingly.

"Keep calm," he said to me in a low voice.

I realized I was in trouble but couldn't guess what was about to happen. Yang Guang brought me to the stockyard on the other side of the road, seated me on a stone stool, and took a photograph of me. After that, he took a photograph of Guan Jingkong, a blast furnace worker. Smiling slyly, Yang Guang waved his hand and told us to return to our dormitory.

Walking down the road, I saw Commissar Mu sitting in the pavilion by the tracks to the ore milling factory, jubilantly reciting a poem by Mao Zedong. Jingkong came to ask me what I thought about the matter. I just shook my head and didn't say a word. By then, I had been put under constant surveillance, with no chance of an escape. But nothing happened right away. For a whole week everything was quiet.

18

Inferno

(1968–1969)

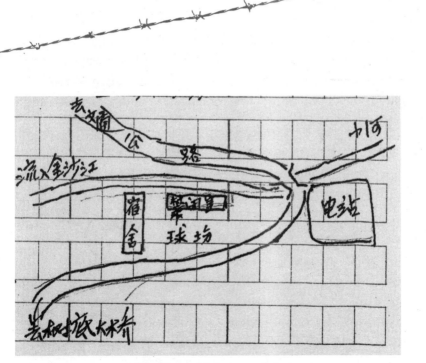

The venue of the arrest meeting

On the morning of August 22, 1968, we were marched to Shudi for a meeting and seated on the basketball court near the four solitary confinement cells, one of which held Wencan. A large number of armed police and cadres swarmed in. Yang Wei, the Public Security Bureau officer in charge of the labor camps, whom we had not seen in a long time, stood in front of us dressed in a brand-new blue uniform, a pistol strapped to his waist, murder written on his face.

"Today we have convened an arrest meeting, to arrest those recalcitrant, irredeemable reactionary elements. Xu Hongci. Stand up!"

The day long anticipated had finally arrived. Casting aside the low wooden stool that had accompanied me for seven years, I walked up to the front. Several big Public Security Bureau officers grabbed me and tied my hands tightly behind my back. I wasn't afraid, just angry at myself for not having been decisive enough to make my escape in time. Now I was in big trouble.

Scanning the assembly, I felt a puzzling calm. Some of the detainees looked frightened; some were enjoying the pleasure of my calamity; others wore blank expressions on their faces. As the old saying goes, "Deploy your troops with no route of retreat, and they will fight for their lives." With things having come to this, I had no choice but to struggle to the end.

"Guan Jingkong. Stand up!"

"Ding Yongcheng. Stand up!"

"Yang Wencan. Stand up!"

Jingkong and Yongcheng stood beside me and also had their hands tied behind their backs. The cadres opened the door to Wencan's cell, dragged him to the front, and tied his hands too. His face was covered with a beard. He was ghostly pale and had lost a lot of weight.

Two horse carts arrived. Handcuffed, the four of us were seated on one of them, guarded by Yang Wei, who kept a close eye on us and prohibited us from speaking. The horses lumbered up the mountainside, heading toward Lijiang.

The four of us sat silent and forlorn. None of us knew which law we had broken. In the past, a crime had been something clearly defined: murder, theft, rape, arson, fraud, and so on. We had done none of these. We hadn't even committed a political crime, such as organizing a counter-revolutionary uprising or providing intelligence to foreign organizations.

I looked back down at Shudi with loathing. The place had brought me nothing but suffering and humiliation. I hated it. I hated every scoundrel there. I never wanted to see the place again. As I sat on that horse cart, the escape plans floating around in my head crystallized into a sharp, hard, irrevocable resolution: I would regain my freedom or die fighting for it.

When the horse carts reached the Lijiang labor camp's brick kiln east of the town, Yang Wei ordered the four of us to get down and walk with our bundles to the prison. Probably, he didn't want the residents of Lijiang to see lowly, despised convicts riding comfortably on a horse cart into the prison. I had too many things, too many books in particular, and couldn't possibly carry them all by myself. Frowning, Yang Wei finally asked two detainees working in the brick kiln to help me.

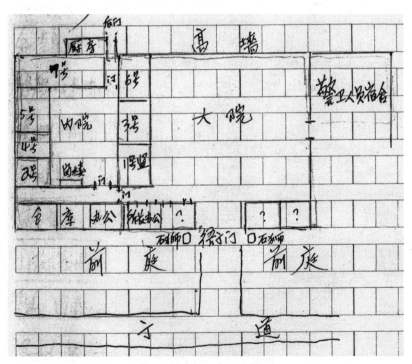

The Lijiang Subprefectural Prison

Starving, trudging with heavy steps, we didn't reach the Lijiang Subprefectural Prison until 4:00 p.m. It wasn't the old prison I had seen in 1960. From the outside, this place looked like a *yamen*, a government office from the feudal era. As we entered the outer yard, two guards stepped forward. Yang Wei disappeared into a building for a moment, then departed.

We were left sitting in the yard for a long time, right by the door to the prison commandant's office. It was strange. The door was open, and there was nobody inside. Peering into the office, I saw a big map of China hanging on the wall. The three escape routes shot to mind. My brain worked intensively, mulling over the options, weighing the pros and cons. I still felt the route to Mongolia held the greatest chance for success. But how was I going to break out of this prison?

At dusk, the prison commandant brought us to the inner yard, the prison itself, which was separated from the outer yard by two doors. His name was Li. Of medium height, with a full beard and a serious demeanor, he walked heavily, his body tilted forward, as he spoke sternly in the Huaping dialect.

I caught sight of my old friend Zhang Manjie, the former KMT officer who had been rearrested at the copper mine in December 1966. The only prisoner in sight, he greeted us with a fleeting smile and helped us carry our things. Because we were being watched by guards, we weren't able to speak but communicated by exchanging glances.

After a thorough inspection by Commandant Li, I was taken to cell number five. Not having eaten all day, we were finally given a bowl of rice. There were only two meals per day in this prison, with a daily grain ration of a mere seven *liang*. A new round of punishment by hunger and starvation was about to begin.

During Commandant Li's body search, I had managed to hide my thirty yuan in my sleeve. Now I carved out a crack in my soap bar, stuffed in the bills, filled the crack with soap slivers, and smoothed the surface with saliva. This would be a temporary storage place, to have the money ready at hand in case of an emergency.

There were four other prisoners in my cell: Yang Shan, Xie Yiren, Peng Yunhong, Li Shoucheng. Yang Shan was a good-natured Naxi youth who stuttered and knew little Chinese. According to hearsay, he had participated in an attack on Lijiang's revolutionary committee. Xie Yiren was a cross-eyed, smooth-talking geologist from Jiangsu Province serving time for lechery. Peng Yunhong, a moody, melancholy local cadre with the air of a small-time intellectual, and Li Shoucheng, an instructor at the Lijiang Party School, had also been sentenced for sexual misdemeanors.

They were all friendly toward me, which gave me some consolation and comfort. I was surprised to hear Yunhong say that many people in Lijiang knew my name. Formally rearrested, I waited for my official interrogation. Wencan, Yongcheng, and Jingkong were all called in, but not me. I found the arrest unnerving: No interrogation, no confession, what were they planning to do with me?

Our prison block was partitioned by a double fence, with a long, narrow strip between the two fences called the *waikao*, "outer basket." During the day, we had to sit in this *waikao*, allowing the guards in the sentry tower to keep an eye on us. At night, the double fence was locked. The windowpanes in our cell were out, and the cold wind pierced our bones.

The guards in this prison practiced a special kind of punishment. If you happened to incur the anger of a guard, he would order you to stretch your arm out through the fence of the *waikao*, then he would grab and twist it. As you turned your body to reduce the pain, he would continue to twist your arm until you screamed for mercy. Every newcomer was warned by the others not to offend the guards.

Each morning and afternoon, when we were allowed to sit in the yard for an hour to take in the sun, we would watch a convict drag his heavy chains in circles. It was Zou Zhiyun, whom I had known in the processing factory back in 1966. He seemed to have been here for a long time. His face was covered with a beard. But the shackles hadn't broken his feisty spirit, and he continued to curse the Communist Party in the most colorful, unsparing language.

Catching sight of me, he nodded and shouted out loud the saying "Bai lian cheng gang!" "Hardship makes you strong!"

Rearrested, Manjie had been in this prison for almost two years, and was still awaiting his resentencing. He took care to follow all the rules and had won the trust of Commandant Li, who had assigned him to the job of turnkey. Sometimes, Manjie exchanged a few sentences with me through the fence, trying to keep my spirits up. His kind words meant a lot to me. But I couldn't understand why he wasn't more worried for himself. Had Commandant Li given him a hopeful hint?

It was possible to communicate with the prisoners in cell number four through the cracks in the *waikao*'s wooden boards. Mostly I spoke with a young man by the name of Li Changbao. He had a round face, a strong physique, and intelligent eyes. Only twenty-two years old, he had come from Kunming to take part in rebel activities and had been jailed for concealing a pistol, but would soon be released and said he had a plan to get me out of this place.

To discuss this matter in more detail, we volunteered to take part in digging a well by the entrance to the courthouse in Lijiang. I had never actually seen the town before and was impressed by its ancient architecture. There were many small stone aqueducts, and all the cobblestoned streets were lined with freshwater gutters where women washed clothes. The houses were two-story wood-and-stone structures with black tile roofs. Half of the people on the streets were Naxi women dressed in sheepskins.

The court's chief justice, Feng Longxi, was a *zouzipai*, "capitalist roader." Every day, he arrived at work punctually with two red paper banners pinned vertically to his Sun Yat-sen uniform, with the characters "日本走狗!" "Japanese running dog!" written on one and "汉奸!" "Traitor to the Chinese!" written on the other.

The paper banners rustled in the light wind. Feng Longxi walked slowly, carefully protecting them, afraid that they would tear, his thin face empty of any expression. Presumably, people had already grown accustomed to this humiliating punishment, because nobody paid any attention to the banners.

As Changbao and I dug the courthouse's well, we made sure the guards were not paying attention and continued our discussion.

"As soon as I am released and get back to Kunming, I'll get some people together and spring you out of this place. We'll have weapons and cross over into Burma," he said.

"Springing me out of this prison would be too dangerous," I told him. "We have to use our wits. We should forge documents ordering me to Kunming for interrogation, and you can spring me along the way there."

Changbao agreed and said that he would discuss the matter with his comrades.

"As soon as we get you onto our truck, we will drive straight south and get out of this country. Anybody who tries to stop us will be shot dead with a machine gun."

Changbao was not all empty boasting. At the time, the factional battles in Yunnan were fierce, and a lot of weapons were disappearing from the Haikou munitions factory. His rebel faction was a group of real, fearless fighters. But as the political landscape of the Cultural Revolution shifted, their spirit was blunted, and their movement petered out.

The verdict of my young cellmate Yang Shan was handed down from the military control commission of the Lijiang People's Court: seventeen years at hard labor. Without a word, he was taken away and sent to the *laogai*.

By the end of that year, I had still not been interrogated once. The other three from the copper mine had all been questioned and submitted their confessions. Nervous, I asked Commandant Li to be interrogated, but he ignored me. All I really wanted was to dig a hole under the wall and flee to freedom. But we were heavily guarded, and an escape was impossible.

One day, I was amazed to see two ten-year-old boys put into one of the prison cells. One boy's name was Wang Guilin. He looked just like a little girl, with white skin, delicate features, and gentle manners. Apparently, he had been arrested for scribbling "Down with Mao Zedong!" on a toilet wall. The other boy, He Zhongxiang, was dark and thin, with brusque movements. Early that spring, he had carved "Down with Mao Zedong!" into a young pumpkin. As the pumpkin grew over the summer, the characters had become visible, and he had been arrested. With the oldest prisoner over sixty and the youngest ten, we were now a real *santongtang dajiating*, "big, three-generation family under one roof."

I was prohibited from sending and receiving letters, and knew Mother must be worried. One day, I wrote a short letter to her on a piece of yellow paper that I had picked up from the ground, squeezed the letter through the crack to Changbao, and asked him to send it when he got out of prison. Changbao folded the paper carefully, but we had been seen by Duan Shaoxun, who immediately reported the matter to Commandant Li.

As punishment, I was moved to cell number one, and the soap bar with my thirty yuan was confiscated. This cell was right beneath the sentry tower, and the guards could see everything. Later, Yunhong told me that Changbao had acted quickly, swallowed the letter, and admitted to nothing. I was nervous: if Commandant Li found out about our escape plans, we would be executed on the spot.

On January 16, 1969, I met Li Faxiang by the latrine.

"There will be a verdict meeting tomorrow," he told me.

The next morning, we were given an early breakfast and not allowed to take the sun in the yard. Extra guards had been posted in the sentry tower. Everybody was scared stiff, fearing that he or she would be the meeting's target, and no one dared say a word. Not even the crashing of Zhiyun's chains was heard.

At around 2:00 p.m., the terrifying silence was broken. The door to the inner yard was opened, and Commandant Li and a group of guards entered. Unlocking my cell door, he told me to step out. Altogether, some twenty prisoners were called forth, among them Wencan, Jingkong, Yongcheng, and the two young boys. I realized that I was the main target of this verdict meeting.

The guards brought us to the outer yard, where a large contingent of soldiers was waiting. Three or four surrounded me, tied my hands behind my back as hard as they could, and forced me to lean forward. My mind was completely blank. With me first in line, we were marched out through the main gate, past the party school, heading west toward Democracy Square.

The streets were lined with people. Earsplitting loudspeakers screeched, "Navigating the seas, we rely on the Helmsman!" Bent forward, my head lowered, I walked with heavy steps, squeezed between two soldiers. The rope obstructed the blood in my arms, and a piercing pain spread from my fingers and wrists to my shoulders. I could hardly breathe. My head felt as if it would explode. My eyes went black. On the verge of collapsing, I was struck violently with a rifle butt in my back, regained my senses, and used every last drop of my strength to keep moving forward.

Approaching the square, I saw a sea of people, red banners fluttering in the air, a mad clamor of slogans rising in crescendo. More than ten thousand people must have attended that rally. Escorted by the guards, we made our way through this human wall to the podium, in front of which there stood some twenty large *baxianzhuo*, traditional square tables.

The guards lifted me up onto the first table to the right. There were a lot of military officers and revolutionary committee members seated on the podium. Screaming into a microphone, one of the cadres led the masses in reciting quotations by Chairman Mao on class warfare and singing sayings from his Little Red Book, skillfully whipping the crowd into an ecstatic, delirious, bloodthirsty insanity.

After some twenty minutes of mayhem, the cadre declared the verdict meeting opened. My body couldn't take it any longer. My head dropped closer and closer to the ground, but the soldier behind me grabbed my hair and jerked my head, then shoved his knee into the small of my back and shouted to me to stand straight. My hands hurt with an unbearable pain. I was on the verge of screaming out loud. After another five minutes, I started slumping over again.

My verdict came first: "Xu Hongci was branded a Rightist in 1957, refused to reform himself, planned to betray the motherland and join the enemy, and was sentenced to six years. Having served his sentence, he continued to engage in counterrevolutionary activities as a post-sentence detainee and has consistently opposed our most beloved great leader, Chairman Mao, opposed all of our party's policies for building and reforming socialism, sung the praises of U.S. imperialism and Soviet revisionism, and mongered fear of nuclear war. His crimes are grave and he is hereby sentenced to—"

I was absolutely sure the next word would be "death." Then "twenty years" struck my eardrums. My mind was completely blank. It was as if my body no longer belonged to myself. I couldn't feel anything. If I had been sentenced to death, pinned to the ground, and finished off with a bullet to the neck, it wouldn't have been at all painful. That shrill voice continued to assail my ears: "Guan Jingkong, twenty years! Li Zengjun, eighteen years! Yang Wencan, fifteen years! Guo Peiliang, fifteen years! Ding Yongcheng, eight years!"

After all the verdicts had been announced, an officer from the military subcommand gave a speech, repeating all the hackneyed balderdash about the Cultural Revolution, Mao Zedong's thought, class war, smashing the enemy's conspiracy to restore the old order, consolidating the dictatorship of the proletariat . . .

We had been standing on the tables for more than two hours. I could no longer feel my hands. My head reeled, and my vision blurred. I couldn't hear what they were saying and just hoped that everything would be over as quickly as possible. A bullet in the neck would have been pure relief. Now and then, I caught a glimpse of the raving, idiotic faces beneath the podium and recalled the words of the purged defense minister Peng Dehuai: "The Chinese people prefer death to waking up!"

After the officer had finished his speech, the chairman declared the verdict meeting closed. "Parade the criminals through the streets!" he yelled.

I was pushed down from the table and almost collapsed to the ground. Grabbing the rope tied around my arms, the soldier pulled me up straight again. As we were led through the crowd, people threw mud and small rocks at us. I heard one man shouting, "This villain even has the arrogance to wear a leather jacket."

Indeed, on that day I was wearing a black deerskin jacket that Mother had sent to me. We were paraded through Lijiang's main street, where the insults, humiliations, and abuses continued. At the end of my physical and mental tether, I walked slower and slower as the soldier kept striking me in the back, prodding me to hurry up.

After being paraded along the streets for more than an hour, we finally returned to the prison, where the soldiers untied us. If anything, the pain in my arms was even more excruciating. I thought I would be crippled for life.

I was put back in cell number one, where my cellmate Mu Biaosheng helped me roll out my mattress and lie down. My hands were swollen to the size of boxing gloves. Each finger was as thick as a carrot, and the skin had turned purple. I turned onto my side and asked Biaosheng to examine the damage from the rifle butt. Horrified, he told me that my back, buttocks, and thighs had been beaten into a ghastly pulp of black and blue.

Once again, I had been given an unforgettable taste of Mao Zedong's "revolutionary humanism." This primitive barbarity was his so-called socialist civilization. That evening, Commandant Li brought me to his office. In the dimly lit room, I saw a cadre waiting for me. He handed me the official court verdict and asked me to sign my name on it.

I looked at the verdict and sneered, "You haven't even given me a trial. On what basis have you sentenced me to twenty years' imprisonment?"

The cadre stared at me angrily through his glasses and replied impatiently, "We know everything about your case. There was no need for a trial."

I stood in front of him, hesitating.

"Are you going to sign it or not?" he asked angrily.

"I'll never find justice here. I have to get to the labor camp as soon as possible and find a way to escape from there," I said to myself. Gnashing my teeth, I held the pen with my swollen hand and signed a name I couldn't recognize, then threw down the pen, turned around, and walked out.

The horrible pain kept me awake all night. I thought about many things. Although the Communist Party had treated me with such sadistic brutality, I had taken its abuse and insults lying down. From now on, there was nothing more to be said. There remained only one path: to fight to the bitter end. I wanted to get to the labor camp as soon as possible and make my last stand.

On January 27, 1969, Wencan, Jingkong, Yongcheng, Zengjun, and I were sent to the processing factory to begin serving our sentences. I said goodbye to Manjie.

"Don't worry. Later, when my case has been clarified, I may be sent to the processing factory to continue as a post-sentence detainee. I'll look after you," he said with his special eagerness.

I thanked him and told him to take good care of himself. Even more naive than I, he was confident that he would not be resentenced. It was the last time I saw Manjie, this brave KMT officer who had fought well against the Japanese.

19

The Art of War

(1969-1972)

By 1969, Lin Biao was firmly ensconced as Mao's No. 2, and the party apparatus had been staffed with his army cronies. China and the Soviet Union were on the brink of war, and the whole country was militarized. But as Lin Biao's power grew, so did his and the PLA's ambition and insolence. "A certain person is very anxious to become state chairman, split the party, and seize power,"* Mao told local cadres during his inspection tour of southern China in late August 1971. The chairman now moved to thwart Lin Biao, who responded with a plot to assassinate him. In the small hours of September 13, 1971, following an aborted attempt by Lin Biao to air bomb Mao's private train, Lin and his family boarded a Trident plane destined for the Soviet Union but ran out of fuel and crashed in the grasslands of southern Mongolia.

Two months earlier, Henry Kissinger, Richard Nixon's national

---

Jianguo yilai Mao Zedong wengao (Manuscripts of Mao Zedong since the founding of the People's Republic), 13 vols., ed. CCP Archive Study Office (Beijing: Zhongyang Wenxian Chubanshe, 1987–1998), 13:244–45

security adviser at the time, had made a top secret journey to Beijing to pave the way for a visit by the president, who, in an incongruous exception to his staunch anti-Communism, sought to exploit the Sino-Soviet rift to win the Cold War and wanted to open China's door with a brilliant feat of diplomacy. For his part, Mao wanted a seat at the UN and Western technology. The historic meeting between the two men took place in Beijing on February 21, 1972. In his counsel to the president, Kissinger had called Mao and the other Chinese leaders "a group of monks . . . who have kept their revolutionary purity" and who might "challenge us in a moral way."*

I had been through "collective training" at the processing factory in the summer of 1966, so I was familiar with the place. But this time I was a resentenced convict and held in a different part of the prison complex called the inner yard: a ten-thousand-square-foot space with three prison blocks on its western side and a sentry tower at the southern end.

We arrived in the afternoon. The convicts were working, and the inner yard was deserted. I put down my bundle and sat on it, waiting for a cadre to give us instructions. I saw a short man standing in a doorway looking at me with an ironical expression. It was Kuang Zhong, the Cantonese doctor from the third detachment of the construction brigade. I nodded my head in recognition.

After half an hour, the prison commandant appeared. He was my height and wore an old cotton military uniform and a military cap. He was swarthy in complexion, with a long face, uncreased eyelids, and a mean look, and he appeared extremely confident and proud. I knew him from my last stay at the processing factory. It was the notorious Li Guangrong.

Holding the list, he called my name. I stood up and responded. He

---

*Nixon Project, Memoranda for the President's Files, Box 85: Briefing of the White House Staff, July 19, 1971, p. 4; and Box 88: Cabinet Meeting, February 29, 1972, p. 18.

measured me up with a fierce glance, then ordered Kuang Zhong to inspect our belongings. I realized that Kuang Zhong had served his sentence and was now a post-sentence detainee, one step above me in the pecking order.

Except for Mao's *Selected Works* and a copy of his Little Red Book, all my books were confiscated.

"You've read too many books," Li Guangrong said to me. "The more you read, the more confused you are. The more you read, the more reactionary you become."

I asked if I could at least keep the works of Marx, Engels, and Lenin.

"No," Li Guangrong replied. "Here, you are only allowed to read the books of Chairman Mao!"

I watched the toadying Kuang Zhong carry my beloved books into his clinic and throw them under his bed. It was like saying goodbye to my closest friends. But a steadfast conviction told me, "China cannot continue to live by the five books of Mao Zedong alone. One day, at long last, the Chinese people will have freedom of speech, and I will have all the books I want."

Granted the status of a local, state-owned enterprise, the processing factory had changed its name to the 507 Agro-machinery Factory, taking the number of its postal box. The factory produced small electric motors, hay cutters, and threshing machines, made wooden furniture, and repaired vehicles. With the negligible cost of forced convict labor, it was considered a money tree in the *laogai* system. On average, the prison held about 110 convicts, all serving heavy sentences ranging from fifteen years to death row, as well as some 30 post-sentence detainees.

As a high-security prison, the 507 Agro-machinery Factory employed about fifty guards, equipped with trained dogs. The perimeter wall was ten feet high, topped by a thirty-inch electric fence and wide enough for the sentries to patrol with their dogs. By the inner yard's gate, there was a high-pressure quicksilver lamp mounted on a thirty-foot-high pole that lit up the entire yard as bright as day. Nobody had ever escaped from this prison.

Wencan and I were assigned to the metalworking team. On the first night, the members of our team gathered by a bonfire in our block for study and discussion. With four fires burning at the same time, the block was filled with smoke, and the walls and ceiling blackened with soot.

Wencan and I sat quietly listening to the other prisoners, all well versed in the works of Mao Zedong. Not only were they able to recite the *Lao san pian*, "The three old articles," they even knew the *Lao wu pian*, "The five old articles," by heart, and the quotations from Chairman Mao rolled off their tongues like well-cooked melons.

Unable to recite *Lao san pian* from memory, I was given three days by the team leader, He Yutang, to memorize the three articles. I'm terrible at rote learning, and the order put me on the spot. But to adapt to this new place, I forced myself, reading the articles aloud over and over again, until finally I could parrot them like a robot.

On our first day in the metalworking shop, He Yutang pointed to a six-inch-thick steel cylinder and instructed Wencan and me to saw it into four-inch sections, to be used to make wheel gears. Because we had never done this kind of work before, it took us two full days of pulling and pushing a metal saw back and forth to saw off a single section.

I sat with Wencan outside the shop, sawing patiently and chatting. He told me about his love affair with Li Guojun—the real reason for his fifteen-year sentence. The crime stated on his official verdict, "opposing Vice-Chairman Lin Biao," was a completely fabricated charge. In 1968, the central leadership in Beijing had issued its "Six Public Security Articles," according to which anyone who opposed Mao Zedong, Lin Biao, or Mao's wife Jiang Qing could be sentenced to a long prison term, and it was this new "law" that the Lijiang People's Court had used to wreak the party's wrath upon Wencan and me.

"They are even more fascist than the Fascists," said Wencan.

"What can you do?" I replied.

"I'm going to appeal."

"Appeal to whom?"

"To the revolutionary committee of the Lijiang People's Court."

"That was the court that sentenced you. It's not going to change its verdict."

"No matter what, I'm going to appeal," he said. "What about you?"

"Trying to reason with these people is like asking a tiger for his skin. I'm not going to waste my energy."

During our group discussions, He Yutang told me to examine my crimes and apologize to Chairman Mao.

"I haven't committed any crime, and I will make no examination," I replied.

My attitude infuriated Li Guangrong.

"I warn you!" he shouted. "If you continue to maintain your reactionary position, you will be smashed to pieces by the iron fist of the dictatorship of the proletariat."

Recalling my history of escapes and the money I had concealed in the soap bar, he reminded me, "Nobody has ever escaped from the processing factory. Anybody who tries will be shot dead on sight."

One day, He Yutang overheard Wencan and me exchange opinions about another convict in our block and reported the matter to Li Guangrong, who immediately reassigned Wencan to the electric work team and prohibited us from talking with each other. He Yutang was a cunning, merciless operator.

As a newcomer to the metalworking shop, I started with simple tasks such as drilling holes and making nuts. Of the various processes in metalworking—sawing, chiseling, filing, boring, and leveling—I found filing the most difficult. But I was a quick learner and received a lot of help from Old Liu, a skilled metalworker who taught me everything he knew.

My first independent job was to make an iron door for the Lijiang Middle School. Having finally managed to cut all the pieces according to measurement, I brought them to the vehicle repair shop, where the welder Liu Zhaolong soldered the pieces while I held them in place. Ignorant of the danger of the welding arc, I didn't protect my eyes, which swelled up and ran. No eyedrops helped. But I kept on working, and after one week the swelling disappeared.

As expected, Wencan's appeal was denied, but instead of being discouraged, he went from begging to fighting and, after putting out a couple of preliminary feelers to make sure he could trust me, asked me to stage a breakout with him. Initially, we were still able to meet in public, even smoke a cigarette together. But He Yutang was keeping a constant eye on us and reported everything he saw and heard to Li Guangrong.

Inexperienced, having never made an escape before, Wencan was even more eager than I. In our discussions, we summarized the lessons and mistakes from previous failed attempts, including my own. First, escapees had lacked money and grain ration coupons, and had not carried authoritative identification and travel documents. Second, they had sought shelter and/or food from ordinary people. Third, the time span between their escape and its discovery had been too short, allowing search dogs to pick up the scent. Fourth, they had kept to main roads, and been caught at bus stations or river crossings.

"If there is only one hour between our escape and its discovery, the enemy simply has to draw a circle with a radius of three miles, call every people's commune within that circle, and we will be caught. If we have eight hours before our escape is discovered, this radius becomes twenty-five miles. At that distance, the people's communes will be less zealous and might even ignore orders to search for us," I said to Wencan. "But we must be patient and not make any attempt before the right opportunity presents itself."

Every day, I passed the official announcement of my sentence pasted on the wall by the carpentry workshop. It had probably been posted in every little town in Yunnan, perhaps all of China. I was thirty-five years old, but the verdict mistakenly stated my age as thirty-three. Again and again, I read the five "crimes" for which I had been sentenced to twenty years of hard labor. Scorched by the sun, torn by the wind, this piece of paper disintegrated slowly, finally disappearing without a trace. But I will never forget the injustice it stood for.

In low spirits, I tried to manage my present situation and gradually settled into work. During our study sessions, I was now able to regurgitate the *Lao san pian* without hesitation and learned how to heap abuse and criticism upon myself. I followed every rule, never took any liberties, and reduced my contacts with Wencan to a minimum to blunt He Yutang's vigilance and dispel Li Guangrong's suspicions.

Bound by our common fate, Wencan and I became brothers in arms, sworn to live and die together. Occasionally, we would squat on the latrines in the narrow passage behind the prison blocks and chat for a few minutes, but most often we wrote notes to each other. We signaled one another by running our hands through our hair. Seeing Wencan do this, I followed him to a place where nobody could see us and he'd slip me a note. Later, we left notes for each other in a hole at the foot of the wall by the latrine, covering it with a rock and grass. This was safer, and by communicating in this manner, we managed to solve several problems.

First, we abandoned the idea of escaping to Burma, because as soon as our breakout was discovered, the Public Security Bureau would seal off every border pass and river crossing. Our only possibility, we agreed, was to make a big roundabout maneuver, traverse all of China, and escape across the border to the Soviet Union or Mongolia. Consequently, with the harsh winter in these northern countries, we would have to make our escape in the summer.

The first few hours after our escape would be crucial. We discussed heading south from Lijiang to Heqing County, then southeast into the Yunling Mountains, on to the town of Duomei on the banks of the Golden Sand River. Making a sweeping circle south then east, we would pass through the town of Jinjiang, head south to Pianjiao on the Yong-Bin highway, turn east onto the Burma Road, and get out of Yunnan as quickly as possible.

For now, we agreed to work quietly and make the necessary preparations. I assumed the dangerous responsibility of forging the documents. We exchanged information about Li Guangrong, He Yutang, and others, in order to know their movements and take the appropriate precautionary measures.

I wrote a letter to Mother, explaining to her briefly that I had run into trouble and been resentenced and imprisoned, and asked her to send me five yuan per month—the maximum amount of pocket money allowed in the prison. Anything more than that had to be deposited in the bank. I also asked her to send me national grain ration coupons whenever possible.

But the most difficult task was to forge the documents. In the spring of 1969, making use of the midday siesta, I slipped into one of the empty cells on the opposite side of the inner yard, where I carved wooden blocks of type in the official Song style in the same manner as I had done back at the copper mine. While doing this work, I always kept Mao's Little Red Book beside me. As soon as I heard any noise, I hid my tools and held up the book as if reading it.

Having created three official documents with the letterhead "Revolutionary Committee of Yun County, Yunnan Province" (云南省云县革命委员会), I then carved the corresponding official seal and imprinted the seal on the documents. We now had three empty, official documents that we could fill in by hand as the circumstances required.

I rolled up the documents and put them into a glass bottle, dug a hole in the dirt floor by my bunk, and buried the bottle there. I also hid the type blocks and my tools but threw the official seal into the fire. Completing this work in one month, I informed Wencan that our protective "talismans" were ready to go.

By then, we had identified the convict Yuan Yicheng as the zealot of zealots, the man most trusted by Li Guangrong and most hated by the prisoners. About forty years old, he had a triangular face alight with shrewd intelligence. His fealty to Li Guangrong was flabbergasting. For example, as soon as Li Guangrong announced one of his many campaigns, Yuan Yicheng was able to write a ten-thousand-character self-criticism in a single night and then conduct a model self-examination at the next day's rally.

He was equally adept at attacking other convicts, his choice of words acrid and his analysis deep, and he was constantly and intentionally putting people in dangerous situations. In several of the campaigns, he served directly as Li Guangrong's agent, controlling the flow of information up and down and always making his influence felt.

At the end of April 1969, the Communist Party held its Ninth Congress in Beijing. Lin Biao was appointed vice-chairman, and the new party program clearly anointed him as Mao Zedong's successor, while the Gang of Four—Jiang Qing, Yao Wenyuan, Zhang Chunqiao, Wang Hongwen—became members of the Politburo. This was big news, especially for Li Guangrong and the other cadres, who hastened to express their allegiance to this new order, constantly assembling us in the inner yard to listen to live broadcasts from Beijing, decorating the main gate with lanterns and colorful streamers, and plastering every wall with the latest slogans.

On the eve of the May 1 celebrations, a ceremonial arch was erected outside the 507 Agro-machinery Factory's main gate. Li Guangrong was so dizzy with excitement that he even asked me to help, forgetting his suspicions of any escape plans on my behalf. From the town, we often heard the roar of gongs and drums and people shrieking Mao's directives at the top of their lungs.

"Ecstasy is the mother of tragedy," Wencan whispered. "In the end, we will see who judges whom."

Although spoken in anger, his prediction proved accurate. A couple of years later, Lin Biao was killed, and the Gang of Four was eventually toppled. History has no mercy.

At the time, Lijiang suffered from a severe lack of electricity, especially during the two last months of the dry season, May and June, when the reservoir of the Guanpo hydroelectric plant was at its lowest. Sometimes, there was a power outage during the day, forcing us to work night shifts instead. Sometimes, there was a blackout at night, which made the prison leadership nervous with regard to security. New sentry posts were added, and zealots were deployed to keep a close eye on reactionary elements like me.

"Should we make a go for it?" Wencan asked me.

I said no for a simple reason: the enemy was in the highest state of vigilance, and there was no hope of success. Usually, after finishing work at midnight, we were brought back to our blocks and given a meal before going to sleep. If there was an outage, the leadership assigned several zealots in each block to watch us. Kerosene lamps were kept burning through the night to monitor our movements, leaving us no option but to behave ourselves.

I examined every corner of our block and took note of all activities during various times of the day. We were under constant surveillance, sometimes simultaneously by several people from different angles. Darkness, our best friend, was not to be had. Devising an escape was the most difficult problem I had ever tried to solve.

Back in 1965, upon my request, Mother had sent me a copy of *Hong yan*,* "Red cliff," which had become a prohibited book during the Cultural Revolution. Knowing that it would be confiscated at some point, I had given the book to a fellow convict. I recalled a few insights I had gleaned from *Hong yan*. In such a heavily guarded environment, we must not only devise the best possible escape plan but, even more important, have the wits, courage, and determination to act decisively when the window of opportunity presented itself.

Through long and careful observation, I knew that three of the prison's four sentry towers were manned around the clock, while the sentry tower by the latrine in the northeast corner of the main yard was only manned temporarily, on those occasions when we had to work

---

*A novel written by the party cadres Luo Guangbin (1924–1967) and Yang Yiyan (1925–), *Hong yan* describes the events leading up to the successful mass prison break staged by members of the Communist underground from the KMT prisons Dregs' Cave and White Mansion in Chongqing in 1948, on the eve of the infamous November 27 Massacre, when, with the PLA closing in on the city, some two hundred Communists were executed by the KMT. The book was published in 1961, had a total print run of some 10 million copies, and enjoyed great popularity for several years. But following the outbreak of the Cultural Revolution, the fact that Luo Guangbin had survived the massacre was turned against him. When Luo and Yang refused the request of Mao's wife Jiang Qing (who was obsessed with covering up her bourgeois past as an actress in pre-revolution Shanghai) to rewrite the book with her as its heroine, she had it banned and instigated the persecution of its authors. On February 10, 1967, Luo Guangbin, held captive by Red Guards in Chongqing, either jumped or was pushed to his death.

during evenings and nights. Accordingly, I concluded that the only place to scale the perimeter wall and make an escape was by the willow tree behind the latrine in that northeast corner. But how were we going to get there?

As prisoners in for the long haul, with no freedom foreseeable on the distant horizon, we actually enjoyed a few privileges. Ordinarily, we received three meals per day, and every two weeks we had a small feast, at which each convict received half a *jin* of cured meat. In the wintertime, the team leader Wei gave us cow and goat offal purchased from the local slaughter grounds, which we, escorted by guards, washed in a nearby creek and cooked several times a week. Goat eyes, I discovered, are a delicacy.

There was a water pump in our block, and the two large pools were often filled with water so we could wash our clothes and keep a decent level of personal hygiene. On Sundays, we rested, and the guards allowed everybody to go to the main yard to play basketball or stay in the inner yard and have a haircut, mend clothes, or play chess.

Most surprisingly, we were not required to shave our heads. Apparently, the prison administration felt so confident of its security measures that it saw no harm in allowing us to keep our hair. And from my first day in the *laogai*, I had never worn a prison uniform. The cadres had always told me that because I had my own clothes, the state's uniforms should be saved for the poor prisoners. Aside from the leather jacket Mother had sent me, I had a cotton-padded jacket that I had worn for more than ten years. My underwear had been patched and repaired over and over again, and I had become quite skilled with needle and thread.

Our numbers were written directly on our civilian jackets and pants with white paint. My number was 13022. The number 13 referred to the thirteenth *laogai* brigade of Yunnan Province, and 022 was my individual number. Naturally, this number would be a big problem for our escape, but when the time came, I would find a way to solve it.

Since the beginning of the Cultural Revolution, the reading room had been closed, and we were only allowed to read the works of Mao Zedong. Every team received a copy of the *Yunnan Daily*, each block a copy of the *People's Daily*, and the broadcasts crackled from early morning until late at night.

Every other month, we were shown a movie, usually a propaganda documentary or one of the *yangbanxi*, "model movies" depicting the perfect Communist man. Before each meeting, we had to sing a few revolutionary songs to whip up an appropriate atmosphere of class hatred, which always filled me with conflicting emotions and instilled a lifelong aversion to singing, whatever the song.

To hide my agitation, I often sought out Zi Genlin for a game of chess and made sure all my actions were quiet and steady, giving no cause for suspicion. Unable to guess my intentions, fearing dereliction of duty more than anything, the cadres grew uneasy, and at the sight of me a strange apprehension clouded their faces.

In the north, Jade Dragon Mountain towered above us. Every day, I stopped several times to enjoy its beauty and always felt a bit depressed when it was hidden behind clouds. Everything about Lijiang was bloodstained, barbaric, and humiliating. Jade Dragon Mountain was clean and noble. Sometimes, I dreamed that if I managed to escape but had nowhere to go, I would climb that mountain and kill myself there. I couldn't understand how people who had lived for generations in the presence of such awesome majesty could behave with such smallness and venality.

Around this time, the two little boys from the Lijiang prison were sent to the 507 Agro-machinery Factory to serve their sentences for scribbling and carving graffiti against Chairman Mao. Wang Guilin had received seven years, He Zhongxiang ten.

The rainy season arrived. Dictated by the seasonal winds of the Indian Ocean, Yunnan's climate is clearly divided into a dry and a rainy season, and during the latter it rains almost every day. With torrents of water gushing down from the Himalayas, the hydroelectric plants once again generated electricity at full capacity. There were no more power outages, and at night the whole prison area was lit up as bright as day, making an escape more impossible than ever.

In November 1969, the leadership announced a new campaign

dubbed *sanjiao*, "the three confessions," and demanded that we own up to our reactionary thinking, counterrevolutionary sabotage, and other crimes. Naturally, I was one of the main targets. By now, Li Guangrong was convinced that I was planning an escape and he used every bluff he could think of to force my hand. Superficially, he held the trumps, but as long as I didn't flinch before his intimidations and threats, there was nothing he could do.

Using the old Communist control method of *renren guoguan*, "letting people through the gate one at a time," Li Guangrong ordered everybody to write a self-criticism and then divided the prisoners into two groups, those who had "passed the gate" and those who had not, using the former group to attack the latter. The whole process was extremely long and tedious, and interspersed with constant struggle meetings. I wrote several self-criticisms, but they were all rejected, and I was ordered to write a new one.

Because they suspected Wencan and me of secret activities, the leadership's strategy was to separate us, keep us under close surveillance, and sow seeds of distrust between us, with the ultimate aim of destroying us. But they never discovered our little hole by the latrine, where we constantly exchanged notes to ensure that we were acting in unison.

With only some ten people who had not "passed the gate" remaining, the psychological pressure on Wencan and me was ramped up to the bursting point. Faced with the risk of imminent exposure, which meant a bullet in the neck for both of us, we decided to disperse the zealots' energy by providing them with a fall guy.

There was a former KMT soldier from Jiangxi Province named Li Di, about fifty years old, who was serving a twenty-year sentence. In truth, he had been good to me. He had many fond memories of life before the Communist takeover—eating, drinking, whoring, and gambling—and loved to talk about them. People often saw us smoking a cigarette together, chatting and joking, and knew that we were friends.

In my final self-criticism, I confessed to some things Li Di and I had said to each other, such as expressing nostalgia for life in the old days, which implied a desire to restore KMT rule. This put Li Di in a tight spot and, exactly as we had foreseen, gave Li Guangrong an opportunity to extricate himself. Having at least managed to ferret out the reactionary memories skulking in Li Di's brain, he was able to keep face before his superiors and could unwind a bit. Both Wencan and I were allowed to "pass the gate," and the campaign was concluded.

After a short lull, there was a new round of struggling and infighting. From that time on, the political campaigns followed one another in unending succession, and virtually every day passed in a state of high tension. Fortunately, we were old hands and able to parry the maneuvers and machinations. A newcomer would have been scared stiff.

One day, all our belongings were removed from the blocks, placed in rows in the inner yard, and inspected by the team leaders, who focused on Mao's Little Red Book.

"How many Little Red Books do you have?" He Yutang asked me, leafing through my copy.

"One," I replied.

I learned that the convict Wang Wenlong had found a crumpled page from the Little Red Book with Mao's portrait on it in the latrine, covered with excrement, and reported his finding to the prison administration. This actually happened several times. But how were they going to find the culprits?

I was punished for pasting a postage stamp with Mao and Lin Biao on its side. For this, I had to write a several-thousand-character-long self-criticism and endure three days of questioning and denunciation by my team. If I had pasted it upside down, I would have been done for.

On the morning of April 30, 1970, we received terrible news: Zhang Manjie had been executed on Lijiang's Democracy Square. According to eyewitnesses, he was shot once in the chest and once in the neck. My old friend Manjie, who had promised to take care of me. According to the execution decree, he had conspired to organize a prison uprising during those tense weeks in April 1969 when the Soviet

Union's invasion of Zhenbao Island on the Ussuri River in Manchuria had brought our two countries to the brink of war, but in reality the charges were a shameless fabrication by the authorities.

His real "crime" was simply that he had been a KMT soldier. But whether or not he had fought against the Communists during the civil war, he was a Chinese citizen, and the regime had no right to put him to death. Even Li Guangrong and the other cadres were conscience-stricken. Manjie's execution notice was not posted in the prison, and his case was only mentioned in the most perfunctory, fleeting manner.

"It's time to make our move," Wencan said to me.

"We have to be one hundred percent sure of success."

"Yes, let's leave them gaping," he replied.

As in the previous year, the dry season in May and June 1970 brought empty reservoirs and constant power outages. Extra guards were added, and zealots assigned to watch over the convicts.

Impatient, Wencan proposed sneaking out of the processing factory hiding under a truck. But every vehicle leaving the prison was inspected at the main gate, and the guards would get down on their knees to make sure nobody was hiding in the chassis. I told him to keep his cool and work with me to devise the best escape plan.

At the time, a 12,000-ton hydraulic press had been built in Shanghai. Inspired by this feat, and craving glory and merit, Li Guangrong decided to demonstrate the strength and ability of the 507 Agromachinery Factory by building a 660-ton screw press. We were marched to an old electric power station on the other side of town, where we worked all day dissembling a steam engine, gathering the metal parts to be used in making the screw press.

The key component of this machine was a triple-screw copper spindle, about ten inches in diameter and twelve feet high, made by Lu Guocai, a master lather from Shanghai. Lu Guocai had been severely persecuted during the Cultural Revolution. The logic of Mao's cronies had always been "When we need you, we will use you. When we don't need you, you don't exist."

Working at the lathe for a full month, his face covered in a white beard, Old Lu finally completed this part so coveted by Li Guangrong. I admired his patience and ability and mourned the low status of skilled workers in our country. As fellow Shanghainese, we were good friends, and whenever I ran into technical problems at work, he was always eager to help me.

After six months of heroic efforts, at a cost of 200,000 yuan, Li Guangrong finally had his 660-ton, fifteen-foot-high screw press. The leadership boasted that it was the only machine of its kind in western Yunnan. The only problem was that it didn't work. It wasn't even able to press an engine shell. Useless, it stood there as a monument to the Communist Party's folly and reckless waste of the people's blood and sweat.

Wencan told me that a 50,000-kilowatt hydroelectric power plant was being built in Lijiang.

"When it is finished, there will be no more power outages. We have to make our escape as soon as possible," he said.

I took his point but I argued that we still didn't have enough grain ration coupons or money. Of the five yuan Mother sent to me every month, I had to use some and was only able to put away two yuan. How long a time would it take to save a hundred yuan?

Pondering the problem, I told Wencan to find a way to get sent to the infirmary, contact his wife, who lived nearby, and ask her to procure the necessary grain ration tickets and money. Wencan agreed to the plan, but to get sent to the infirmary, you had to be seriously ill. Our hope lay in pulling off a *kurouji*, "ruse of suffering flesh"—that is, to win the enemy's sympathy with a self-inflicted wound.

Two days later, Yang Wencan sought me out. "Can you get me blood?" he asked. "Chicken blood, pig blood, goat blood, any blood will do."

After waiting for an opportunity for a few days, unable to find any animal blood, I decided to use my own. One day in August 1970, I made some excuse to take a day's sick leave and, hiding under my mosquito net, strapped a belt tightly around my calf. Piercing a bulging vein with a knife, I filled a 100-cubic-centimeter bottle half-full with blood, stuffed some rice straw into the bottle, and shook it in order to deactivate the blood-clotting fibrin, then sealed the bottle tightly and dressed my wound.

In the afternoon, I transferred the bottle to Wencan. The next morning, hiding in the latrine, he poured my blood into his mouth and returned to the electric workshop, where he coughed blood in front of everybody, falling onto the ground and rolling his eyes until the whites showed. The team leader had him taken to the infirmary, where the doctor admitted him. I congratulated us on our successful completion of this first step.

Two weeks later, I saw Wencan walking into our block carrying a hemp bag with dried mushrooms and snuck out to see him. He told me that his wife had visited him but that she was in a bad way and in no position to help. To extend his stay in the infirmary, he needed to vomit blood once more. I told him to borrow a syringe from Yu Xingzhe and extract some of his own blood or steal a syringe if necessary.

Then he asked me for money. Reluctantly, I gave him five yuan. I was very unhappy with him. The whole purpose of his getting into the infirmary had been to procure money. We had to save every yuan for the right moment. Still, I placed my hopes in him and gave him twenty yuan in all, even though he probably used it to buy cigarettes.

Early one morning before National Day, the convict Liu Xiangchun escaped over the perimeter wall but was caught by guard dogs at dawn. Fitted with shackles, Xiangchun was paraded around the inner yard by Commissar Du, who made a point of giving me a fierce look. Subsequently, all the infirmary patients, including Wencan, were temporarily sent back to their cells. Nothing was allowed to go wrong on National Day.

During the festivities, everybody had a good time, relaxed, and lowered their guard. Wencan found an opportunity to meet me by the latrine. He told me that since his wife came from a family of rich peasants who had been classified as counterrevolutionaries, she was a target of the proletariat's dictatorship, had no income, and even had to ask for grain from their people's commune. I promised Wencan I would be responsible for procuring the money and the grain ration tickets and said that we couldn't afford to waste another yuan.

One Sunday afternoon shortly after National Day, Li Guangrong convened some thirty zealots in the foundry workshop for a meeting. I stood by the gate to the inner yard, observing the workshop at a distance. Although Li Guangrong was constantly convening meetings, this one was obviously different.

"Probably a new campaign," Wencan said to me.

I nodded my head.

"Keep an eye out, and stay cool," I said.

The meeting did not break until the evening meal, when the zealots emerged with unusually excited looks on their faces.

As expected, work was suspended the next morning and a new campaign was announced: *sicha pingshen*, "the four investigations." As he spoke, Commissar Du searched for me among the convicts assembled in the yard, and when our glances met, I felt the fire of his wrath.

Machine guns were mounted in the sentry towers, and the atmosphere was tense. Everybody knew another round of calamities was about to commence. Who would be the sacrificial lamb this time?

That afternoon, Hong Xuan posted a *dazibao* accusing me of corrupting the young convict Wang Guilin, trying to steal him from the proletariat, engaging in counterrevolutionary conspiracies, refusing to acknowledge guilt, making secret plans to escape, toadying to foreign countries, and more.

Hong Xuan was an intelligent man. Well aware I had seen him talking secretively with Li Yinyue in our block, he was terrified that I would expose him and had decided to launch a preemptive attack.

To defuse Hong Xuan's momentum, and without mentioning his name, I posted a small *dazibao* asking everybody to expose and criticize my mistaken words and actions and help me to reform myself. By adopting this soft attitude, I managed to win the sympathy of a lot of people, who saw hidden motives in the aggressiveness of Hong Xuan's attack. Even Li Guangrong nodded his head and smiled.

Forced to retreat, Hong Xuan did not say a word at the evening session. I sat calmly to the side, polite and respectful, and let everybody state their opinions. That night, I received a note from Wencan by the latrine. Praising my clever move, he admonished me to keep my cool, not fall for the temptation of exposing Hong Xuan, and ride out the storm by remaining impassive.

But Li Guangrong was a shrewd fox, not easily outwitted. Deploying the team leaders, he urged everybody to criticize both me and Hong Xuan, and within a couple of days the inner yard was plastered with *dazibao* attacking both of us in the most vicious language. To help the illiterate convicts, Li Guangrong ordered the *dazibao* to be read aloud at mealtime, which turned the tide of public opinion against me once again.

The *sicha pingshen* campaign harped on for two months but failed to break the mental defenses of a single major target. Unhappy with the meager results, Li Guangrong launched another frontal attack on Hong Xuan. At this time, I saw the opportunity to extricate myself by making Hong Xuan the number one counterrevolutionary and joined the general onslaught with a large *dazibao* titled "What Are Hong Xuan and Li Yinyue Discussing?" At the same time, I was modest and polite with Li Guangrong and wrote endless self-criticisms.

Around the Chinese New Year of 1971, the suicide of a convict named Li Jinxian finally brought the campaign to a close. Shamed by the revelation of his homosexual relationship with the young Tibetan convict Yong Chu, Li Jinxian nearly severed his own head in the narrow alley by the post-sentence detainees' dormitories and was found dead in a pool of blood. Sexual relations were prohibited in the prison, but human nature could not be extinguished, with sodomy an inevitable outcome. Chu and Jinxian were not the only couple, and it was their bad luck to have been caught in the act.

That spring, Li Guangrong ordered the construction of four minute solitary confinement cells, each one measuring three feet three inches wide, four feet eleven inches high, and five feet three inches long. A prisoner locked in one of these concrete boxes could not stand straight, could barely turn his body, and had to sleep curled up. Sometimes he was even fitted with shackles and handcuffs. Li Guangrong had several reasons for building them. First, campaigns and struggle meetings were short-lived and unable to break the convicts' will. Second, killing convicts outright had a negative political effect, so Mao's followers had come up with this method of destroying their enemies slowly. Third, a prisoner locked up in one of these cells had a strong intimidating effect on the rest of the convicts.

Since my incarceration in the processing factory, my correspondence with Mother had been limited. Unable to tell her what had really happened, I preferred to say nothing at all. Doing everything she could to help me, in addition to the monthly five yuan, she also sent me clothes and shoes and a new cotton-padded jacket to replace the old one I had worn for ten years. Worried that my stubborn character would lead me to my death, she urged me to bear my hardship with patience. And during all my years in the *laogai*, she instilled in me a steadfast faith: "Where there is life, there is hope."

My younger brother, who returned to Shanghai in 1970, sent me ten yuan to show his sympathy and support. My two sisters, however, were angry for the trouble I had brought upon the family and refused to have anything to do with me.

National Day on October 1, 1971, was strange. There were no mass parades on Tiananmen Square, and Lin Biao's name was nowhere to be seen. Subsequently, Li Guangrong ordered all Lin Biao quotations and slogans painted on the walls to be scrubbed off with lime. Obviously, Lin Biao had run into some kind of trouble, but none of us knew what had happened.

On the afternoon of National Day, in violation of our rule to not speak to each other in public, Wencan asked me to meet him in the carpentry workshop. Seeing his agitated expression, I nodded my head in a sign for him to go there first, then walked a lap around the yard to make sure nobody was watching, before stepping inside.

"During the inspection yesterday, He Yutang found a note I had written to you in one of my books. I didn't have time to remove it," Wencan said.

We were finished. I wanted to slap his ears.

"It didn't say anything about our escape," Wencan continued. "I was just telling you that I saw Yuan Yicheng bugger Yang Lunyuan in the small cell opposite block three."

"Why did I need to know that? Are you absolutely sure the note said nothing about an escape?"

"Yes."

"Now listen to me," I said. "If Li Guangrong questions you, you must tell him that you were trying to frame Yuan Yicheng."

Afraid that we would be seen, I told him to leave the workshop first. After he left, I sat by the machines for a while, mulling over the matter. My thoughts drifted back to my escape from the White Grass Ridge labor camp with Xiangzai in 1958. "Wencan is just like him," I said to myself.

The next day, Wencan asked to speak with Li Guangrong but was told that there was nothing to talk about.

"He is waiting for us to panic and confess," I told Wencan. "Because he has refused to speak with you, pretend as if nothing has happened, and wait for his next move. From now on, you must follow me to the letter. If we are divided and begin to blow our own horns, we will be annihilated."

Around October 10, the prisoners were informed of Lin Biao's attempted coup, defection, and plane crash in Mongolia but prohibited from discussing the matter. It was a resounding defeat for Chairman Mao. Under ordinary circumstances, the news would have overjoyed us, but the inadvertent discovery of Wencan's note to me had put a damper on our spirits, and we were in no mood to celebrate.

On the evening of October 15, Li Guangrong summoned Hong Xuan, Ding Yongcheng, Shen Shangwu, and me to a meeting in his office. It was the first time I had been called to a "small" meeting. Everybody found it odd.

"We're holding a small meeting here tonight," he said. "Don't be nervous, there is no specific topic. We can talk about the progress that has been made since the *sicha pingshen* campaign and any problems that still remain. You may also discuss your opinions and feelings since learning of the Lin Biao incident."

Based on my long experience with struggles, I determined that the purpose of this meeting was to make us own up, but I didn't know which method Li Guangrong intended to use. Yongcheng spoke first, hypocritically criticizing himself and thanking the government for saving him, as Li Guangrong listened smugly. Hong Xuan and Shangwu kept up the farce. Speaking last, I said the *sicha pingshen* campaign had done me good by making me realize what a bad, guilty person I was and that I would reform myself with a steady, focused heart from now on. Finally, I stated a sincere opinion: "When there were no parades on National Day, and Lin Biao's name did not appear in the newspapers, I knew something had happened with Lin Biao. But I could never have guessed that Lin Biao would commit such a grave error. Lin Biao has caused great damage to our country."

And I added in my head: "You sentenced Wencan to fifteen years for the crime of opposing Lin Biao. Now you can rehabilitate him."

Li Guangrong was not pleased with my speech.

"Xu Hongci," he said, looking at me sternly. "You've made progress in reforming yourself these past few years, and your work has been good. But we know there are people who are trying to turn you back onto your former path of resisting reform. You must draw a clear line and expose these people. Otherwise, all your achievements will have been wasted. I will give you one day to think this matter over and hope that you will make a report of your own accord."

Pretending there was nothing unusual, I simply nodded my head.

"The decision is yours," Li Guangrong continued, angered by my feigned indifference. "If you come clean, we will treat you with leniency. If not, take a good look at the beard Hu Naiming has grown in solitary."

That night, I met with Wencan by the latrine.

"Li Guangrong knows that your note was intended for me," I told him. "Now you will have to write two more notes predating it. You will give them to me here tomorrow morning before roll call, and I will show them to Li Guangrong."

I told Wencan what to write in the two notes. My strategy was to rub Li Guangrong the right way and create confusion by mixing truth with falsehood. The first one was to precede the note about Yuan Yicheng's buggery with Yang Lunyuan by two months and state that Wencan had seen Li Zengjun stealing cured meat from the storage room. The second one was to predate the intercepted note by two weeks and say that we needed to deflate Yuan Yicheng's growing arrogance.

Reading these notes, Li Guangrong would try to connect the dots and find comfort in thinking he knew what we had been up to. This, in turn, would reduce Wencan's crime to the small matter of fabricating rumors and eliminate the risk of a major disaster.

The next morning, I received the two notes from Wencan by the latrine, crumpled them up, and hid them in my toolbox. Having waited the whole morning for me to make a clean breast of things, Li Guangrong finally lost his patience and summoned me to his office. "This is your last chance," he said angrily. "Are you going to confess or not? If you don't, you know what is waiting for you."

"I have considered this matter carefully," I replied calmly. "Actually, it is no big deal. Yang Wencan wrote two notes to me."

"Where are the notes?" Li Guangrong asked, unable to hide his glee.

"In the workshop."

"Go get them right this moment."

I turned around and returned to the workshop, retrieved the two notes from my toolbox, then hurried back to Li Guangrong.

Grabbing the notes, he studied them with a cold sneer, then snorted, "You cunning rascal. Go back to your block and write a self-criticism!"

I left Li Guangrong's office with a sense of victory. Just as I had predicted, the two notes had taken the edge off Li Guangrong's bluster, and I had been let off the hook with a mere self-criticism. Close call!

At the same time, I was forced to reconsider my whole relationship with Wencan. I still trusted him politically. But his lack of willpower and other flaws filled me with deep misgiving.

About one month later, I had finished work and returned to my block for mealtime when Wencan approached me.

"I have broken a punching die," he whispered. "There might be trouble."

At first, I didn't get his meaning. "Just make a new one," I said to myself. But sure enough, right after mealtime, Li Guangrong summoned everybody to a meeting at which he accused Wencan of deliberately breaking the punching press, sabotaging production, thereby causing a loss of several hundred yuan. He then added that Wencan had fabricated rumors against a trusted zealot, refused to relinquish his reactionary thinking, and must be severely punished.

"Put Wencan in shackles," he ordered the blacksmith.

This time there was nothing I could do to save him. I had told him to be more careful in his work, but he hadn't listened to me. Watching him drag his chains toward the solitary confinement cell, I bid him a silent farewell. From that moment on, I became a complete loner, with nobody to speak to and share confidences with, and would have to rely solely on myself in all matters.

Wencan's first week in solitary was extremely cruel. At mealtime, his handcuffs were not opened, and he was fed through the cell door's window by a kitchen worker. The sight thrust a knife into my heart. I felt sorry for him and blamed him at the same time. He was a bungler. But I wasn't afraid that he would expose me. We were in too deep, and it would mean the end of us both.

Knowing Li Guangrong, I guessed Wencan would be locked up for at least a year. His confinement was a time bomb that could blow up in my face at any time. I had to make my escape now—or never. But the swelling of my scrotum, which I had suffered from for a long time, was getting worse, and because an escape would mean trekking hundreds of miles, I had to cure this problem first.

In January 1972, as I was being attacked and beaten giddy during a new campaign, I faked a collapse and told them that I had to have surgery. The prison doctor, Zhang Wenxuan, took one look at my scrotum and immediately asked Li Guangrong to send me to the infirmary for an operation.

After making careful consultations and arrangements, Li Guangrong finally agreed. His cold, sharp glance warned me that any attempt to escape would spell my death.

Zhang Wenxuan operated on me right away, and after one and a half hours I was resting in the spartan ward. But only four days later, at risk of rupturing my unhealed wound, I was ordered to return to the 507 Agro-machinery Factory. After three days, Zhang Wenxuan inspected my wound and removed the stitches. I still remember his kindness with deep gratitude.

During the dry season in May 1972, the electric supply continued uninterrupted, with no outages. How I prayed for a blackout! After three years of careful observations, research, and contemplation, in a moment of sudden inspiration I had finally hatched the perfect escape plan.

During an evening blackout, I would avail myself of the momentary disorder after the 9:00 p.m. roll call and not return to my block but cross the yard and hide in the bed of dahlia shrubs by the door to the kitchen workers' prison cell. By doing this, I eliminated the risk of being shot by the guards in the southern sentry tower while crossing the yard. After everybody had fallen asleep, I would crawl to the end of the building, turn right into the blind corner by the door, scale the ten-foot wall separating the prisoners' inner yard from the post-sentence detainees' yard, enter their canteen, follow the wall around the main yard, and then scale the perimeter wall behind the latrine by the willow tree in the northeast corner of the prison complex.

As I waited for a blackout, my preparations went into high gear. First, I successively bought some forty pieces of *shagao*, a traditional Lijiang snack made of soybean flour, corn flour, and sugar, which each cost a one-*liang* grain ration ticket and one jiao, and hid the cakes under a double bottom in my toolbox. This would be my dry food on the road. Second, I scraped off the convict number painted in white on my leather jacket, then treated the whole jacket several times with black shoe polish. I also faded the number painted on the sleeve of my sweater with gasoline and sewed a patch over the number beside my pants' pocket.

Third, one piece at a time, I hid these clothes and everything I was going to bring in the metalworking shop. Fourth, I ground a sharp, triangular knife. Fifth, I made a small pocket at the bottom of my trouser leg where I could hide my money. Last but not least, I prepared myself mentally and steeled my resolve. Every day, I repeated my motto: "Be brave. Keep steady. Stay calm. Think quick."

In the midst of these preparations, I received a note from Wencan in our hole by the latrine. With no hope of being let out from solitary in the foreseeable future, he told me to go it alone. I admired his fighting spirit and wondered how he had been able to find a pencil and paper. But having considered the matter seriously, in order to maintain absolute secrecy, I didn't respond and didn't receive any more notes from him.

On July 6, 1972, the labor camp administration assembled all convicts and post-sentence detainees of the 507 Agro-machinery Factory and the Dayan Farm for a meeting in the newly built garage. Although the theme of this new campaign appeared to be economic, I was still on high alert, because there was always a political aspect to every campaign in the labor camps.

Speaking about the need to increase production and reduce waste, Commissar Du urged everybody to expose wastage and destruction of state property, promising leniency to those who came clean and severe punishment of those who hesitated.

In passing, he mentioned that the Americans had gone to the moon in 1969. Although this lunar landing had taken place three years earlier, I had never heard of it. Commissar Du treated the achievement with disdain, adding that there was nothing special about the United States. But I thought that the Americans had done something incredible. It also made me deeply aware of the Communist Party's policy of block-ading information to keep us ignorant, blind, and deaf.

After the meeting, we formed discussion groups, and everybody was ordered to write a self-criticism. Since my arrival at the 507 Agro-machinery Factory, I had never made a rejected product, and the only error I had ever committed was to make a small hole in the platform bed of a drill. If the Communist Party had been as magnanimous and benevolent as it loved to boast, it would have disregarded this trifling matter. But instead of forgiving me, not to speak of giving me credit for my hard work, it seized upon this little mistake with its ingrained meanness and used it as an excuse to settle old accounts.

The zealots He Yutang and Li Gui were deployed to attack me for sabotaging production. A condemned rapist, Li Gui was particularly eager to gain merit, even if it meant sending me to my death. His evil motives filled me with hatred. Well aware that he had hidden many rejected products under his bench, during rest time I gathered them into a pile by the entrance to the drafting room for everybody to see, affixing a note on top: Li Gui's rejected products.

This move caused a commotion and succeeded in taking Li Gui down a peg. To my surprise, it also moved my former enemy Hong Xuan, who declared that our past arguments had been a misunderstanding and offered to be reconciled. But in the heat of my anger, I had forgot-ten that Li Gui was Li Guangrong's hatchet man and that an attack on him was tantamount to an attack on the prison leadership.

Having learned of my reconciliation with Hong Xuan, Li Guang-rong decided the time had come to squash both of us once and for all and began assembling every scrap of incriminating evidence he could find, scouring the records of our evening study sessions for reactionary utterances.

Here's what he could find: I had said that the factory had wasted 200,000 yuan to manufacture a screw press that hadn't been used in production for two years. I had claimed that Bangladesh had become an independent country after the capitulation of the East Pakistan army to the Indian army, which, because China and Pakistan were allies, was considered a reactionary opinion. I had attacked the Communist Party by allusion, saying that while China was doing class war, the West was doing business. Finally, I had linked up with Hong Xuan of the Great Harmony Party and attacked Li Gui, who was reforming himself diligently.

On August 2, Deng Juqing whispered in my ear, "He Zhongxiang has snitched on you for giving him grain ration tickets and money to buy *shagao* cake."

The noose around my neck was tightening every day.

20

Endgame

(August 6-September 10, 1972)

On August 6, Li Guangrong went into action. That morning, more than a hundred *dazibao* denouncing me were put up on the prison walls, and the metalworker Yang Xijing was assigned to read them aloud to set the prisoners' hatred roiling. The accusations were venomous: counterrevolutionary, turncoat, traitor, conspirator, scum, serpent . . . Virtually every poster demanded the death penalty.

I purchased a pack of cheap cigarettes, put the tobacco in my metal mug, and soaked it in boiling-hot water to draw a thick juice, then poured the liquid into a small glass bottle. This was my poison—concentrated nicotine. If my escape failed, I would end my life with it.

At lunchtime, Wencan, let out of his cell, was squatting on the ground, eating his gruel. Seeing him drag his chains, his hair dirty and disheveled, his bearded face as pale as death, I wanted to give him wings so that he could fly away to freedom. He scanned the yard, looking for me, then ran his hand through his hair. It was our old sign. I knew what he was trying to say: "Go!"

He was right. I did not have much time left.

In the evening, Li Guangrong convened all the prisoners in block one. I sat at the back with my head lowered, thinking, "Will he put me in solitary tonight?" Seated by the Ping-Pong table, Li Guangrong began his lecture. He didn't call out my name and pretended nothing special had taken place during the day. Instead, he talked about general things like study and reform, admonished us to continue our efforts to reduce wastage and identify errors in production, and urged everybody to put forth proposals for consideration.

Feinting was one of Li Guangrong's old tricks. Without warning, he changed tack and began criticizing Yuan Deli for preferring to practice calligraphy instead of studying the works of Mao. During his two years in solitary, Deli had become a changed man. He never spoke, and whenever he had spare time, he put on his old glasses and practiced calligraphy with a fountain pen. I think it was a kind of mental comfort for him. As long as he didn't make trouble, why not just leave him alone? But Li Guangrong was too mean even for this.

Suddenly Yuan Deli stood up and pointed at Li Guangrong. "Execute me, Commandant Li, execute me right away! If you don't execute me, you're a coward!" he shouted.

He had come to the end of his tether and decided to make a clean break with this inhumane system and seek liberation through death. Although I thought he was being stupid, I was also inspired by his courage. "If Yuan Deli is determined to die, I shall be equally determined to live," I said to myself. Li Guangrong and the others were dumbstruck.

"Execute me! Execute me right now!" Deli shouted again.

However despotic, Li Guangrong didn't dare to put a bullet in Deli's neck there and then. On the other hand, if he didn't execute him, he would lose face in front of all the prisoners. Regaining his composure, Li Guangrong sent Yuan Yicheng to fetch the guards.

Deli laughed and continued shouting, "Execute me!"

He had gone mad and gave vent to every last drop of his pent-up despair and rage, throwing all caution to the wind. The guards dragged him away to the number four solitary confinement cell, where he continued to shout in a hoarse voice: "Commandant Li, execute me! If you don't execute me, you're a coward!"

It was a miracle. Li Guangrong had been saving the number four solitary confinement cell for me. Now Yuan Deli had forced him to change his plans, and with all solitary confinement cells occupied, somebody would have to be released before I could be locked up. Who? Definitely not the newcomer in number one. It would have to be either Wencan or Naiming. But neither of them had made a thorough confession, and it would take time to reach a decision on whom to release.

The next morning, I was working on the construction of a high-voltage transmission tower when my friend the blacksmith Wang Zhiwen walked over.

"Li Guangrong has ordered me to make a pair of heavy shackles. I think they are intended for you," he said in a low voice.

It would be a matter of days, or even hours, before Li Guangrong roped me in. Then, around 10:00 a.m., the electricity went dead. The new fertilizer factory nearby had triggered a blackout, and we were informed that the power wouldn't be back on until 6:00 the next morning.

"Everybody who uses electricity in their work shall go to the foundry workshop to do cleaning. Those who do not use electricity shall continue their work as usual," we were told.

It was another miracle. The day I had waited for so long had finally arrived. I immediately went to the carpentry workshop to fetch two seven-foot poles, five foot-long pieces of wood, and some short stumps of hemp rope and placed these materials in the gutter along the wall by the blind corner, where there was already a lot of rubbish lying about.

I then filled an old, high basket with long pieces of scrap metal and placed it by the door to the kitchen personnel's prison cell, to enlarge the shadow as I crawled to the blind corner that night. During the midday break, I put all the things I was going to bring with me in the metalworking shop. My official verdict was a souvenir I had to bring along. I folded it neatly and fixed it with starch paste to the inner side of a round cardboard box, then filled the box with needles, thread, and other articles. In the afternoon, I dug up the three fake permits, the wooden type blocks, and seventy-eight yuan and sewed up the money in the small pocket at the bottom of my trouser leg.

After the evening meal, I hid under my mosquito net and filled in my first fake permit with a Chinese writing pen—*Comrade Ling Yun is traveling from Lijiang to Binchuan to visit relatives*—then threw away the pen. With all preparations in place, I lay down and pretended to sleep. He Yutang returned from a meeting with the prison leadership, and our group members gathered by a kerosene lamp to study.

"I am not feeling well and ask to be excused," I said to He Yutang.

Thinking that I was in a bad mood after having been struggled with, he allowed me to continue resting. I heard him say, "This campaign will intensify. Every person guilty of destructive behavior and actions will be criticized until he recants and submits."

At that time, my bunk had been moved to the wall facing the inner yard. Across the aisle to the right was Zi Genlin's bunk, while Gu Yuheng slept at a perpendicular angle at the foot of my bunk. Both of them were simple, honest men who took no interest in politics and didn't participate in schemes and conspiracies. They even had a bit of sympathy for me and walked with light steps in order not to disturb my rest.

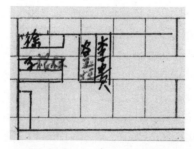

This drawing shows the placement of Xu Hongci's bunk at the time of his escape: Xu Hongci (top left), Zi Genlin (bottom left), Gu Yuheng (second from right), Li Gui (right).

At 9:00 p.m., the roll-call whistle sounded. I got out of bed and quickly stuffed some old clothes under my blanket to make it look like a sleeping person, then put the mosquito net in order. This was done in darkness and was not noticed by anybody. The last person to enter the

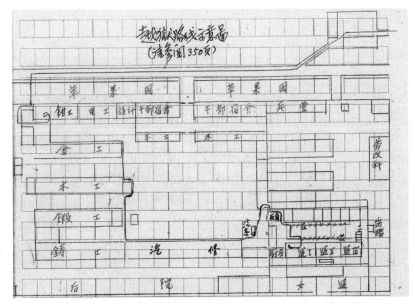

The 507 Agro-machinery Factory with Xu Hongci's escape route penciled in

yard, I stood in my usual place. Lan Wenguang, a life prisoner in the metalworking group, held up a kerosene lamp for the guard, who shouted our names.

"Xu Hongci!"

"Here!"

With all prisoners accounted for, the guards could relax, and we were dismissed. Everything proceeded according to the ordinary routine. Some people went to the boiler to salvage the last drops of hot water to wash their feet; some went to the latrine. To maintain order, the guards in the sentry tower only allowed five people to go at a time. When they had returned and reported, another group of five was allowed to go, while the others, some thirty or forty prisoners, stood in line, smoking and chatting.

Lan Wenguang placed the kerosene lamp by the boiler, but the wind blew out the light, and the yard went pitch-black. It was the first quarter of the lunar month, and people, moving in all directions, stumbled in the darkness. These few chaotic minutes were a golden opportunity. Gritting my teeth, I began to move. After the roll call, I had walked toward my canteen table, as if to get something. When the kerosene lamp went out, I immediately ducked and hid among the dahlia bushes by the tables, six feet from the kitchen personnel's cell.

Squatting among the bushes, I surveyed the yard and could only see the kitchen worker Peng Zixian fetching water by the boiler. Some prisoners had returned to their cells, and I was anxious to get going, but I could hear Peng Zixian, Yu Longcai, and Yang Caifeng talking and had to restrain myself. I waited for about twenty minutes, incredibly nervous, cursing them between my teeth. Yang Caifeng got up and went to the latrine, then returned.

I squatted among the bushes for a full hour until everybody had gone to sleep. Under the cover of the basket with scrap metal, I crawled the twelve feet to the blind corner. The distance between me and the sentry tower was more than 150 feet, and in the darkness the guard couldn't see me, especially because his attention was focused on the gate.

Out of the guard's line of vision, I stood up, retrieved the materials from the gutter, and tied them into a ladder, finishing the work in about thirty minutes. I heard somebody report for a visit to the latrine and had to wait. When that person returned to his block, I placed the ladder against the wall separating our yard from the post-sentence detainees.

Twelve feet long and ten feet high, this wall was the weakest point in the whole prison. Why had Li Guangrong been so careless? The answer was simple: he had not thought anybody would dare cross the inner yard under the muzzle of a machine gun to reach this blind corner. Carefully, I climbed up to the top crosspiece. The ladder was too short for me to get my leg over the wall.

I felt caught like a turtle in an earthen jar. I looked around and discovered two carrying poles lying about, which I used to extend the legs. The ladder was long enough now. I straddled the wall, pulled up the ladder, and placed it on the other side. My heel struck a shingle. It fell to the ground with a thump, sending a flash of terror through my body. Luckily, all the post-sentence detainees were asleep, and the guard in the sentry tower was at a safe distance.

I carried the ladder into the post-sentence detainees' canteen and, crouching, entered the main yard, where a truck was parked. Quickly, I crossed the yard and crawled under it, hiding between its front wheels.

When I lifted my head, I could see Wang Wenkui, one of the post-sentence detainees, walking over to the kitchen door and poking about some cinders. After a few minutes, he walked over to the truck and took a piss, splattering my face. I pressed myself to the ground, not daring to breathe. Wenkui returned to his dormitory to sleep. Close call!

I waited for a while and, making sure nobody was up and about, crawled out from under the truck, pulled out the ladder, scurried along the wall of the vehicle repair shop, turned the corner by the foundry workshop, opened the window to the metalworking shop, jumped in, changed clothes quickly, and gathered my food and other things in a string bag.

Taking one last look around, I said goodbye to the workshop where I had toiled for three and a half years under the gaze of the old Mao poster. I wanted to destroy it, but reason held me back.

I jumped out through the window, closing it after me, entered the latrine, stood the ladder against its rear wall, and climbed it, then descended to the edge of the cesspit on the other side, bringing the ladder with me. Following the cesspit to the gable of the metalworking shop, I reached Wencan's beloved willow tree, its branches stretching into the prison from outside the perimeter wall.

I climbed up and straddled the dead electric fence, throwing my string bag onto the ground outside. I wanted to bring the ladder with me, dissemble, and dispose of it, leaving Li Guangrong with no clue as to how I had escaped. But the barbs of the electric fence held my clothes. The thought shot through my head: "What if the electricity comes on!"

I jumped down, hitting the ground with a thud that broke the stillness of the night. My whole body was shaking violently; my heart racing as if mad. I retrieved my string bag and ran through the narrow apple orchard to the main road. I had made it! I had left the bloodstained 507 Agro-machinery Factory behind me once and for all! The time was about 11:30 p.m., August 7, 1972. I had six and a half hours until the morning roll call.

Jumping a ditch, I hurried south along the road to Lijiang, shaking my fist in triumph at the prison's main gate. But I had celebrated too soon. A flashlight shone straight upon me from behind and refused to let go. I didn't turn around or start running but continued walking in my original direction. It was the prison's patrol guard. If I started to run, I would be shot dead on the spot. After about ten seconds, there was a side road to the prison's garage. I turned onto it without hesitating and entered the garage through the back door.

Probably, the patrol guard, seeing that I was wearing a leather jacket and leather shoes and appeared unperturbed, had taken me for a driver. I hid behind the door, waited, watching the flashlight flicker about. A couple of minutes later, everything was darkness. The guard was gone.

I tiptoed through the garage and exited through the half-open main door. In Lijiang, I passed the local party committee and the Public Security Bureau, then turned right toward Democracy Square, where so many people had been sentenced to death and executed. Remembering my own trial on that square three and a half years earlier, I couldn't help lobbing a ball of spit in its direction.

I walked as fast as I could to get as far as possible from Lijiang before daybreak. But I hadn't had exercise for a long time, and after about two hours I was exhausted. I sat down by a stream to rest and strengthen myself with some *shagao* cake, moldy but still edible. It was pitch-dark in all directions, and I could see almost nothing of the surrounding landscape.

In one village, I heard the voices from a movie emanating from a house and, listening carefully, recognized the dialogue from the Korean movie *A Time to Pick Apples*.

"Do the peasants of Lijiang watch movies in the middle of the night?" I asked myself.

Up ahead, I could see bright lights and hear the deep rumbling of engines—the Guanpo hydroelectric power station. Descending from the Lijiang Plateau, I continued walking south as fast as I could, everything around me once again silent, as if the world were dead. Darkness was my best friend.

But soon the sun would rise. When my fellow inmates discovered that I was gone, the whole prison would be in an uproar. Li Guangrong would direct the chase, ask all people's communes to send out search parties and set up roadblocks, and dispatch cars, motorcycles, and guard dogs to hunt me down. If I continued walking on the road, sooner or later they would catch up with me.

I turned off the road into a pine forest and sat down on a stone to rest. Both my ankles were terribly swollen. I estimated that I had covered about twenty miles.

I wanted to find a place to sleep but was afraid I would be discovered by peasants going up into the mountains and decided to keep going. My ankles were painful, and after walking a short distance, I had to rest again. I walked and rested, walked and rested, making slow progress. Suddenly I came upon a peasant picking mushrooms.

"What are you doing here?" he asked with a strange look.

I thought he was going to interrogate me, but he didn't stop and simply continued on his way. I ate my cake and drank water from a stream. Although exhausted, I was full of fighting spirit. I guessed the prisoners would not be put to work that day and that everybody would be interrogated. The guards would search the perimeter wall to find my point of escape. How far could the dogs trace me? How would Li Guangrong explain himself to the higher authorities? What would the other prisoners say? I was both elated and anxious and had only one thought in my head: to get out of Lijiang County as fast as possible.

I crossed a dam. In the distance, I could see a funeral procession approaching and sat down to wait until it had passed. Around noon, the forest came to an end. An open, gentle slope rose in the distance. I surveyed the landscape carefully. I was in the middle of a long *bazi*, one of those enclosed mountain plateaus typical of northern Yunnan. To the west there was a high, denuded mountain range. If I walked in that direction, it would be possible to be seen from a long distance. The gentle slope in the south was also bare, but the mountains to the east were forested.

Passing through several villages, I walked east on a horse cart road toward the forested mountain. I realized the road would lead me to Heqing County, part of the Dali Bai Ethnic Minority Autonomous Region, which was outside the jurisdiction of Lijiang. As soon as I reached Heqing, the danger would be cut in half. I had followed the route Wencan and I had plotted, without deviation. If he betrayed me, it would be easy for the Public Security Bureau to track me down. But I knew he wouldn't.

The pain in my ankles subsided, and I was able to walk at a slow but steady pace. The horse cart road brought me to a village where some peasants were playing basketball. Seeing me walk with confidence, neatly dressed, they took no note of me. A sign on the door of a building said "Lijiang County, Wufeng People's Commune." So I was still in Lijiang County. When would it end? But I felt sure Heqing couldn't be far off.

I passed more villages. Dusk descended. I walked until it was so dark I couldn't see the five fingers of my outstretched hand. There were no villages or people. I found myself a patch of grass, spread the blue plastic sheet I had packed in my string bag, and lay down to sleep but was attacked by mosquitoes. I hadn't slept for almost forty hours, was exhausted, and finally dozed off.

In the middle of the night, I was awakened by thunder. As I was worrying about this, the peasants in a nearby village began shooting fire arrows toward the clouds. At least one hundred arrows exploded, illuminating the night sky. The peasants often used this method, believing that it would disperse the clouds and prevent the hail from ruining their crops. I had always doubted its efficacy, but in any event it didn't rain. I thanked the peasants of the Wufeng People's Commune for saving me from the thunderstorm.

I fell asleep again, but my brain was in a state of high alert and I soon woke up. At dawn, I packed my string bag, placed the small knife in the lining of my trousers, and put the bottle with concentrated nicotine into my pocket. I discovered that I had lost the cardboard box with my official verdict. Perhaps it had fallen out of the bag when I had thrown it to the ground from the wall. I washed my face with water from an irrigation ditch, ate some *shagao* cake, and continued walking south.

August 9: The mountains were shrouded in clouds. It seemed it would rain. The horse cart road shrank to a small path, and the villages grew sparser. A gentle slope rose before me. I guessed that Heqing County would be on the other side. At about 10:00 a.m., a goat shepherd approached me.

"Where are you going?" he asked.

"To Binchuan," I replied.

"Why don't you take the bus?"

"I have to go to Duomei to take care of some business first. After that, I will go to Binchuan," I said.

He didn't ask to see my documents, but merely said, "That's a long way. You'll have to walk several days."

"Shouldn't take me more than three or four days," I replied.

Because I had learned to speak the local dialect, he was not particularly suspicious and allowed me to continue on my way. At noon, I finally reached the top of the hill. Below me lay another beautiful *bazi* dotted with villages. I felt sure it must be Heqing County.

I came upon a large complex surrounded by a high wall, with orderly rows of buildings and sentry towers in each corner—a *laogai*. My heart began pounding, and I started walking faster. Passing the camp, I crossed paths with some people who looked like cadres, but fortunately they didn't stop me.

At about 4:00 p.m., I finally found the departure point for the horse caravan road up the mountain. A caravan overtook me.

"Comrade, where are you going?" one of the drivers asked me.

"Duomei."

"That's two days' walk," he said, and drove on.

I was thirsty. Having found a stream, I drank the cold water and ate some cake. I found some trees to sit down and rest among. The mountain was serene, with not a human being in sight. Gradually, I allowed myself to relax. I recalled my escape, the anguish and the excitement, and couldn't help feeling proud. "Where are you now, Li Guangrong?" I thought. I wondered if he had executed Yuan Deli. If he wasn't able to catch me, he would undoubtedly find somebody to pour out his anger on.

I missed Wencan. But I knew that if we had made our escape together, our chances of success would have been virtually nil. Again and again, I told myself, "Stay away from people. No matter what, don't even think about a bed and a roof over your head." Darkness fell. I spread out my plastic sheet. There were fewer mosquitoes here, and after three days of physical and mental strain I finally got a good night's sleep.

August 10: In good spirits, I followed the horse caravan path toward Duomei. Descending for roughly an hour along the winding path, I came to a large village with a brick kiln and many neat dwellings. There were few people about. Afraid of meeting somebody, I hurried out of the village and down to the river. I thought it might be the Golden Sand River, but this river flowed north. "It must be a tributary," I said to myself.

A stone bridge appeared up ahead. By it, a peasant and his wife were roasting a chicken over a campfire. They observed me carefully and seemed a bit suspicious. I hurried up on the bridge and crossed the torrential river, heading east and making about six miles before nightfall, when I lay down to rest in some woods.

At night, the valley was filled with the strange shrieks and howls of wild animals and birds. The peasant couple roasting a chicken lingered in my thoughts for a long time. Some people were allowed to live in peace, carefree and content. I felt like a hunted animal, with the hand of death in close pursuit.

August 11: Here and there along the path, I saw a beautiful mushroom called *jizongjun*, white, about four inches in diameter. "With a place to cook, I could have a feast," I thought.

At dusk, the path branched at the foot of a high mountain. I wanted to turn right but hesitated and asked some peasants for directions. They told me to take the left path to get to Duomei. The right path led to Songgui, a large town on the road from Heqing to Dali. Several *laogai* convicts on the run had been intercepted in Songgui, and if I had taken that path, I would have delivered myself into the hands of the Public Security Bureau. Without knowing it, those peasants saved my life.

August 12: I hit the road again and walked until I heard a familiar roar—the Golden Sand River. Having lived beside this mighty river for five years, I was overjoyed at the thought of seeing it again.

"Long time no see. Wish me good luck!" I said, waving to the river.

The town of Duomei was still nowhere in sight. Some peasant girls walked by.

"How do I get to Duomei?"

"You have walked too far," they said, pointing to a dirt path at the foot of the mountain. "Take that path. Duomei is not far."

I thanked them and walked back toward the path but hadn't made it more than a hundred feet when I heard people behind me shouting. Two men were talking to the girls and then started running toward me.

"The People's Militia," I said to myself.

By the path, there was a thatched shack with a pile of mud bricks. Trying to act normally, I walked into the shack, sat down on the mud bricks, and lit a cigarette. The two young men approached me. One of them, a man in his thirties with an intelligent face, was wearing a gray Mao uniform. The other man was younger, looked earnest, and wore a blue uniform.

"Comrade, where are you going?" the man in gray asked me.

I removed the cigarette from the corner of my mouth, exhaled a puff, and answered, "To Binchuan. I have a permit."

Knitting his eyebrows, he examined the document carefully. "All permits are letterpress printed. But this one . . ."

He looked at the seal on the back, trying to find something wrong with it. I sat smoking, feigning indifference. Turning the piece of paper over again and again, he looked at me with suspicion, then handed it back to me.

"You have taken the wrong path," he said. "Go back and take that path up the mountain."

Rejoicing quietly, I thanked him, picked up my string bag, and started walking toward the path. Looking back, I saw the two men heading in the direction of the riverbank. I walked as fast as I could, reaching Duomei by noon.

I had heard many things about this famous, picturesque town, situated on the western bank of the Golden Sand River. It was a busy place, with several stores. I found a small restaurant and had two big bowls of rice with tofu soup for just five jiao.

On the bank of the river, I sat down on my haunches and washed my face with the muddy water, drinking a mouthful to pay my respects.

"Where are you going?" a peasant woman asked me.

"To Pianjiao, and then Binchuan," I replied.

"There are torrents coming down the mountain all the way. You have to walk a bit higher," she said.

I thanked her for the information and climbed until I reached the third path running along the mountainside. At this altitude, I had a better view of the landscape. The mountains were dotted with villages, with rice paddies down by the riverside. There were a lot of people up and about, everybody busy attending to their livelihood.

By nightfall, I had still not reached the third bend in the river. I found a flat spot to lie down on for the night. The sky was clear, and the mosquitoes few, but the roaring river kept me awake as bad memories from my prison years replayed themselves in my head. The more I thought about it, the more I valued freedom. I would rather die than lose it again. Finally, I fell asleep and dreamed about Li Guangrong directing the hunt.

August 13: The sixth day of my escape. At 9:00 a.m., standing on the mountainside, I finally saw the third bend in the Golden Sand River, which made a ninety-degree turn toward the east. Up ahead, a tributary blocked my path. In a long, narrow cotton field, two peasants, one older and one younger, were hoeing weeds.

I passed them and walked up to the tributary, which was about ninety feet wide, its muddy water tumbling down from the mountainside with great force. I stood on the bank for a long time, wondering whether I should ford the river or make a big detour upstream but couldn't decide. I walked over to the peasants.

"Is there a boat?" I asked.

"It's been washed away," they replied.

"How deep is the water? Is it possible to ford the river?"

"Can you see the willow tree on the other side? Aim for it. That's where the water is the most shallow."

Thanking them, I walked back to the river and, facing the willow tree, took off my shoes and clothes, put my bundle on my head and stepped into the water. It became deeper, until it reached my waist. The current was swift and relentless. I trod with great care, struggling to keep my footing. As soon as I lifted one foot, the rushing water took hold of me with all its might. The water was up to my neck, and if the river continued to deepen, I would be washed away and drowned. Summoning all my strength, I took another step. The bed was even. Thank God! After a ten-minute battle, I emerged from the swirling eddies, drained but overjoyed.

I stood in the high grass by the steep bank and dried myself. The current had pushed me sixty feet downstream of the willow tree. Seeing me disappear into the muddy, swirling water, the two peasants had rushed to the riverbank. I smiled and raised my clasped hands. They smiled back, waved, and returned to their hoeing.

I walked east on a road being built along the river. Touched by the two peasants' kindness, I thought about the other people who had helped me during my escape and felt a strong conviction that human nature, in its essence, is good. People become evil at the enticement of others. If there hadn't been a Mao Zedong, I'm sure there wouldn't be lackeys like Li Guangrong either.

The sun scorched my head. Drenched in sweat, I slowly made my way forward. Sometimes the road ran alongside the river; sometimes it turned up into the mountains. I was thirsty and needed something to drink but couldn't find a potable stream. Finally, a large village appeared up ahead. Without further thought, I entered one of the houses, where a lot of people were discussing some matter in the main hall. A peasant woman in her forties stood up and asked, "What do you want?"

"*Dama*, can I have some water, please?"

She led me out through the main gate around the corner and in through a side entrance. From a vat, she filled a gourd with water and handed it to me. I drank it all down in one gulp. She filled up the gourd again and again, until my thirst was quenched. I thanked her, passed the gate carefully, and hurried on my way.

I soon arrived at the road between Yongcheng and Binchuan. I was happy. Everything was going according to plan. But the topography of Yunnan is unforgiving. To cross a river, you have to descend three thousand feet and then climb another three thousand feet of mountain, in seemingly endless succession. I walked until nightfall without reaching Rehe Village, the village of Wang Jinru's wife, Hu Mei.

I found a dry spot for the night among some house ruins by the side of the road, but the mosquitoes made it impossible to sleep. In the middle of the night, it started raining. I gathered my belongings and started walking again, forced by the rain to keep going. In the blackness, I discerned the characters for Rehe Village painted on the wall of a house. The rain beat through the cracks of my plastic sheet, soaking my body. I was like a robot, moving forward one mechanical step at a time, my mind blank with fatigue.

August 14: At noon, I reached Lijiao, a place I had heard a lot about but never visited. This small town had a style of its own. It was neat and clean, and the stores were full of merchandise. If there had been a national competition, Lijiao would have placed right up at the top. I treated myself to a meal in a restaurant, and threw away the remaining, moldy *shagao* cake.

By dusk, I reached Niujing, the county seat of Binchuan County. Niujing was a prosperous town with a large population and bustling markets. At night, I lay down in a forest of poplars about two miles outside the town. The sky was clear, and I slept well.

August 15: At noon, I reached the old seat of Binchuan County—Zhoucheng. Some fire trucks were doing drills, racing back and forth, adding to the lively atmosphere. In contrast to the Naxi of Lijiang, the people appeared content and forthcoming, which I thought might be related to the region's rich agricultural production and well-developed communications.

August 16: I emerged from the hills of Ludian, following the winding road. The mountains retreated, and the road drew close to a large, beautiful lake. Now and then, I could hear the sound of airplane engines. I recalled hearing about a military airport in Xiangyun and realized that I must be near that town.

At 11:00 a.m., I walked into Xiangyun. The buildings were old, and the town couldn't compare to Niujing. But there were a lot of people in the busy market. Feeling sure that Li Guangrong wouldn't be looking for me here, I strolled about in the town and had a meal in a peasant restaurant, but the soup was so salty I could hardly swallow it.

In the afternoon, I reached the Burma Road* and stepped up my pace, heading east. It started raining again. I covered my head with the plastic sheet, praying it would not rain all night. It rained harder and harder. A young man approached me and tried to strike up a conversation, which I did my best to muddle through.

"I live in the village up ahead. Why don't you spend the night in my house?" he said, pointing to a mountain path.

Struggling with myself briefly, I declined his invitation and continued walking. It was dark. It rained. I walked. I was exhausted but continued walking. My brain was sleeping. Only my feet were moving.

---

*Seven hundred and seventeen miles long, the Burma Road runs from Kunming in Yunnan Province to Lashio in Burma (now Myanmar). Its main sections were built in 1937–1938, and the road served as an important conduit to China in the beginning of its war against Japan. After Japan's occupation of Burma in 1942, the road was closed, and its reopening was an important part of the American general Joe Stilwell's strategy to help China defeat Japan.

I walked all through the night until the break of dawn, when it finally stopped raining. Bone weary, I sat down on a rock outside a walled village. Two young men approached, observing me.

"I wonder who he is?" I heard one of them say.

I cast a sidelong glance at them but said nothing. They stood there for a while and then left. Afraid they had gone off to report me, I hurried on my way.

August 17: I had been walking for twenty-four hours straight, without a minute's sleep, and continued east on the Burma Road at a steady pace, squeezing the last drop of stamina from my body. Even more important was my steadfast will. Throughout the escape, I had stuck to my rule of staying away from people, walking and sleeping in pouring rain rather than seeking shelter among human beings.

The day was clear but not too hot, and although I was walking under the sun, I didn't break a sweat. The Burma Road was even steeper and more winding than the Yong-Bin Road, and there were more vehicles. I kept a special eye out for buses, in case there was a *laogai* cadre from Lijiang traveling on it. Each time I saw a bus approaching, I sat down with my back toward the road until it had passed.

I had heard that the railroad between Kunming and Chengdu was already in service. The town of Guangtong in Chuxiong County was a junction station on this line, where people from western Yunnan going to Sichuan changed trains. Hoping to get out of Yunnan Province as fast as possible, and thereby greatly reduce the risk of being caught, I made Guangtong my goal.

In the afternoon, the Burma Road wound itself up a mountain, and by dusk I had arrived at the small town of Pupeng. I ate a meal there, and continued my climb. I hadn't slept for thirty-six hours, but with my life at stake I struggled on, reaching the top of the nine-thousand-foot Fuziling Mountain late at night. At this altitude, the weather was crisp and pleasant. I found a spot of grass by the side of the road and lay down to rest. There was no rain that night, and few mosquitoes. I fell into the sleep of the dead and got a good night's rest.

August 18: In the evening, I finally reached Nanhua County, had a meal in the local hostel, and washed myself. I really wanted to use my fake document to stay in the hostel for one night, but after fighting with myself briefly, I dropped the idea. Instead, I spent the night in a wooded area not far away.

Although I had been on the run for eleven days, I knew Li Guangrong would never give up the chase and might have dispatched his people to intercept me at distant checkpoints. Pondering the matter, I thought he would probably focus on Xiaguan, the Gongguo Bridge, Heqing County, Jianchuan County, and other such places. Or perhaps he believed that I was hiding out in the mountains, in which case he would ask the people's communes to dispatch search parties. Only one thing was for sure: Li Guangrong was after me. The sooner I got out of Yunnan Province the better.

August 19: In the afternoon, I reached Chuxiong, a large town with a busy market. I went to a bathhouse and washed myself, lingering there for a long time, drinking tea. After an evening meal, I walked back up the mountain to a pine forest and found an undisturbed place to spend the night.

August 20: I bought a bus ticket for one yuan from Chuxiong to Guangtong, arriving there at 11:00 a.m. It was a small town, but there were a lot of travelers on the move.

"When does the train to Shanghai arrive?" I asked the ticket seller at the railroad station.

"The southern line via Kunming arrives at midnight. The northern line via Chengdu is due to arrive now," he replied.

"How much are the tickets?"

"Forty-five yuan for the southern line. Forty-six fifty for the northern line."

"One ticket for the northern line," I said, to get out of the province as soon as possible.

The train arrived at 11:45. There were a lot of people boarding, and squeezing myself into a wagon, I managed to find a seat. As the train pulled out of the station, my nerves, strung up like piano wires for twelve days, gradually began to unwind. "No matter how smart Li Guangrong is, he'll never find me here," I told myself.

Looking back at the past two weeks, I felt proud of myself and grateful to Wencan. During our friendship, I had absorbed much of his wisdom and courage. He hadn't betrayed me, and he silently supported my action. I felt sure that he was rejoicing in my success at this very moment.

With its countless tunnels, the Kunming-Chengdu railroad is an impressive engineering feat, made possible by the backbreaking labor and self-sacrifice of hundreds of thousands of workers. As we rode past the many graves dotting the track's embankment, I remembered the victims of the Lamagu copper mine and felt an aching sorrow at the disregard for life so often seen in China. If life had been respected and valued, the necessary safety measures would have been put in place, and all those senseless deaths could have been avoided. Just to be sitting on that train on that day, I was the lucky survivor of a great calamity.

It was ironic. Thirteen years earlier, I had fled from Shanghai to Chengdu. Today, I was running away from Yunnan to Chengdu and back to Shanghai. My escape plan fell into three parts: escape from jail; return to Shanghai and see Mother; then seek refuge in a foreign country.

I was now on the second leg. If Li Guangrong had made plans to intercept me in Shanghai, I ran the risk of falling into his hands. I didn't have to return there. But Mother's unswerving love and support over the years made it impossible for me not to see her one last time before setting out on my final leg. Although this decision greatly reduced the odds of my success, it was something I had to do, whatever the consequences.

August 21: At noon, the train pulled in to Chengdu station. Because the train to Shanghai wasn't leaving until midnight, I deposited my bag at the station and walked into Chengdu with free hands to visit the city I hadn't seen for thirteen years.

My train was scheduled to arrive in Shanghai at 6:00 p.m. on

August 23. This was bad timing for me, because there was no way I could knock on Mother's door. If I couldn't go home, where would I sleep? The safest way to see Mother would be to stand by the Lihong Bridge early in the morning and wait for her to go to work or to the market to buy vegetables. After making sure she hadn't been followed, I could then step forth and greet her.

As the train departed from Chengdu that night, I decided to disembark at Nanjing, wait there until late in the evening, then take an overnight train to Shanghai so that I would arrive at the North Station around 5:00 a.m. and reach the Lihong Bridge around 6:00.

August 23: I arrived at Nanjing in the morning, spent the day strolling around this historic city, paid my respects at the grave of Dr. Sun Yat-sen, and visited the Biyun Temple and the Yangtze River Bridge. Tasting watermelon for the first time in fourteen years, I gorged myself on this delicious fruit. That night, I boarded a train to Shanghai. The thought of seeing my family again after all these years made me extremely agitated and nervous, and I couldn't sleep.

August 24: At 5:00 a.m., I returned to my hometown after fourteen years' separation. I exited the North Station, terrified that somebody would recognize me. But everything was quiet. Shanghai looked just about the same. I spent four jiao for a pedicab and told the driver to take me to the small market by Sanjiaodi. From there, I walked to the Lihong Bridge, sometimes waiting on the bridge, sometimes waiting by the stop for the number nineteen tram, which Mother took to and from work.

But she was nowhere to be seen. Torn with anxiety, I didn't know what to do. I waited until 7:00 a.m. If I waited longer, I would attract people's attention. I was sure that Mother was at home. Racking my brains, I decided to go to Suzhou and find my maternal grandfather's mistress and ask her to tell Mother to come to Suzhou.

I returned to the station and bought a train ticket to Suzhou. There, after many twists and turns, I found her apartment building at 33 Shengjiadai. I knocked on the door. A man in his fifties opened. Hurriedly, I explained the purpose of my visit.

"What is your relation to her?" he asked with a Ningbo accent, measuring me up.

"I am Wang Zilin's grandson."

"Oh! I see! I see! She is not at home. Because she is a Christian, she is under surveillance and has to work every day over at No. 29. You have to go there to see her. As long as you don't talk about politics, it should be all right to visit her."

That would be too risky. I thanked him and walked past No. 29, afraid to even look, leaving the place as fast as I could.

"What should I do?" I asked myself. Having weighed my options for a long time, I remembered Xi Junfang, the mistress of my mother's brother, Wang Bing. In 1959, she had helped me and proved to be trustworthy. I hurried back to Shanghai, reaching Xi Junfang's house after dark. I had left the 507 Agro-machinery Factory with seventy-eight yuan in my pocket. I had only three yuan left.

I walked to 92 Beijing West Road Alley 707 and fumbled my way in the darkness up to the third floor. The south-facing room was brightly lit. Xi Junfang's younger sister and her husband, Zhang Zhonghu, saw and greeted me. I smiled back, then turned around and entered the northern room. Xi Junfang was shocked to see me. Quickly, she locked the door, told me to wash my face and sit down. She poured me a glass of cold water and asked if I had eaten.

"Are you out on leave?" she asked finally.

"No. I have escaped."

She stared at me, terrified.

"Don't be afraid," I said. "Please ask Mother to meet me and to bring some money for me. I am broke. After I have the money, I will leave Shanghai."

Xi Junfang was now an elderly woman, sixty-seven years old, but she was brave and told me to wait at the entrance to the Ping'an cinema while she went to Hongkou to get Mother. She told me to leave first to avoid arousing the suspicion of the neighborhood watchman. I left in a hurry, sauntered about the China-Soviet Friendship Building on Nanjing Road, then waited at the tram station on Shaanxi North Road.

Xi Junfang and Mother didn't arrive until 10:00 p.m. Seeing them disembark from the tram, I jumped up to greet them. Mother and I embraced, overcome with emotion. With nowhere to go, we strolled around the Wangjiasha area on Nanjing West Road, talking. Mother told me she had been at work when Junfang had come to get her and that it was her granddaughter Wang Ou (by then fourteen years old) who had gone to the factory and told her to come home. She had asked for two hours' leave and had to be back on time to avoid suspicion. I told her I had been resentenced, that I had been cruelly persecuted in prison, and all about my escape.

"Where are you planning to go?" she asked me.

"To the Soviet Union or Mongolia."

"All your escapes have failed."

"I will make it," I said. "Anything is better than this kind of life."

"Our family has been classified as a target of the people's dictatorship, and our bank account has been frozen. This is all the money I have. Take it!" she said, handing me a hundred yuan.

I thanked her from the bottom of my heart. Mother told me that in order not to make life even more difficult for me, she had concealed Father's true fate all these years. In October 1958, Father had been sent to a *laogai* in Menyuan County, Qinghai Province, but Mother hadn't been told to send warm clothes and a blanket with him, and he had died of the cold a few days after his arrival in Qinghai. Having branded me a Rightist, this is how the Communist Party had driven Father to his death, on the grounds of his having worked one year for Wang Jingwei's puppet government. Father was fifty-three years old when he died.

"I had guessed that Father had met an unfortunate fate, but I didn't know that he died so cruelly," I said.

"It's my fault," Mother replied. "I should have sent the warm clothes and blanket immediately after his arrest. It is too late to be sorry now."

"I've seen many people die in the most horrible manner. Their last thoughts are always with their families and hometowns. I know the agony Father must have gone through before he died."

"Soon after he had died, his mother died of grief."

"Our family has been broken up and destroyed."

"I have one other terrible regret. All the thousands of Father's photographs were confiscated by the Red Guards. Our family's memories have been burned," Mother said. "In 1960, Tang Ximeng came to our house and asked to have the photographs of you and her back. She has hurt you."

Thinking I didn't know about the Lin Biao incident, Mother told me all the news. Time passed quickly, and she had to go back to work.

"Xi Junfang is your savior. Never forget her," Mother said.

She asked to see me one last time the next morning at 6:00 at the Post and Telegram Office on Sichuan North Road. She warned me not to stay in a hostel, but to walk on the streets, have a meal at an all-night restaurant, and keep an eye out for inspections by the People's Militia.

After Mother had left, I accompanied Xi Junfang back to Beijing West Road. It was already midnight. Following Mother's advice, I walked around the Huangpu District, ate some food in different restaurants, and whiled away the night.

August 25: At about 5:00 a.m., I waited for Mother by the number nineteen tram stop on Tiantong Road near the Post and Telegram Office. Gazing up at the Tiantong Building, I thought of an old comrade who lived there, Wang Yanxiong, wondering what kind of work he was doing and how life had treated him, but scolded myself for daydreaming. Who in the whole world would acknowledge me as a "comrade"? I, an "enemy of the people," a "criminal deserving the death penalty." At a quarter to six, Xi Junfang, alone, stepped down from the number nineteen tram.

"I wish you good luck," she said.

Tears welled up in my eyes. I held her hand tightly and thanked her. Without another word, we crossed over to the other side of the road, where I helped her board a tram in the opposite direction. Seeing her thin, weak body, I said to myself, "You are really my savior. I will never forget you."

Mother arrived at 6:00 a.m., carrying a vegetable basket.

"I brought a basket so people would think I was going to the market," she explained.

She gave me another forty yuan and some grain ration tickets.

"Take some more, just in case."

We walked side by side on Sichuan North Road.

"We haven't seen each other for fourteen years," she said. "I should have asked you to stay for a few days and cooked a meal for you, but I haven't been able to do this. Please forgive me. Now you must leave Shanghai as soon as possible. Every minute counts. Your clothes are dark. People in Shanghai will become suspicious. Buy a white T-shirt,* and change right away."

We walked north, passing Haining Road.

"Does Hongming know that I have returned?" I asked.

"She sometimes does things to ingratiate herself with the government. I would never tell her," Mother replied.

We walked to the Wujin Road crossing, then turned right toward Wusong Road.

"Don't go back to the North Station. It is full of plainclothes policemen who might recognize you. Take a bus to Zhenru and get a train from there."

I nodded my head.

When we reached Wusong Road, Mother said, "We are close to home. I'm afraid we will run into an acquaintance. Don't follow me, just go. Don't write me until you reach your goal. And take care!"

We embraced again and bade farewell. I turned around and walked away without looking back. I was waging a life-and-death struggle and

---

*At the height of the Cultural Revolution, white shirts and blue, gray, or green jackets and pants were worn by virtually everybody.

could not let sentimental thoughts about family and home blunt my resolve. I had never thought that I would value freedom this much. Following Mother's advice, I changed clothes, caught a bus to Zhenru, and from there continued by train to Nanjing.

When I arrived, it was already late afternoon. Not having slept all night, I was tired and found a secluded place by the Xuanwu Lake to lie down and take a short nap but fell into deep sleep. In the middle of the night, I was awakened by somebody prodding my side with his foot. Two soldiers stood above me and shined their flashlights into my face.

"Who are you? Show us your documents!"

Shocked, I sat up, pulled out my second fake document, which said that I was traveling from Yun County to visit relatives in Shanghai, and handed it to them. They examined it carefully under the flashlight.

"From Yunnan, eh?" one of the soldiers snorted, handing the document back to me. "You're not allowed to sleep here. Hurry up! Get your things together and go find a hostel."

Once again, my forged documents had saved my life. With no choice but to return to the train station, I immediately bought a ticket to Xuzhou.

August 26: I reached Xuzhou in the morning. At the train station, I witnessed policemen and railway personnel maltreating and beating passengers. I rested for a long time in a bathhouse near the train station, then caught a train to Jinan in the afternoon. There, I wanted to get a train to Beijing right away, but the ticket seller asked to see my papers.

"Your document is not valid. It says you are going to Shanghai. You are not allowed to buy a ticket to Beijing."

"I just want to see our capital," I pleaded.

"No," the ticket seller replied.

I left the station, sat down under a streetlight, and filled in the third forged document, stating that I was on my way from Yunnan to visit relatives in Inner Mongolia, then returned to the station and bought a ticket to Tianjin.

August 27: After arriving in Tianjin at noon, I immediately boarded an express train to Beijing. Wandering about a bit at will, I found myself on the famous shopping street Wangfujing, where I walked into the Xinhua Bookstore. Ever since Li Guangrong had confiscated my books and prohibited me from reading anything except Mao's *Selected Works*, I had been starved for a good read.

I browsed every shelf with fascination and discovered that even if Mao Zedong had caused immense damage to China's cultural life, it was gradually reviving. The number of people jostling to purchase the complete set of Sima Qian's *Records of the Grand Historian** was proof of this. Leaving the bookstore, I felt a tap on my shoulder.

"Aren't you Xu Hongci?" a voice asked.

I steadied myself, turned around, and looked at the familiar face.

"Guess who I am?" the man said, smiling.

But no matter how hard I tried, I couldn't place him.

"I'm Li Weizhen," he said finally.

I recalled him. He was a classmate from middle school. We had shared the same bench. I shook hands with him warmly.

"Where do you work?" he asked.

"I am a doctor in Yunnan," I replied.

"Are you married?"

"No."

"We won't get any younger. It's time to tie the knot," he said.

I smiled bitterly and said nothing. Sensing my reserve, he spoke about himself.

"After graduating from the Shanghai University of Transportation, I was assigned as a lecturer to the Liaoning School of Telecommunications and married a sports teacher there. We have two children, a son and a daughter. Since the Cultural Revolution, I've been standing on

---

*Sima Qian was a historian who lived during the Western Han dynasty (206 B.C.–A.D. 25). His *Records of the Grand Historian*, spanning over two millennia, is considered one of the outstanding achievements of Chinese historiography.

the sidelines and only recently found work. My father is retired and lives in Beijing. I'm here to visit him."

"Have you been back to Kunshan?" I asked him.

"Not for a long time," he replied.

He asked about my family. I lied that everything was fine. He invited me to his home, but I was afraid that if we spoke for too long, I would give myself away and hurried to decline the invitation. When we had said goodbye, a heavy weight was lifted off my chest. In my situation, I couldn't trust anybody or count on help from any other person. I actually knew quite a few people in Beijing but couldn't visit any of them; they were all party members.

I lingered about Tiananmen Square until late in the evening, then lay down among some bushes on the western side of Zhengyi Road and caught some sleep, rising at the crack of dawn. I was familiar with Zhengyi Road, because the Youth League's offices were located there, and during the second National Youth Congress in 1953 I had gone there almost every day. Little did I know then that nineteen years later, I would be spending a night among its bushes as an escaped *laogai* convict.

August 28: Feeling strangely confident, I visited the Forbidden City, Zhongshan Park, and the other famous sites of Beijing, which I hadn't seen since that wonderful trip in August 1956, when I had traveled to meet Lan Cheng and other friends in the capital. I made a special point of having lunch in Beihai Park, remembering when I had treated Jiang Weiyu to a meal there, watched her eat pork, and made fun of her for being a phony Hui Muslim . . . Lan Cheng taking a photograph of us by the side of the lake . . . the memories were like fish returning upstream against the river of time to their magical birthplace. Here I was, almost forty years old, without an accomplishment to my name. Would I still have time to achieve anything? I spent another night sleeping among the bushes on Zhengyi Road.

August 29: Taking in the view of Kunming Lake from the Buddha Pavilion at the Summer Palace, I pondered my next move. I didn't have much money left, definitely not enough to get me to Hailar and over the border to the Soviet Union. The route from Erenhot to Mongolia seemed more realistic. After reaching Mongolia, perhaps I would be able to make it from there to the Soviet Union.

My biggest challenge was to make it across the border. I was less worried about whether Mongolia or the Soviet Union would take me in. Because of the tense relations between China and the Soviet Union at the time, I was confident that the Soviets and their Mongolian satellite would help me. Only later would I learn what a complicated matter political asylum is.

Beside me in the pavilion, an old military man and his daughter discussed history and literature. Spellbound, I eavesdropped on their conversation, envying their family happiness. The sun set, and the father and daughter left, leaving me alone in the Buddha Pavilion. Gazing in all directions, I sank into gloom. In a few days' time, I would be fighting a battle with only two possible outcomes: life or death.

August 31: Having taken the night bus from Beijing's Yongdingmen, I arrived in Jining at 11:00 a.m. At the train station, I learned that the train to the border town Erenhot had already departed and that the next train wouldn't leave until 9:00 a.m. the following day, meaning I would have to spend twenty-two hours in Jining.

To kill time, I strolled about the town and lingered in teahouses nursing a cup. According to the official propaganda, Jining was supposed to be a modern, model city, but in reality the infrastructure was poor, with old, dilapidated buildings, garbage everywhere, and unpaved streets that turned into mud porridge when it rained. Although the town lay in the Inner Mongolia Autonomous Region, I saw few Mongolians, and the only language I heard was the Shanxi dialect.

After whiling away the whole day, I returned to the train station, where people were lying on their bundles everywhere, smoking, eating, chatting, and sleeping. I found a chair and tried to get some sleep.

"Ticket inspection!" the station master shouted. "Everybody without a ticket must leave the station."

Luckily, they only wanted to see our tickets, not our documents. Everybody got up and submitted themselves to the inspection, and people without a ticket were thrown out, which caused some arguments. I showed them my ticket from Beijing to Jining, but although it had already been used, I was allowed to stay. *Amituofo!** I spent the night sleeping on that chair, awaking around 4:00 a.m.

September 1: The train tickets from Jining to Erenhot, situated right on the border with Mongolia, went on sale at 8:00 a.m. Based on my past experience at the Burmese border, I knew that all borders in China were restricted areas, and that a special permit would be required to buy a train ticket all the way to Erenhot. Therefore, I would have to get off the train at the last station before the restricted zone. To find out the name of that station, I lingered by the ticket window for about twenty minutes making observations and learned that the last station you could travel to without a permit was Saihantala, which lay about seventy-five miles southeast of Erenhot. From there on, I would have to walk.

I bought a train ticket to that town. The train departed at 9:00 a.m. Gradually, the landscape was transformed from the wheat fields and adobe houses of Shanxi into a barren wasteland, and after Tumu'ertai there was nothing but the endless Gobi Desert. The train stopped at every station, taking more than eight hours to cover the 130 miles from Jining to Saihantala.

I got off the train late in the afternoon and walked into the town— a dirt road with a few shops and official buildings. My plan was to walk toward Erenhot along the tracks during the night, and rest in hiding during the day. To pass the time, I had a meal in a Hui restaurant, then ate again in a Han restaurant. Some of the customers were insulting the waitresses, and there was a big fight. It grew dark. I left the restaurant at about seven. Just before the train station, I took a side road to the tracks and followed them heading north.

The sky was pitch-black, without a speck of moonlight or stars. In

---

*The Amitabha Buddha, "the immeasurable," often used as an incantation with the meaning "Thank God."

the vast, bleak Gobi Desert, I seemed to be the only creature stirring. I walked for about two hours. It started to rain. The rain grew in strength. The wind rose from the north, and the temperature dropped sharply. My plastic sheet was useless in such a storm. I was soaked, the cold cutting straight to my bones. My whole body shivered, my teeth clattered, and my feet kept slipping on the sleepers.

Suddenly I twisted my right ankle. The pain was excruciating, but I forced myself to keep going. After a while, I came to a small station. I shone my flashlight on a sign and saw that it was Chulutu, seven miles out of Saihantala. I needed to find a place to rest my foot. About three hundred feet before the station building, there was a small, deserted house full of garbage. I was about to seek shelter there but hesitated, afraid that I would be discovered by a night patrol.

Speak of the devil. From the north I saw a red light approaching. I scurried down from the embankment and hid myself in a depression some hundred feet from the tracks, holding the fruit knife I had bought in Beijing, prepared to defend myself if needed. Looking back, I saw the red light swinging to and fro right by that little house. Indeed, it was a night patrol who had caught sight of my flashlight. He looked around for a couple of minutes before continuing on his way.

With the patrol at a safe distance, I climbed up on the embankment again. The rain and ice-cold Siberian wind grew in strength. I tried to keep going, but the pain in my ankle made it impossible. If I continued farther into the desert, I would freeze to death. Finally, I decided to return to Jining, give my foot time to heal, and then attempt to make it to Mongolia along the same route. I started walking back in the direction I had come from, making slow progress. Along the way, I had to hide from another patrol heading north along the tracks.

September 2: I came to Saihantala around 4:00 a.m., found a half-finished house under construction, and took shelter from the rain there. At dawn, I went to the train station to rest. The train back to Jining did not depart until 9:00 in the evening. I went to a restaurant and drank half a *jin* of rice vodka to warm myself, then went to a store and bought a woolen sweater for thirteen yuan, put it on, and returned to the station.

September 3: Back in Jining, crackling loudspeakers on every street corner filled the morning air with an earsplitting, histrionic voice. The whole town was headed in the same direction—the execution grounds. On a billboard, I read the official verdict of the person about to be shot. He was a Mongolian shepherd living on the Chinese side of the border, sentenced to death on the charge of treason for attempting to cross over to Mongolia.

The mad clamor unsettled me, but I had reached the point of no return and could no longer feel fear. If my escape failed, I would die standing. Using my last fake document, I took a room in the Jining No. 1 People's Hostel. After washing up, I went to a nearby hospital to see a doctor for my foot. He gave me electric acupuncture,* which was effective. After only one treatment, the pain was reduced, and I didn't have to return on the second day. I wanted to get going again without further delay, but I was exhausted and decided to have a good rest. I still had thirty yuan in my pocket and would make full use of it before escaping across the border.

September 7: After resting in the Jining People's Hostel for four days, I returned by train to Saihantala. That night, I once again walked north along the railroad embankment, passing Chulutu. On the morning of September 8, I reached a small station, Guo'erbenaobao, and turned off from the railroad tracks, walking west for about one mile.

By this time, it was already light, and I was visible in the midst of the Gobi Desert's open expanse. Unable to find a hiding place, I had no choice but to lie down flat on the ground. As long as I lay still, I knew I would be safe. I fell asleep. When I awoke in the afternoon, a herd of goats was grazing nearby, and the herdsmen were galloping around on their horses. I was becoming nervous that they would see

---

*A type of acupuncture in which the needles are connected to a power source that transmits a weak electric current.

me when the sky turned dark, a strong wind blew up, and thunder rumbled on the horizon. With rain approaching, the herdsmen drove their herd back toward their yurts. It never rained, and the goat herd disappeared in the distance.

I relaxed again. Studying the Gobi Desert, I discovered that it was covered by stone plates, with sparse tufts of grass and other plants growing in the cracks. In scattered places, the vegetation was more abundant, providing forage for goats and other animals. All around me, small creatures scurried in and out of their burrows, darting here and there, jumping about. These little mammals were the size of a rat and had a long tail that stood straight up, with a wisp of hair at the tip. As soon as they sensed danger, they disappeared into one of their many holes, which pockmarked the hard ground. I tried to catch one for fun, but it was too quick.

After nightfall, I returned to the tracks and continued north. On the way, I encountered several patrols and had to keep hiding as they passed. Around midnight, a huge black shadow came upon me so quickly that I only managed to jump aside at the last moment. Shocked, I realized that it must have been a camel. Later, I learned that the Gobi Desert was populated by more lethal animals—wolves.

Fortunately, it had been raining, so I was able to find water and fill my bottle, otherwise I would have died of thirst during those few days. I walked all night and reached Qiharigetu, a somewhat larger train station, before dawn. There was a military train standing there, loaded with tanks and artillery guns. Strangely, the train was not guarded, and I walked right beside it without anybody seeing me. I continued another two miles until the sun rose and found a good place to hide for the day.

September 9: My hiding place was in a depression surrounded by high grass, so there was no danger of discovery. I slept all day, until the whistle from a train heading north woke me up late in the afternoon. Surveying the landscape, I felt more confident. With so few people around, it seemed that if I could only make it to the border, it would simply be a matter of walking over into Mongolia. The actual crossing would be the easiest part. The hard part would be getting close to the border. I walked along the railroad tracks for another full night. The sky was clear, and the North Star shone brightly, keeping me company.

September 10: In the morning, I reached Xili, the station before Erenhot. I hid in a thicket of cocklebur bushes about one mile northwest of the train station. The cocklebur plant is common in Jiangsu, but I was surprised to find it in the Gobi Desert. I slept until late in the afternoon. When I awoke, there were hundreds of camels all around me. A Mongolian horseman appeared in the west, galloping in my direction, before veering off only a few hundred yards in front of me.

That night I continued walking north along the tracks. Up ahead, I could see the glaring, cold white lights of the Erenhot train station and, with victory in sight, stepped up my pace. All along the way, the eerie sounds of Mongolian herdsmen goading their creatures punctured the stillness of the night. The lights from Erenhot came closer and closer. I entered the town. West of the tracks, there was a paved, parallel road. I turned onto it.

The road and the tracks were separated by concrete piles and an iron fence. After about five hundred yards, I came to a crossing in front of the train station lit up by a powerful mercury-vapor streetlamp. About sixty feet before it, I stopped and urinated, wondering whether I should avoid the bright light. As I stood there hesitating, the streetlamp went out. I was jubilant. It was as if God were right there by my side. Later, I realized that the light was probably turned off at midnight and that I had arrived at just the right moment.

Crossing the intersection, I ran into a man heading west, but he ignored me. I continued north on the road, with the tracks to the right and a row of railway workers' dormitories to the left. "Chong guoqu!" "Keep going!" I told myself. I increased my pace, heading north as if I had already reached no-man's-land, not even worrying whether there were border patrol guards up ahead waiting to arrest me. After some 250 yards, I passed the last dormitory build-

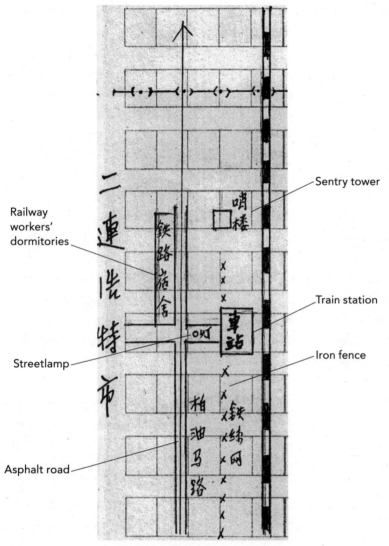

Sentry tower

Railway workers' dormitories

Train station

Streetlamp

Iron fence

Asphalt road

Map of the border crossing to
Mongolia at Erenhot

ing, and after another 500 yards the paved road abruptly ended, leaving nothing but the Gobi Desert ahead. Off in the distance, I could see streetlamps glowing faintly in the Mongolian border town of Zamyn-Üüd.

I stopped and took stock of the situation. It was pitch-dark. Who would be able to see me? Without any more hesitation, I ran toward the border. Suddenly the ground descended, and I came into a depression—a perfect hiding place. I sat down, got out my dry food and water bottle, and filled my stomach. I rested for about twenty minutes, put my things in order, and ran toward the lights of Zamyn-Üüd. The lights came closer and closer, while the lights of Erenhot faded behind me. Comparing their distances, I realized I was in Mongolia. As I later learned, I had actually crossed the border within sixty feet of a sentry tower equipped with a radar able to detect even goats. By incredible luck, I had passed so close to the tower that I had been within the radar's shadow.

I turned around and looked back, torn by a storm of conflicting emotions. I was overjoyed to have escaped once and for all from the grim, merciless clutches of the Communist dictatorship. On the other hand, I was heartbroken over having been forced to flee my country, the people who had borne and raised me, the land of my forefathers.

I squatted on the ground a few minutes, bidding my weather-beaten, grief-plagued motherland farewell. I didn't shed tears. I was just sad and angry, confident that sooner or later the Chinese people would rise up to cast off the yoke of Mao's tyranny and establish a democratic nation.

I told myself, "On that day, I shall return."

Epilogue

Entering a fire station, Xu Hongci was taken into custody by the Mongolian border patrol and explained himself by tracing his route on a map. He was told to strip naked, searched, and given a Mongolian army uniform to wear. In his pocket, he had nine yuan. After a doctor bandaged his bloodied feet, Hongci was brought by jeep and train across the Gobi Desert to the capital, Ulan Bator, four hundred miles northwest of Erenhot.

There he was locked up in the central prison and interrogated. Details of his account were verified, such as the lunar phase on the night of his prison break, and he was asked to carve a seal. To prove his identity, Hongci told his interrogators to look for the article about his case published in the *People's Daily* on August 2, 1957, which they were able to confirm. Finally, the authorities informed him that if he had a Mongolian acquaintance who could vouch for him, he would be set free. But Hongci knew nobody in Mongolia, and so he was charged with illegal entry into the country, then sentenced to two years in prison. Asked to speak, he told the judge, "I could not continue living in my country, and I thank the Mongolian people for granting me asylum. Mao Zedong sentenced me to twenty years. In comparison, two years is a bargain."

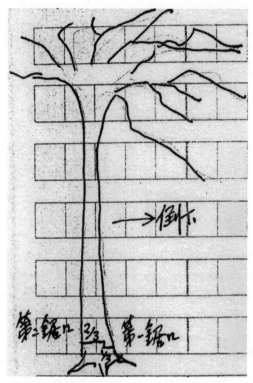

Drawing showing how Xu Hongci and his comrades felled trees

Hongci spent the winter as a labor camp convict in Züünkharaa in the northern province of Selenge, felling trees in temperatures that dropped below minus forty degrees Fahrenheit. There was little political indoctrination in the Mongolian camps, but the conditions were extremely harsh, with heavy drinking and frequent brawls. In the summer of 1973, Hongci was hospitalized with broken ribs after a fight with a guard.

One year later, on August 27, 1974, he was put on the night train to Ulan Bator as a free man, then transferred to Tsetserleg, the capital of Arhangay Province, a town of fourteen thousand people three hundred miles west of Ulan Bator, where he was assigned to metal-working at the local transportation station with a monthly salary of four hundred tugrik. Later, he worked in construction during the summers and shoveled coal in the boiler room of the local middle school during the long, freezing winters.

At the end of 1974, Hongci wrote a letter to his father's old friend Lu Liangbing, who, having retired from the airfreight business in Hong Kong, had immigrated to Canada and was living in Vancouver. Liangbing forwarded the letter to Hongci's mother, who finally learned of her son's successful escape. In her return letter sent via Liangbing, she told Hongci that the Lijiang Public Security Bureau had dispatched two officers to Shanghai to arrest him. After interrogating her, they had traveled three thousand miles to the border town of Yining in Chinese central Asia to question Hongci's sister Yunqing with the hope of catching him there.

The following year, Hongci returned to Ulan Bator to seek treatment for an inflammation in his right eye. At the hospital, he met Sukh Oyunbileg, an orphaned twenty-one-year-old nurse who took care of him. They fell in love, and upon the completion of Hongci's treatment she returned with him to Tsetserleg.

In 1976, China was rocked by a string of momentous events. In January, Zhou Enlai, China's prime minister and Mao's second-in-command during the entire Chinese revolution, passed away. At his wreath-laying service at Tiananmen Square on April 5, riots erupted and the mourners were evicted from the square by force. On July 6, the legendary general Zhu De died, and twenty-one days later one of the most devastating earthquakes in history struck the city of Tangshan, 120 miles east of Beijing, killing some 250,000 people. Then, on September 9, Mao Zedong died of heart failure. Around the world, more than fifty nations, including West Germany, Canada, and France, flew their flags at half-mast for a man historians say was responsible for the deaths of more people than Hitler and Stalin combined. One month later, the Gang of Four was arrested.

Listening to Radio Beijing in Tsetserleg, Hongci and his fellow

Chinese exiles celebrated the tyrant's death. In March of the follow-ing year, his and Oyunbileg's first son, Anjir, was born. Hongci spent the summer months of 1977 working in construction. Their second son, Buyant, was born in August 1978. When the Sino-Vietnamese War erupted in February 1979, the Mongolian government, fearing an expansion of the conflict, put the country on war alert and repa-triated many Chinese exiles. But Hongci had behaved well, married a Mongolian woman, and started a family, so he was allowed to stay.

In the winter of 1981, he received a letter from his mother: the party committee of the Shanghai No. 1 Medical College had issued a *gaizhengshu*, "notice of correction," in his case, removing his official classification as a Rightist from his dossier. The following year, the Shanghai Public Security Bureau reversed his *laojiao* sentence, but Hongci still required the same kind of notice from the Lijiang Interme-diate Court to be able to return to China without fear of arrest.

It snowed in Tsetserleg on June 19, 1982. That day, Hongci finally received news from his mother that the Lijiang Intermediate Court had repealed his verdict. "I could not believe my eyes," he writes in his memoir. "For me, this was not a mere piece of paper. This was the conclusion of a lifelong struggle: I was an innocent man. That had always been the case. But for the Communist Party to acknowl-edge my innocence was as if heaven and earth had been turned upside down."

After arranging a passport and conducting the necessary for-malities, Hongci departed Ulan Bator on May 7, 1983, for a two-month visit to Shanghai. His mother, white-haired and aged, was waiting for him in the alleyway to her house. He got out of the taxi and held her hands. She lifted her eyes to inspect his weary face: "You're home!"

That night, Hongci shared a meal at home with his mother for the first time in twenty-five years. He also was reunited with his sister Hongming, his brother-in-law Wang Bin, and their children, Wang Ou, Wang Ying, and Wang Wei. Hongci showed them photographs of his wife and children and talked with his mother until the early hours. Once again, she told him the story of his father's death, Tang Ximeng's visit to retrieve their photographs, and the house searches and confiscations by Red Guards during the Cultural Revolution, somberly turning the pages of the past years' tumultuous events. But when Hongci told her about his experience during the mass verdict rally in Lijiang in 1969, at which he had been sentenced to twenty years' hard labor and paraded through the streets, her eyes filled with tears.

The next day, Hongci visited with Wang Yanxiong, his old friend from the underground organization in Kunshan, who recorded thirty hours of interviews with him in preparation for a book about his life. At the Shanghai No. 1 Medical College, the head of the party committee's United Front apologized to Hongci and gave him three hundred yuan. In all, 157 students and teachers at the college had been classified as Rightists during the Anti-Rightist Campaign of 1957. One had died, and 155 had already received their "notice of correction." "You were the only one we couldn't find. Most people thought you were dead," they told Hongci.

Hongci also met Tang Ximeng, who, after spending the Cultural Revolution in the city of Jiading, had become head of the Department of Surgery at Shanghai's Yuanyang Hospital and had recently been inducted into the Communist Party. She was married to Bao Yougen and had two daughters, one of whom had immigrated to the United States.

I sat by a long table by the entrance reading a newspaper, patiently waiting for Tang Ximeng. I had my back to the door, and the first thing Ximeng would see of me was my white hair. Nervous and agitated, I tried to keep my eyes on the paper. Memories and scenes from our love sorrow flashed across my mind, as sharp and painful as if they had all taken place on the previous day.

I heard somebody entering through the door and turned around. It was Ximeng. I stood up and held out my hand. She smiled uncomfortably. Our hands touched for the first time in twenty-five years. She was a little bit plumper than before and not as dazzling in her beauty, but she looked at least ten years younger than her age. In comparison, I was an old man. We sat down beside each other on a bench. She seemed upset, sat silently with her head lowered, waiting for me to speak.

"Ximeng, have you been well all these years?" I said finally.

She nodded her head.

"How are your parents?"

"They are fine."

"Do they still live on Lintong Road?"

She nodded her head, then asked me, "How are your parents?"

"Father died in 1958. Mother is still living in Hongkou."

"How about your sister?"

"She has been working in the Culture Palace in Changning District ever since she graduated from the Shanghai Theatre Academy."

We fell silent again, crushed by the weight of emotions. What more was there to say? I broke the silence again: "Do you know what happened to me?"

"Shen Limei has told me some."

"I did nothing wrong. You remember I told you history would prove me right, even if it took three hundred years. Not even thirty years have passed, and the verdict has already been issued."

Ashamed, Ximeng said nothing.

"I remember the last time we saw each other on the street, at the beginning of 1958. You hated me then. I never told anybody about us. But you told them everything."

I had said what I wanted to say. Ximeng lowered her head. To make her feel better, I showed her photographs of my family.

"I didn't marry until 1975. This is my wife, Oyunbileg. These are my two sons. This is my family."

"Your wife looks very young."

"She was born in 1954, the year we started college."

Ximeng did not speak of her family.

"I am lucky to be alive," I said. "I never thought we would see each other again."

"We should thank the great wisdom of Deng Xiaoping for that," Ximeng said. "It's not only you. My whole family has also been rehabilitated."

Xu Hongci returned to Tsetserleg in July. Later that year, the Mongolian government notified him of its decision to allow the whole family to move to Shanghai. Their daughter, Esenya, was born in February 1984. On April 1, Hongci, his wife, and their three children stepped off the train in Shanghai to start a new life.

Hongci eventually found a job as an instructor at the Shanghai Petrochemical Company in Jinshan, sixty miles south of Shanghai, where he taught management, psychology, and other subjects. Through a colleague, Hongci was put in touch by phone with Chen Xiangzai, with whom he had made his first two escape attempts and who had surrendered himself to the Public Security Bureau in Chengdu shortly after their separation in 1959, then been sent back to the White Grass Ridge labor camp. When Hongci told him his story, Xiangzai could not believe his ears, but he was too ashamed of his conduct back in Chengdu to meet with Hongci in person.

Hongci retired in 1993 at the age of sixty. It was around this time that he began to pen his detailed, extensive memoir—572 hand-written pages with some 380,000 Chinese characters. In 1998, the family moved from Jinshan back to Shanghai, where Hongci made several unsuccessful attempts to publish his book. At a gathering of old Rightists in 2005, he met the journalist Hu Zhanfen. Most of the old men attending the meeting had spent more than twenty years in the labor camps. They had never heard of anybody else who had made a successful escape and agreed that of the 550,000 men and women officially sentenced as Rightists in 1957–1958, Hongci might have been the only one to win his freedom in this manner.

Hongci and Hu Zhanfen decided to collaborate on a book about Hongci's life based on his oral account, but the manuscript was rejected by mainland Chinese publishing houses due to its sensitive nature; fifty years on, Mao Zedong's Anti-Rightist Campaign remains an unhealed wound in the Chinese collective psyche and a virtually taboo subject under Communist rule. Instead, *Escape from the Laogai* was published in Hong Kong by Art & Culture, one of the numerous small publishing houses there that make full use of the former British colony's threatened but still vibrant freedom of speech, enshrined in the Basic Law signed by China and Great Britain at the handover in 1997.*

Shortly after the book's publication in March 2008, Hongci was diagnosed with kidney cancer. He passed away later that year.

---

*In recent years, these brave publishers have paid a steep price for upholding the freedom of the press solemnly pledged in Article 35 of China's constitution. In 2014, the seventy-four-year-old Yiu Mantin, a Hong Kong publisher of books on contemporary Chinese politics, was arrested in China and sentenced to ten years in prison on trumped-up charges. In the winter of 2015–2016, the publishers Gui Minhai, Lam Wing-kee, Lui Bo, Cheung Jiping, and Paul Lee disappeared in succession, making headline news around the world as "Hong Kong's missing booksellers." The latter four have since been conditionally released by the Chinese authorities, while Gui Minhai remains imprisoned.

Final Thoughts

The Anti-Rightist Campaign was a turning point in modern Chinese history. Ever since then, the Chinese Communist Party has been in steady decline. The main reason for this was the inability of Mao Zedong, steeped in the mentality of ancient China, to listen to dissenting opinions, in particular to correct opposing views. This deprived the party of a mirror capable of reflecting its true nature, as well as the medicine needed to treat its afflictions, and allowed it to fall deeper and deeper into evil ways. Of even graver consequence, the party has wiped out a vast contingent of outstanding comrades and patriots who possessed both mental acuity and a spirit of innovation. Instead, it has made use of yes-men who do not strive for progress, even of toadies with a particular flair for tricks, games, and flattery. Gradually, these people have set the standard for cadres, sapping the party's strength and will to fight for its ideals. Today's Communist Party is not the party we knew before 1957. Politically, it is old and feeble, stuck in a rut of ingrained bad habits. I gave everything I had to improve and strengthen it, but all I got in return was calamity. The party's tragedy lies wholly in its failure to establish a truly democratic system.

I am one of the tens of millions of victims of its countless political campaigns, and an incredibly lucky survivor. Looking back at my bitter experiences, remembering all the tribulations and misfortunes, I can only draw this conclusion: under Mao Zedong's dictatorship, the Chinese people had no human rights. My history is a good example of this.

XU HONGCI
Jinshan
1993–1995

Appendix 1: A Foul Wind in the Department of Medicine

Fifty-One Articles by Xu Hongci, Niu Zhikui, and others

Weng Fuping has said, "The 'airing of views' among university students is not a problem."

In reality, this is not the case.

1. No philosophy exam (we have already taken the dialectical materialism exam and have studied the historical materialism course several times). [The exam for] public hygiene should be changed to an assessment. The radiology course exam should only encompass X-ray images.
2. We oppose the vilification of Rudolf Virchow, August Weismann, and Thomas Hunt Morgan.* They should be evaluated correctly.
3. We oppose the dogmatization and vulgarization of Pavlov's theory.

---

*Rudolf Virchow (1821–1902), a German doctor known as the "father of modern pathology," August Weismann (1834–1914), a German evolutionary biologist, and Thomas Hunt Morgan (1866–1945), an American geneticist awarded the Nobel Prize for medicine in 1933, were subjected to the particular ire of the Soviet and, subsequently, Chinese Communist regimes, which denounced the three scientists as "reactionaries" and "bourgeois."

4. Our college organizes too few academic activities, and the students' knowledge is too shallow.

5. We oppose the mechanical aping of the Soviet Union. We should be learning from all advanced countries.

6. The level of the teachers in the Marxism study group is too low.

7. At the university level, our political class should only cover dialectical materialism. There is no need to study the other topics.

8. Discontinue the Friday political activities. These should be organized after class.

9. The level of the students is too low. For example, having taken the general surgery course, they are not even able to drain an abscess.

10. The anatomy course should focus on morphology, not phylogeny.

11. The foundation for the internal medicine course should be changed to physiological and laboratory diagnoses.

12. First-year students should be allowed to choose their own foreign language (English, Russian, German, Japanese, and so on).

13. Strengthen the core subjects (especially physics).

14. Our college should liaise with the other medical colleges in the city and increase the number of internships.

15. The social standing of our professors and lecturers should be respected, and their compensation should be improved.

16. The [new] library must be built.

17. The college's leaders and cadres should meet with the people, try to understand their problems, and not only listen to one side of the story.

18. The canteen's accounts should be made public.

19. The college's administrative cadres, especially the cadres in the student section, should come down from their tower. Students are afraid of the student section! Lecturers are afraid of the personnel section!

20. The sanitary conditions of the college are poor.

21. The public transportation company on East Temple Bridge Road should be taken over by the college. The fetid gutter by the physiology building should be filled in.

22. We oppose the political evaluation of students!
   [Note: Article 23 is missing.]
24. Revoke the special privileges of party and Youth League members!
25. Who selected Jia Tingzhen to participate in the National Student Federation's congress? The four opinions are not the students' opinions. Who chose Guo Xuexun and Jiang Zhangying as the representatives for the condolence delegation to Zhejiang? Why was this decided from above?
26. Who selects the student representatives for international activities? Are they really students?
27. We oppose the Youth League committee's monopoly over the student union. The student union should be the highest student organ on campus.
28. First Appeal: Establish a national university student publication. Second Appeal: Issue a student publication for our college.
29. Why has the Youth League's work come to a standstill? Open the door!
30. What is the Shanghai Student Federation up to? Who chose them? Are they student princelings?
31. Implement a rotation system for class-level cadres. The class monitor should not be appointed by the leadership!
32. The student representatives' meeting is a pure formality and does not solve any problems. "Be a socialist university student" is an empty slogan.
33. Movie theaters off campus offer a 30 percent rebate, but our college's movie theater charges a tax!
34. Youth League members should come down from their tower to participate in the "airing of views" and not just be bystanders. We oppose the way in which certain individuals attack others!
35. Reinstate compensation for intern doctors.
36. Lecturers' fees should be paid from the account for education expenses!
37. The "general" elections are not democratic. We oppose single-candidate elections. Candidates should be generated from the

grassroots level and up, meet with voters, give election speeches, and conduct election activities.

38. The Campaign to Eliminate Counterrevolutionaries was a mistake, and [those disciplined] should be rehabilitated.

39. How is the Hu Feng clique* really being treated?

40. Why are the democratic party factions† not allowed to establish organizations among university students?

41. Upon graduating, university students should be allowed to choose their job freely.

42. Chairman Mao is too secretive during his inspection tours around the country. He should have more meetings with the people.

43. The Eighth Party Congress only reported the good news and none of the bad and was lacking in a spirit of self-criticism.

44. Why has the Communist Party's work come to a halt in 1957? Outstanding students are being shut out.

45. The salary system needs to be thoroughly reformed. Professors, doctors, and primary school teachers should be given higher salaries.

46. An examination system should be implemented for the promotion of cadres.

47. When national leaders participate in physical labor, there is no need for the newspapers to provide excessive coverage.

48. Students at different universities are treated differently (why do we have to pay tuition when the students at the teachers college don't?).

49. Primary school teachers should be given better political treatment and higher pay.

50. We should not invite experts only from the Soviet Union. We should also invite professors and researchers from all other culturally and scientifically advanced countries.

---

*See footnote on p. 44.
†See footnote on p. 33.

51. We should not send students only to the Soviet Union and other socialist countries. We should also send students to capitalist countries.

Li Jing, Zhou Qinzong, Niu Zhikui, Chen Minwen, Yang Jianzhong, Gan Haining, Xu Naijing, Wang Xinsheng, Xu Hongci, Qiu Xinhuang, Wang Ping, Tang Keqiang, Yu Meixiang, Zhou Ziwen

Appendix 2: A Rightist Pawn Attacks the Party

Xu Hongci's Shameful Betrayal of the Party

Liberation Daily, July 23, 1957

Braving the sweltering summer heat, the student body of the Shanghai No. 1 Medical College has congregated on successive days to expose and denounce the Rightist Xu Hongci's antiparty and antisocialist deeds.

Xu Hongci is a third-year student in the Department of Medicine and was originally a Communist Party member. During the Rectification Campaign, he drew together a group of muddleheaded students and posted the [college's] first *dazibao* with fifty-one preposterous articles, such as "revoke the special privileges of party and Youth League members," "the 'general' elections are not democratic," "the Campaign to Eliminate Counterrevolutionaries was a mistake," and "the Eighth Party Congress only reported the good news and none of the bad and was lacking in a spirit of self-criticism." Launching a brazen attack on the party, he claimed that he wanted to "puncture the stifling atmosphere and mobilize the masses for the 'airing of views.'" When his *dazibao* was criticized by the Party Branch Organization, he shouted,

"The Party Branch Organization has isolated me!" When rebuked by fellow students, he posted another *dazibao* titled "Sincere Advice," accusing certain students of "double-dealing." After that, he mobilized the third-year students in classes 11 and 12, organized two forum meetings to "sweep aside all obstacles," and invited certain members of the democratic party factions on campus. In his invitation letter to them, he wrote, "I hope that you will support my actions, sweep aside the party committee's resistance to the 'airing of views,' and do battle with the party committee." At the meetings, he told his fellow students, "The party committee is being hypocritical. It talks about the 'airing of views' but actually does not support it," and, "The Party Branch Organization has isolated me, Party Committee Secretary Li has given me the cold shoulder," madly fanning the students' hatred of the party. To stir up students unhappy with the Campaign to Eliminate Counterrevolutionaries, attacking party members and zealous elements, he also fabricated stories, stating things like "During the Campaign to Eliminate Counterrevolutionaries, I held to the left of the party committee's directives, not to the right."

Xu Hongci's antiparty actions were praised and supported by Fan Rixin, another Rightist [at the college]. At one of the forum meetings to "sweep aside all obstacles," Fan Rixin called Xu Hongci a "model party member" and told him, "Don't be afraid. Keep going. The more noise, the better. You are young. I am old and have more experience than you." Guided by Fan Rixin, Xu Hongci continued his mad attack on the party. He was about to announce his withdrawal from the party, encouraged the "most vigorous" Youth League members to quit the league, planned to set up a separate political group to rally round the "Fifty-One Articles," and urged the students to continue the "airing of views" and dispatch delegations to other universities to give speeches, vainly seeking to undermine the party.

Xu Hongci's antiparty deeds have provoked the outrage of the whole student body. One after another, the students have stood up to expose and denounce him. Even the small number of students who were hoodwinked by him have regained their senses and distanced themselves from him.

At the big meeting on July 9, attended by the whole student body, eighteen students, including Zhang Quanyi, Yan Kejian, Tu Yijun, and Xu Haowen, exposed Xu Hongci's antiparty deeds and denounced his reactionary lies. Professor Xu Fengyan and Professor Chen Youxin also spoke.

Zhang Quanyi said, "When Xu Hongci saw the speeches by the Rightists at Beijing University and Nanjing University, he said that they resonated deeply with him, and he began his antiparty deeds."

Zhang Quanyi also exposed Xu Hongci's contacts with Fan Rixin.

Yan Kejian said, "During the Campaign to Eliminate Counterrevolutionaries, he [Xu Hongci] did not abide by the party's policy, and adopted the method of 'extorting confessions and believing them,' which had a severe negative effect. Fearing the Rectification Campaign, he took preemptive action by blaming and attacking the party, stating, 'The Campaign to Eliminate Counterrevolutionaries was a mistake, and [those disciplined] should be rehabilitated.' He has also said, 'If there is a Hungarian Uprising in China, I'll be the first to oppose the party.'"

Tu Yijun said, "Although I am not a party or Youth League member, I know very well that party and Youth League members 'put hard work before enjoyment' and do not enjoy any special privileges. While Xu Hongci may say, 'Revoke the special privileges of party and Youth League members,' in my opinion, it is he who sets great store by special privileges. At a cadre meeting, he once said, 'I represent the party; I am the party.' He also used the boast of his 'ten years of party membership' to avoid taking part in collective activities."

Xu Haowen said, "Xu Hongci said, 'The Twentieth Party Congress of the Communist Party of the Soviet Union criticized Stalin's mistakes. The Eighth Party Congress was lacking in a spirit of self-criticism. It only reported the good news and none of the bad.' His evil intention is to split the party and overthrow it."

The student Ya Lu denounced Xu Hongci's lies. He said, "Xu Hongci has said that those disciplined during the Campaign to Eliminate Counterrevolutionaries should be rehabilitated. This is nothing but a repetition of Luo Longji's* absurd 'appeal for leniency' for the counterrevolutionaries." Drawing a vivid comparison between our country's elections and the U.S. elections, Ya Lu explained that [our] "general" elections are true democracy and refuted [Xu Hongci's] lie that "the 'general' elections are not democratic."

A student hoodwinked by Xu Hongci into co-signing the "Fifty-One Articles" also made a confession, exposing [Xu Hongci] and stating that he would draw a clear line between himself and the Rightist Xu Hongci.

The college's three thousand students were unified in their wrath against the Rightist Xu Hongci and determined to continue the struggle against the Rightists until the very end.

Xu Hongci joined the Communist Party in 1948 (he was a candidate member for three years and officially inducted in 1951). He harbored wild personal ambitions, consistently expressed his dissatisfaction with the party, opposed the party, and finally betrayed it.

---

*Luo Longji (1898–1965) was a prominent Chinese intellectual and politician, deputy chairman of the Chinese Democratic League, and one of the four non-Communist ministers in the Communist-led government, serving as minister of forestry. During the Anti-Rightist Campaign, he was singled out as one of the main culprits, denounced, and purged from all his official positions.

Acknowledgments

Xu Hongci and his memoir have made a long, arduous journey across continents, decades, and cultures, and I am sad that he is not here to see its English publication, which has been made possible only with the help of a number of people. Our editor, Sarah Crichton, deserves particular thanks for sharing her rich experience in the art of narrative economy and for shaping the book. I am also grateful to my agents, Peter and Amy Bernstein, for their commitment to bringing this and other important manuscripts of unknown Chinese writers to the world's attention. Marsha Sasmor and Kate Sanford provided invaluable help in keeping the memoir's publication on track, and my copyeditor, Ingrid Sterner, and proofreaders, Judy Kiviat and Ellen Feldman, have done a superb job with their innumerable incisive comments and their meticulous editing. Victor Mair, Andrew Nathan, Frank Dikötter, and Anne Thurston generously took time to carefully read the manuscript and offered their crucial support.

I also want to thank Scott Auerbach, Jo Ann Metsch, and Sarah Scire at Farrar, Straus and Giroux in New York; Judith Kendra at Rider Books in London; and Hu Zhanfen, Sonya True, William

Taubman, Åke Johansson, the late Harry Wu, Carrie Gracie, Piet Gaarthuis, Wang Chengzhi, Stacy Mosher, Geoffrey Wade, Diana Chang, Dermot Tatlow, Colin Ridler, and Kelly Falconer. Other contributors will remain unnamed but not forgotten. A special thanks is due to Paul Lee. He and his fellow publishers have been through some very difficult times in the past year, and our thoughts are with them. Edgar R. Lyle II has been a constant source of encouragement. My dear Kit Ping supported this endeavor wholeheartedly from its inception. Finally, history owes Sukh Oyunbileg and her children a deep debt of gratitude for fulfilling Xu Hongci's heartfelt wish to share this memoir.

ERLING HOH

Index

Page numbers in *italics* refer to illustrations.

A Note About the Author

Xu Hongci (1933–2008), a writer from Shanghai, was branded a Rightist in 1957 and spent fourteen years in Mao Zedong's labor reform camps. Following his escape, he lived first in Tsetserleg, Mongolia, and then in Shanghai with his wife, Sukh Oyunbileg, and their children until his death in 2008.

A Note About the Translator

Erling Hoh is a writer and translator of Swedish and Chinese descent and is based in northern Sweden. A former correspondent for *Archaeology* and the Danish newspaper *Dagbladet Information*, he has written about Chinese history, culture, and politics for numerous magazines, including *Natural History* and the *Far Eastern Economic Review*. His most recent publication is *The True History of Tea*, coauthored with Professor Victor Mair and critically acclaimed by *The Guardian* for combining "a real depth of knowledge with a deft stylistic and organisational touch."